THE COMPLETE STUDY GUIDE FOR SCORING HIGH

PRELIMINARY PRACTICE
for the HIGH SCHOOL EQUIVALENCY DIPLOMA TEST

By

DAVID R. TURNER, M.S. in Ed.

arco 219 Park Avenue South
New York, N.Y. 10003

Fifth Edition (B-2040)
Fourth Printing, 1979

COPYRIGHT © 1975
by Arco Publishing Company, Inc.

Published by ARCO PUBLISHING COMPANY, INC.
219 Park Avenue South, New York, N.Y. 10003

Library of Congress Catalog
Card Number 75-34848

Arco Catalog Number 0-668-01441-5

Printed in the United States of America

CONTENTS

HOW TO USE THIS INDEX
Slightly bend the right-hand edge
of the book. This will expose
the corresponding Parts
which match the index, below.

PART

1

2

3

4

PART ONE

THE HOW AND WHY OF SCORING HIGH

How this book was prepared; what went into these pages to make them worth your while. How to use them profitably for yourself in preparing for your test. The essentials of successful study.

The purpose, meaning, and value of the High School Equivalency Diploma. Simple steps to success. Important information on eligibility requirements, fees, how to apply, when, where and how the tests are given.

Samples of each type of question slated for the test. Forewarned is forearmed with this priceless preview. Plan your study time accordingly.

Master each of these methods — they apply to question types you may meet on your exam. Practice them when testing yourself in this book to insure a top performance on your actual exam.

PART TWO

PRACTICE WITH MODEL TESTS

...continued on next page

CONTENTS continued

PART

Compare scores. If you haven't improved, use your final hours to strengthen weaknesses.

PART THREE

VERBAL ABILITY AND READING

A simplified yet effective way to improve your knowledge and usage of English. Twenty-five English "traps" and how to avoid them. Basic grammar rules. Short tests allow you to measure your ability. Correct answers follow each test.

Getting the "spell" out of spelling. Learning to spell a word. Two tests using words that often cause trouble. Comprehensive lists of words that look easy, but are often misspelled.

Concentration, speed, retentiveness, ability to relate the ideas you read . . . these are the hallmarks of the master test-taker. With such a variety of reading matter as this chapter affords, you'll find yourself flexing your mental muscles and acquiring competence through flexibility.

PART

1

2

3

4

PART FOUR
MATHEMATICS REVIEW
AND FINAL ADVICE

PART ONE

The How and Why of Scoring High

WHAT THIS BOOK WILL DO FOR YOU

*Even though this course of study has been carefully planned
to help you get in shape by the day your test comes, you'll have
to do a little planning on your own to be successful. And you'll
also need a few pointers proven effective for many other good
students.*

If you want to take an exam but are reluctant for fear that you've been away from
school too long, or for fear that your skills are a bit rusty, don't sell yourself short.
You'll get the greatest help from this book by understanding how it has been
organized, and by using it accordingly. Study carefully this concise, readable
treatment of what is required by your exam, and your way will be clear. You will
progress directly to your goal. You will not be led off into blind alleys and useless
digressions.

We believe that you can improve your exam scores measureably with the help
of this "self-tutor." It's a carefully thought-out homestudy course which you can
readily review in less than twenty hours. It's a digest which you might have been
able to assemble after many hundred hours of laborious digging. Since you'll have
quite enough to do without that, consider yourself fortunate that we have done it
for you.

To prepare for a test you must motivate yourself . . . get into the right frame
of mind for learning from your "self-tutor." You'll have to urge yourself to learn.
That's the only way people ever learn. Your efforts to score high will be greatly
aided because you'll have to do this job on your own . . . perhaps without a
teacher. Psychologists have demonstrated that studies undertaken for a clear goal
(which you initiate yourself and actively pursue) are the most successful. You,
yourself, want to pass this test. That's why you bought this book and embarked on
this program. Nobody forced you to do it, and there may be nobody to lead you
through the course. Your self-activity is going to be the key to your success in the
forthcoming weeks.

Used correctly, your "self-tutor" will show you what to expect and will give
you a speedy brush-up on the major problems crucial to your exam. Even if your
study time is very limited, you will:

- gain familiarity with your examination;
- improve your general test-taking skill;

- improve your skill in analyzing and answering questions involving reasoning, judgment, comparison, and evaluation;
- improve your speed and skill in reading and understanding what you read—an important ability in learning, and an important component of most tests.

This book will pinpoint your study by presenting the types of questions you will get on the actual exam. You'll score higher even if you only familiarize yourself with these types.

This book will help you find your weaknesses and find them fast. Once you know where you're weak, you can get right to work (before the exam), and concentrate on those soft spots. This is the kind of selective study which yields maximum results for every hour spent.

This book will give you the *feel* of the exam. Many of our practice questions are taken from previous exams. Since previous exams are not always available for inspection by the public, our sample test questions are quite important for you. The day you take your exam you'll see how closely the book conforms.

This book will give you confidence *now*, while you are preparing for the exam. It will build your self-confidence as you proceed. It will beat those dreaded before-test jitters that have hurt so many other test-takers.

This book stresses the modern, multiple-choice type of question because that's the kind you'll undoubtedly get on your exam. In answering these questions you will add to your knowledge by learning the correct answers, naturally. However, you will not be satisfied with merely the correct choice for each question. You will want to find out why the other choices are incorrect. This will jog your memory . . . help you remember much you thought you had forgotten. You'll be preparing and enriching yourself for the exam to come.

Of course, the great advantage in all this lies in narrowing your study to just those fields in which you're most likely to be quizzed. Answer enough questions in those fields and the chances are very good that you'll meet a few of them again on the actual test. After all, the number of questions an examiner can draw upon in these fields is rather limited. Examiners frequently employ the same questions on different tests for this very reason.

By creating the ''climate'' of your test, this book should give you a fairly accurate picture of what's involved, and should put you in the right frame of mind for passing high.

Arco Publishing Company has been involved with trends and methods in testing ever since the firm was founded in 1937. We have *specialized* in books that prepare people for exams. Based on this experience it is our modest boast that you probably have in your hands the best book that could be prepared to help *you* score high. Now, if you'll take a little advice on using it properly, we can assure you that you will do well.

HIGH SCHOOL EQUIVALENCY DIPLOMAS

Adults who have not completed their high school education now have an opportunity to get a high school diploma without going back to school. All this through a High School Equivalency Diploma, recognized as the equivalent of a four-year high school diploma by business, industry, civil service commissions, U.S. Armed Forces, licensing bureaus, and many institutions of higher education.

This book will tell you what the High School Equivalency Diploma is about and how to prepare yourself for the test. You will find Sample Tests, and answers, to familiarize you with the actual test. You will also find study material designed to make most effective use of your time and effort.

Purpose and Meaning

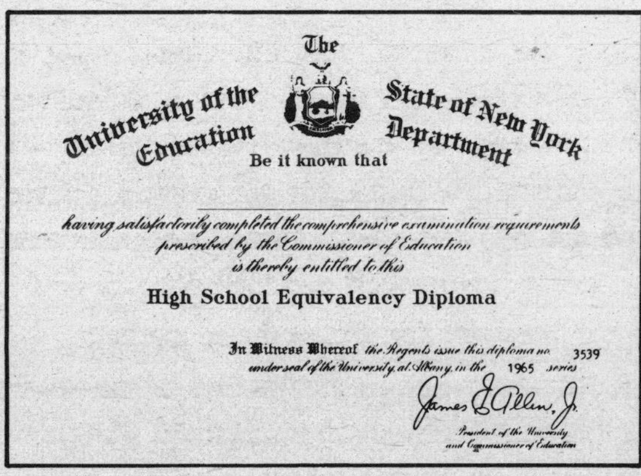

This is the kind of official diploma your State Department of Education will issue to you. It is the legal equivalent of the diploma awarded to students who have graduated from a four-year high school.

HOW IT BEGAN

Many students were forced to leave school during World War II to serve in the armed forces. High School Equivalency Diploma tests were first used in 1945 to give veterans, whose education had been interrupted, a chance to receive high school diplomas. For this purpose the American Council on Education produced the battery of tests called General Educational Development, better known simply as G.E.D. The diploma awarded to those making satisfactory grades on these tests has the same worth as that given to graduates from a four-year high school.

Equivalency programs have now been extended to include civilian adults. Tests are given at regular intervals either by the Education Departments of the different states or by individual high schools, depending on the administrative procedures adopted by each state.

You do not have to attend high school at all in order to get a High School Equivalency Diploma. The age requirement for the examination varies from state to state, but in no state is the minimum age requirement over twenty-one years.

WHY HIGH SCHOOL EQUIVALENCY?

There are great opportunities in our country for those who have educational background. Industry, business, civil service, the armed services, and many colleges extend open arms to those who are educationally qualified. It does not matter whether the educated individual has acquired his education *in* the class room or *outside* the classroom. If he is an educated person, he will be accepted—in fact, he will be welcomed.

The purpose of the High School Equivalency Diploma is to establish that a person who has not attended high school classes has, nevertheless, the educational background of a high school graduate. If he does have that background, in spite of the fact that he has never taken classroom courses, he can now have all the prestige of the high school graduate.

This is as it should be. After all, if a person has traveled widely, and through his travels, has learned quite a bit about history, geography, science, literature, and so many other things that are taught in the classroom, why shouldn't he receive credit and recognition for his ability and achievement?

FAILURE TO GRADUATE

More than half the country's adult population—62 million men and women over 25 years of age—are without a high school diploma. These usually are the people who work at the poorer paying jobs. More and more, the complex society we live in makes it harder for people to get ahead if they lack an educational background. That is the reason the number of people taking the High School Equivalency Diploma Test increases every year.

For one reason or another these people did not finish high school. But now, because of the Diploma Test, it is never too late to make up for it.

HIGH SCHOOL EQUIVALENCY—RECOGNITION AND REWARD

First-rate jobs that are now closed to you because you are not a high school graduate will open up for you the day you receive your Equivalency Diploma. You will be able to advance faster in your present job. You will get into the higher-bracket civil service jobs. You can move up higher in the armed services. You can, in certain cases, enter the college of your choice.

An Equivalency Diploma can actually be measured in dollars and cents. It is often the difference between a good living and a lifetime of struggle.

Since an Equivalency Diploma is considered the same as a four-year diploma, you will also benefit in other ways. You will have the prestige of a high school graduate. You will have the social advantages of being educated. You will gain the increased respect of others. Your personal life, and the lives of members of your family, will be enriched because of the broadening of your educational background.

A great opportunity is open to improve yourself in every way—financially, educationally, socially.

Values of a Diploma

"DO YOU HAVE A HIGH SCHOOL DIPLOMA?" How many times have you heard that question and have had to answer "no"? You probably realize that the lack of a High School Diploma is responsible for holding you back from greater success . . . otherwise you would not be reading this book. Well, the truth of the matter is that a High School Diploma or its equivalent is *one of life's most valuable tools for success*—for it opens up the doors to greater earning power and greater opportunities.

Better, Higher-Paying Jobs

Look around you. A little observation and reflection will quickly convince you that people with High School Diplomas have by far the better positions in all walks of life. The man or woman without a diploma is usually at the bottom of the ladder.

The U.S. Government has made studies which show quite clearly that high school graduates earn nearly $1,000 more each year after the age of 24 than grade school graduates. In plain dollars and cents, a high school diploma or its equivalent can add more than $60,000 to your lifetime earning power.

In Industry

Inspect the want-ad section of the daily newspaper. You will find that the better paying jobs are reserved for the high school and college graduate. A recent study indicates that there are more and more jobs available for the educated person—fewer and fewer jobs for the person who lacks education. Many employment agencies will not even consider an applicant unless he has at least a high school diploma or its equivalent.

In Civil Service

Hundreds of thousands of men and women are needed annually to fill high-paying, secure, lifetime jobs with federal, state, and municipal government units. Firemen, policemen, typists, office clerks, postal carriers, railway mail clerks, etc., are always in demand. A high school diploma or its equivalent is usually required for these positions.

In Our Armed Forces

For anyone in military service, a high school diploma is often an essential for promotion. It is much easier to attain the status of an officer—noncommissioned as well as commissioned—if you possess a diploma. All branches of the armed forces are eager to help servicemen even while they are in service to gain a high school equivalency certificate. The United States Armed Forces Institute (USAFI) has several testing stations just for this purpose.

An applicant who has received a satisfactory score on the High School Equivalency Test while in service does not have to take the test again when he returns to civilian life.

For College Entrance

There are a great many colleges which recognize the High School Equivalency Diploma for college entrance. If you are interested in entering a certain college with your Equivalency Diploma, it would be advisable for you to write to that institution to ask whether it will accept the certificate.

A recent newsletter published by the Commission on Accreditation of the American Council on Education relates the interesting case of a lady from the state of Maryland who says (in her own words): "A few years ago I wrote a letter to the State Department of Education asking them to send me the booklet which explains how an adult may get a high school diploma for college entrance without going to high school. The booklet explained that by passing certain examinations given by the State Board of Education one could get such a diploma. The assumption is that we never stop learning. If you have raised children, the chances are that, without realizing it, you have learned much of their homework by listening to them or helping them. Because of my age, I didn't want to waste time. I studied hard and passed the equivalency examination. With the diploma, I was able to go to college. By this June I shall have earned 107 college credits. I expect to get my diploma from a local university next year, so you see it can be done."

Trade and Vocational Schools

In this age of specialization the skilled person invariably commands a higher salary than the un-skilled individual. Many of the better trade and vocational schools where you can acquire skills that are in demand won't enroll you unless you have a high school diploma.

Prestige

Let's face it—a person without a high school diploma is sometimes looked down at by his friends and his community. This may often be unfair, but the sad fact is that a person who has not gone through high school is supposed to have narrow intellectual interests.

A diploma may make a lot of difference in how people consider you. And it is true—isn't it?—that the effort you put into getting that diploma gives you educational growth and a broader knowledge of the world you live in. These benefits will be with you all the rest of your life.

Richer, Fuller, Happier Life

But, a High School Equivalency Diploma can mean even more. It means you can face life with confidence in yourself and your abilities ... you can meet situations, people, problems without having "two strikes" against you before you start. You will command the attention and respect of others—instead of being overlooked or shrugged off with a "what can he know—he didn't even finish high school." And with the increased earnings and better jobs that go with a High School Equivalency Diploma—you will be able to afford some of the finer things you have always wanted ... find more time for play and relaxation. Think of it! A High School Equivalency Diploma can give you all these things. Can you honestly afford to get along without a diploma any longer? Can you willingly pass up this amazing opportunity to get *your* diploma?

Self Improvement. The Beginning of Better Things.

When you get that High School Equivalency Diploma, you will have the feeling of satisfaction that comes with obtaining something worthwhile. This will be accompanied by an attitude of confidence as well as a desire to continue your education either in the classroom or outside of it. "There's nothing like success to bring success."

Simple Steps to a High School Diploma

You are now aware that you can get a high school diploma (or equivalency certificate) even if you do not have the school credits that are ordinarily required for the diploma. As an adult, if you pass the High School Equivalency Diploma Test, you are able to get a high school diploma—*even if you do not have the school credits*. The High School Equivalency Diploma is awarded to adults who prove that they have the educational level of the average high school graduate—even though they have not gone to high school.

It may very well be that you have the educational background of a high school graduate. If you have traveled, if you have met many different types of people, if you have read books and articles (in English or in a foreign language), if you have had other experiences in life that have broadened you—it is likely that you have more education than your record indicates. That is what the High School Diploma Eqivalency Test is for — to find out whether you deserve to be called a high school graduate even though you do not have the classroom training.

You Can Do It!

Do not be discouraged if you are not ready to take the High School Diploma Test. This book will help you to prepare for it. Let's suppose that your reading, arithmetic, English and spelling levels are somewhere between the 6th and 9th grades. We are going to try to raise your level so that, eventually, you will have a 12th grade ability— then you will be ready to take the High School Diploma Test.

There's plenty of hard work ahead. But you can do it if you are serious. This book will guide you— it will give you light, and it will help you to find your way.

Nationwide Recognition

Every state in the union (and the Canal Zone, the District of Columbia, Guam, and Puerto Rico) issues and accepts an Equivalency Diploma. In all states the examinations for a diploma are based on the G.E.D. tests. The diploma is recognized as a valid high school equivalency credential by all states.

In no state is attendance at school or classes required.

Who Can Take the Test?

Age requirements vary from state to state. There is, of course, no maximum age; an adult man or woman can take it at any time throughout his life The minimum age is never over twenty-one, and in Arizona and Hawaii, for instance, it is as low as eighteen. In a few states and territories the minimum age is lower for veterans than for non-veterans and service personnel.

Fees

Since Equivalency Diplomas are issued by the individual states, there is no set fee throughout the country for taking the test. The fee not only varies from state to state; it sometimes also varies *within* the state, from one testing center to another.

What About Veterans?

A veteran who has taken and passed the G.E.D. battery of tests while in the service will usually receive his Equivalency Diploma without having to take further tests when he returns to civilian life. He should make application for his diploma to his state Department of Education.

For those who pass the test, some states charge an additional fee for issuance of the Equivalency Diploma while others offer this service free.

Testing Centers

Testing agency centers are located in different parts of each state. The chance is that there will be one not very far from where you live.

The addresses of all testing agency centers in your state usually are listed on the application form, which may be obtained from your state Department of Education at your state capital.

When Are the Tests Given?

Since the entire battery of five tests takes ten hours to complete, the examination is always held over a two-day period. Testing time usually starts at 3 o'clock in the afternoon and runs not later than 10 P.M., on the second day it runs from 6 P.M. to 10 P.M.

In large cities, such as New York City, the test is given every week. In less populated areas it is held at longer intervals.

Test Scores

Minimum passing scores are required on each of the five tests as well as a minimum passing average on all the tests. Although the Equivalency Tests are similar in all states, the passing scores differ. They vary between states from a low score of 35 to a high score of 50 required on each test, and from a low combined score of 200 to a high of 250 for the five tests.

In Oklahoma, for instance, a score of 40 or above is required on each of the five tests and an average score of 50—a total of 250—on all five tests. The passing score in Vermont is 35 on each test and an average of 45 is required on all five tests. Virginia and Alaska are among the few states that make no distinction between the passing score in each test and the average score on all five: 40 or above is required in Virginia and 50 or above in Alaska.

When Will I Know?

It takes from six to eight weeks to receive the scores. They are sent directly to the person who took the examination.

Failure Isn't Final

An applicant who fails the Diploma Test may take it again.

Each state has a minimum waiting period between testings. In New York, for example, the waiting time is two months. An applicant must take a different form of the equivalency examination each time he is retested.

A Second State Diploma

In New York State, the holder of an Equivalency Diploma may also go on to earn a Regents High School Diploma. He can qualify for a Regents Diploma by passing Regents tests in all of the following: three units in a major elective subject; either American History and World Background III or American History II and World History; English Comprehensive. Application forms are available at high school offices anywhere in the state.

How to Apply

For an application, write to the Department of Education in the capital city of the state where you reside. Fill out each item of information requested on the application. Follow the directions in regard to the fee and where to mail it.

HIGH SCHOOL EQUIVALENCY DIPLOMA

EXAMINATION FORECAST

Questions That Forecast the Test

If you want a preview of your exam, look these questions over carefully. We did . . . as we compiled them from official announcements and various other sources. A good part of this book is based on these prophetic questions. Practice and study material is geared closely to them. The time and effort you devote to the different parts of this book should be determined by the facility with which you answer the following questions.

A look at the following questions is the easiest, quickest, most important help you can get from this book. These predictive questions give you foresight by providing an "overview" with which to direct your study. They are actual samples of the question types you may expect on your test.

Before you're finished with this book you'll get plenty of practice with the best methods of answering each of these question types. However, you're going to do a little work yourself. You're going to plan your study to make sure that each available hour is used most effectively. You're going to concentrate where it will do you the most good. And you'll take it easy where you have no trouble.

In other words, discover what you're going to face on the test and make plans to pace yourself accordingly.

Tests of General Educational Development
High School Level

There are five tests in this battery, and you will be taking them all in one sitting which will extend over two days. Each test takes two hours, so you will be spending a total of ten hours in those two days.

All the questions are multiple choice. They require that you choose the best possible answer out of several that are presented to you. You can understand from this that you will not be asked to do a lot of writing. You will have to read, to think, to decide, and to mark down the letter corresponding to the best and most sensible choice in each case.

Your answers will reveal the strength and maturity of your thought; the extent to which you have profited from your reading, your observations, and your life's experiences. You will *not* be asked to remember a great deal of specific information in giving your answers. The measure of your maturity will come largely from your ability to understand and interpret various kinds of reading material.

The five tests cover subjects and skills which are taught in all high schools, but you will find as you look over the descriptions and sample questions which follow, that your learning and experience have fairly well familiarized you with them, even though you may never have attended high school classes. And, of course, the later pages of this book will provide all the help and preparation you need to put your best foot forward on the five tests.

TEST ONE — CORRECTNESS AND EFFECTIVENESS OF EXPRESSION

This can be described simply as a test of your working familiarity with the English language.

Part A, which is called *English Usage,* deals with grammar, capitalization, punctuation, and your ability to use words. Although these are indeed high school subjects they need not frighten you because you have undoubtedly mastered most of the questions that will be asked. A little study will provide whatever else is needed.

Part B is a test of your ability to spell. And here again the same advice applies.

Part A: English Usage

In the sample of Part A (which we give you so that you can see for yourself just exactly what you can expect on the test) you will find a reading passage which you are asked to look over very carefully. You will find in the reading passage certain words and expressions underlined and numbered. Refer to the question which has the same number as the underlining. If the underlining is correct as it is, mark the letter A (the NO CHANGE choice). If the underlining has an error in grammar, word usage, or punctuation, mark the letter B or C or D, whichever one gives the correction.

Jane Austen was given birth to in Northern England in the year 1775. She led an uneventful life and never got married.

1. A. NO CHANGE
    B. had birth
    C. was born
    D. had her birth

2. A. NO CHANGE
    B. northern England
    C. northern england
    D. North England

3. A. NO CHANGE
    B. the 1775 year
    C. the year, 1775
    D. 1775.

4. A. NO CHANGE
    B. leaded
    C. lode
    D. had leaded

5. A. NO CHANGE
    B. not ever got married
    C. never married
    D. neither never married

Correct Answers

1. C   2. B   3. D   4. A   5. C

Part B: Spelling Test

Directions: In each of the word groups below, select the misspelled word.

1. A. everywhere
    B. continued
    C. youngest
    D. developement

2. A. offered
    B. rapidly
    C. neccessary
    D. similar

3. A. multiply
    B. senery
    C. requested
    D. decorate

4. A. village
    B. further
    C. improvment
    D. superintendent

5. A. industry
    B. typewriter
    C. surface
    D. tracter

Correct Answers

1. D   2. C   3. B   4. C   5. D

TEST TWO — INTERPRETATION OF READING MATERIALS IN THE SOCIAL STUDIES

This test measures your ability to read and interpret correctly passages in history, economics, and world events.

Reading passages are given to measure your ability to understand and interpret social, political, economic and cultural problems. As an example, here is a reading passage followed by questions in the form of incomplete statements about what you have just read. Each question is followed by five words or expressions. Select the one that most satisfactorily completes the statement in accordance with the direct or implied meaning of the reading passage.

Social Studies Reading Passage

With the fall of Rome, the light that had begun to shine in science went out. The accumulated knowledge of the Golden Ages of Greece and Rome was kept hidden in monasteries. No one studied his environment. Experimentation was unknown. But the sun of knowledge broke through after the rise of Charlemagne in 800 A.D. The Crusades followed. Exploration and trade developed. Men began to observe and invent, and with the invention of printing in 1450 began a great revival of learning, the Renaissance. This period produced some great scientists, whose findings brought advances in industry, government, travel and communication, and made possible a better standard of living.

1. The period immediately after the fall of Rome was
   A. the Crusades
   B. the Golden Ages
   C. an age of ignorance
   D. an age of exploration
   E. the age of Charlemagne

2. The invention of printing helped to bring about
   A. the fall of Rome
   B. the rise of Charlemagne
   C. the monasteries
   D. the Renaissance
   E. the Crusades

3. The basis of scientific development is
   A. environment
   B. light
   C. travel
   D. trade
   E. experimentation

Correct Answers

(You'll learn more by writing your own answers before comparing them with these.)

1. C   2. D   3. E

TEST THREE — INTERPRETATION OF READING MATERIALS IN THE NATURAL SCIENCES

This tests your ability to interpret passages dealing with the different aspects of science encountered in everyday life. It emphasizes your ability to pay close attention to detail and to reason logically.

In the actual test there will be a number of passages designed to test your understanding of facts and opinions in the natural sciences. The sample passage below is followed by incomplete statements about what you have just read. Each of these statements is followed by five words or expressions. Decide which word or expression most satisfactorily completes each statement in accordance with what is actually said in the paragraph or what you think the author is trying to bring out.

Natural Science Reading Passage

Color in nature impresses itself upon the casual observer primarily because of the element of beauty involved. In many cases, though, the distribution of pigment is definitely protective or concealing. For instance, the brightly colored upper surfaces of the wings of the *Kallima* butterfly of India make the insect conspicuous while in flight. When the insect is at rest, however, the under surfaces are exposed and present a striking resemblance to a dried brown leaf. It seems common sense to suppose that, when in this position, the insect is likely to be taken for a leaf by possible enemies and so left unmolested.

1. The function of protective coloration in nature is to
   A. conceal
   B. give variety
   C. produce great beauty
   D. create new species
   E. attract attention

2. The *Kallima* butterfly is protected by
   A. its resemblance to a dried leaf
   B. the size of its wings
   C. a covering of leaves
   D. its rapid motion
   E. its bright wings

Correct Answers

1. A   2. A

TEST FOUR — INTERPRETATION OF READING MATERIALS IN LITERATURE

This test is based on a variety of selections from world literature and emphasizes the ability to interpret figures of speech, cope with unusual sentence structure and meanings, and to recognize mood and purpose.

It consists of a number of literary passages. The answers you give will measure your ability to understand and answer questions about what you read. The sample passage below is followed by statements about it and then by five words or expressions. Choose the word or expression that most satisfactorily completes each statement in accordance with what the author of the passage has written. This is what you will be asked to do on the actual Equivalency Test.

Reading Passage—Literature

Money has now become so important that we often lose sight of what lies behind it. The usual way to regain our focus is to ask a question like this: "If you were without food on a desert island with no chance of rescue for a long time and had to choose between a million dollars in gold or a fifty-pound Wisconsin cheese, which would you take?" I think it is extremely necessary to see clearly and simply what lies behind the dollars. I doubt if we can solve our financial problems unless we see the people, the land, the machines, the houses, the freight cars, the loaves of bread which alone give dollars any meaning. In the long run it is human labor, capital investment, raw materials, mechanical energy and scientific knowledge which form the chief parts of the economic machine.

1. The title that best expresses the main theme or subject of this selection is
    A. solving our financial problems
    B. the real meaning of dollars
    C. Wisconsin cheese
    D. living on a desert island
    E. money and the machine

2. The author suggests that if one were away from civilization
    A. money would be his most important possession
    B. he would miss the economic machine
    C. food would be of greater value than money
    D. it would be necessary to solve financial problems
    E. human labor would be unnecessary

Correct Answers

1. B   2. C

TEST FIVE — GENERAL MATHEMATICAL ABILITY

This is a test in general mathematics, measuring your ability to use those fundamentals of arithmetic that are taught in a high school general mathematics class. Actually, it is a test of problem solving of a practical nature, including such things as the mathematical aspects of life insurance, installment buying, taxes, the ability to estimate costs of simple home construction and repair projects, as well as ordinary arithmetical skills (addition, subtraction, division, multiplication) with whole numbers, percents, fractions and decimals.

For the examples we present here to give you a quick idea of what it's all about work out your answer in the blank space at the right of each question. Below the questions you will find four suggested answers. Select the answer that you have figured out to be the right one and mark it next to the question.

1. What part of a whole pie is left after ⅜ of it is eaten?
    A. ½   C. ⅝
    B. ⅔   D. ⅞

2. Write in Roman numerals: 119.
    A. CLIX   C. MIX
    B. CXIX   D. XIX

3. A plane averaged 360 miles an hour. At this rate, how many miles did it fly in 3 hours and 30 minutes?
    A. 1260   C. 1295
    B. 1280   D. 1305

4. A hiking club walked 3.1 miles one day, 4.3 miles the next day, and 5.8 miles the third day. How many miles did the club hike altogether?
    A. 12.4   C. 13.0
    B. 12.8   D. 13.2

Correct Answers

1. C   2. B   3. A   4. D

Some Good Advice

*How to study for your High School Equivalency Diploma Test.
How to apply yourself to the pages that follow so as to improve
yourself the most in the shortest possible time. How to utilize your
study and practice to achieve the highest possible score on the test.*

You have an important job ahead of you. That job is to prepare yourself for the High School Diploma Test which you are going to take some day. But before you take that test, you must strengthen yourself in the fundamental areas stressed by the test.

The five Sample Tests in this book have just the questions you need to get yourself ready for the more difficult questions in the High School Diploma Tests. That's the reason we call the Sample Tests *Preliminary*.

Each Sample Test follows the general pattern of the High School Diploma Test. Each test will give you a clear picture of the types of questions which you will face on the actual test. The only differences between the High School Diploma Test and the Sample Tests in this book are in time allotment and in level of difficulty. As you already know, each of the five tests is two hours in length. However, in order to keep your study periods down to manageable time limits, the sample tests in this book are all one hour in length. In a sense we have done this to help you firm up your mental muscles for the longer examination. You'll do it by easy steps.

Remember, this is a "practice book." When you have attained the necessary grasp of what is here contained you can go on to more difficult study with HIGH SCHOOL EQUIVALENCY DIPLOMA TESTS, the second and final book in this series put out by the Arco Publishing Company. The material in that second book is a bit more difficult. It is on the precise level of the questions you can expect to encounter on the actual Equivalency Exam. Don't be concerned about this. That's the way the series was planned.

You can take the actual exam after properly studying this PRACTICE BOOK. It is good and sufficient in itself. But you will get additional valuable practice from the second book in the series. If, after finishing this book, you feel confident of passing the test, you needn't spend any more time in assuring yourself of success. If, however, you feel that you need more help, then HIGH SCHOOL EQUIVALENCY TESTS is precisely the book you need.

This book is scientifically planned. Use it properly and you will benefit greatly in your aim of getting a High School Equivalency Diploma some day not too far off.

Take the first Sample Test. When you finish this test, find out where you are weak — Spelling *or* Correct Usage *or* Social Studies Reading *or* Natural Science Reading *or* Literature Reading. In order to strengthen your weaknesses, refer to Part Three of this book which gives you specific tips to improve yourself. After you do this, take the second Sample Test. Again decide on your weaknesses—and again strengthen yourself. Take the other Sample Tests and use the same procedure.

Follow the foregoing plan to the letter and you will take a giant step in successful preparation for that important day in your life—the day that you take the High School Equivalency Diploma Test. You will not find the questions difficult *if you prepare properly*. Every phase of the test is covered adequately in this book. Use the book systematically and you will be amazed (when you take the actual test) at the ease with which you will be able to answer the questions.

The difficulty level of the actual High School Diploma Test is 12th grade—for the *Preliminary* High School Diploma Tests in this book, it is 8th grade.

Put yourself under strict examination conditions while you take the Sample Tests. Allow yourself exactly one hour of working time for each Sample subtest—five hours for the entire battery of tests in each Sample examination. Take a break between one part of the test and another. See the timetable for the exact time that you are to spend on each part of the test.

Tolerate no interruptions while you are taking a Sample Test. Work in a steady manner. Do not spend too much time on any one question. If a question seems too hard, go to the next one. If time permits, go back to the omitted questions provided they are in the same section.

Do not place too much emphasis on speed. The examiners give you enough time so that you don't have to worry about finishing on time. Accuracy and correctness are far more important than speed on the test. Use the Answer Sheet provided just before each Sample Test. These Answer Sheets are very much like the kind that they give you on the actual High School Diploma Test.

NOW PLEASE GET TO WORK!

There is no time limit for the completion of your work in this book. It depends entirely on you: how faithfully you follow the plan of the book—how much time and effort you devote to each section. Most people take three to six months to complete the work outlined in the book. Some take longer. Just be sure that you do a good job!

ABOUT STUDYING

"Overlearning" rather than last minute "cramming" is the best way to study.

Students find it very tempting to stop work when they have once gone over the material before them and feel they have understood it. This is all wrong because of the rapidity with which memory impressions are bound to fade.

Go over the work quickly once more — drive it in and clinch it.

Most students who complain that they don't know how to concentrate deserve no sympathy. Concentration is merely habit and ought to be as readily acquired as any other habit. The way to begin to study is simply to begin.

Don't wait for inspiration or for the mood to strike you, nor should you permit yourself to indulge in thoughts like, "This chapter is too long" or "I guess I could really let that go until some other time."

That type of attitude throws an extra load on your mental machinery, and by making you work against a handicap, makes it harder for you to commence.

Reading aloud is a good device for those whose minds begin to wander while studying. Articulating "sub-vocally" for a few moments is another tonic for drifting thoughts. If this doesn't work you should write down the point or item or principle you happen to be dealing with when your mind "goes off track."

Do your studying alone, and you'll find it much easier to concentrate. If you are certain you need help on doubtful or difficult points, check these points and list them; you can go back or ask about them later. In the meantime, proceed to the next point.

A "little tenseness" is a good thing because it helps you keep alert while studying. Do without smoking, or newspapers or magazines or novels which may lead you into temptation. Studying in one place all the time also helps.

Boiling it all down, the greatest asset for effective studying is plain, garden variety "common sense" and will power.

Comprehension of the general principles of the course will make the remainder of your review easier. During the jig-saw puzzle craze of a few years ago, the people who put their puzzles together most easily were those who first put together the border. When the interlocking border was once assembled completely, the other pieces practically fell into place. Reviewing is analogous. Once you have found the frame within which you can put your facts, you will find that they tend to slip in readily wherever they belong. There will be a place for everything, and everything will be in its place. You will see each fact in relation to the whole, and not as something isolated and unconnected.

To pass the English and Mathematics tests you will need some detailed knowledge. Ability to comprehend the printed page readily and easily is all that is required for the Social Studies, Natural Science and Literature tests. You will notice that this book gives a great deal of emphasis to the subject of "understanding what you read." The book is modelled on the examination, which devotes three entire sections to this type of testing.

Actually, if you have been a constant reader of newspapers, books, or magazines, you should be able to pass the High School Equivalency Test with this simple brush-up course. Subconsciously you will have picked up most of the knowledge which you ordinarily would have obtained from a formal high school course.

There are no questions about subjunctive mood or passive voice. You will not be required to conjugate a verb. But you will be required to know correct usage, correct spelling, the correct punctuation. This book can help with all that.

The Science test requires no pin-point knowledge of leverage or the scarce chemicals and their properties. If you can read the science section of your newspaper or Time Magazine and can understand what the articles are about, you will be able to pass this section of the test. Of course, any readings in elementary scientific subjects will be helpful, not only because they will give you basic background for understanding these sections, but also because they will give you practice with scientific terminology and material.

Similarly, the Equivalency Test will not require you to know the minor dates in history or the theory of comparative costs. If you have followed the newspapers, if you understand the basic problems of the day—the United Nations, immigration, democracy, labor and monopolies, civil rights, etc., you will have little difficulty in understanding the reading materials which are offered in this section. The best preparation you can have is a thorough reading of a good newspaper and a good news magazine for several months. If you can follow the articles and editorials, if you get to understand them, you are preparing for your Equivalency Test in the best possible way.

HOW TO BE A 'COOL' TEST TAKER

1. The best method of preparing for the examination is to do your work conscientiously day by day. It is best to prepare for any test long before the test. Just-before-the-test cramming is a fair help for most fact tests, but tends to clutter up your mind for problem solving. Get your extra study in at least two weeks before the test. Intensive last-minute cramming for the examination will do you little good and is not recommended.

You cannot hope to win a high rating by being only a casual and indifferent reader and then cramming hard the week before the examination. It will not be that kind of a test.

2. Prepare yourself factually. Review the material in a different way than you learned it originally, at least 48 hours before the examination. Memorize first the outline of the subject matter for this will serve to remind you of further details.

3. Prepare yourself physically for an exam. Get a good night's sleep before the test, and take a nap before an important afternoon test. Eat a light, easily digested meal before an exam. Avoid rushing this meal, and relax after it.

4. Prepare yourself emotionally before you take an examination. A certain amount of concern is important, but excessive worry saps your mental energy and keeps you from getting the best grade you can. You should approach any examination as a game, confident that you can handle it.

Why be the frightened kind of student who enters the examination chamber in a mental coma? A test taken under mental stress does not provide a fair measure of your ability. At the very least, this book will remove for you some of the fear and mystery that surrounds examinations.

5. At the examination, read the directions for each part carefully. If you skip over instructions or read them carelessly, you may overlook the main idea of an entire section of questions and thereby lose credit for all of it.

Similarly, read each question carefully.

Be sure you have clearly in mind exactly what is called for before you attempt to answer the question.

6. During the examination, budget your time so that you will be able to complete the examination in the time allowed. Although the test will stress accuracy more than speed, it will be important for you to work steadily.

7. Your score in the examination will be the number of questions you answer correctly. Therefore, answer every question to the best of your judgment. In answering questions about which you are not entirely sure, thoughtful consideration will often help you make a sound choice.

Should you guess, if you are not sure of the answers?

The answer depends on how unsure you are.

In scoring, your wrong answers are deducted from your right answers. This is aimed at offsetting haphazard guessing.

But if you know that one or two of the options offered must be wrong, your chances of selecting the right answer is improved so it may be wise to take a chance.

8. Since time is an important element in your test, it is important that you use every minute effectively, working as rapidly as you can without losing accuracy. If you come to a question which is too difficult, skip it and go on to the next question. If you have time, you may come back to the questions which you omit.

Answer the questions in order, but do not waste time over one or two questions which seem to be especially difficult for you. If you cannot decide on the answer you wish to make to a particular question within a reasonable time, skip that question for the time being and come back to it again when you have completed the examination.

If you complete a section of the test before time is called, it would be wise for you to go back and reconsider any questions about which you were not certain at first.

9. Do not become worried or discouraged if the examination seems difficult to you. The questions in the various fields will purposely be made difficult and searching so that the examination will discriminate effectively.

Remember that if the examination seems difficult to you, it may be even more difficult for your neighbor.

You may find that some sections of this book are difficult and that some sections of the tests you have to take are difficult. It is important not to lose your sense of perspective, not to get panicky. Remember that most tests are "competitive" — that the score is based on what all those who take the test do with the questions. If a test is difficult for you, it is probably difficult for all those who are taking it. The number of questions you get right or wrong is only a raw score which will be translated to a percentile score by comparison with the score of the others taking the test.

On the other hand do not be misled by the comparatively easy questions at the beginning of the test. Tests are usually designed so that the questions grow increasingly difficult. This allows the poorer student to complete as many questions as he is able to answer. Many tests are designed so that practically no one can get a perfect score, and an average score may have only 50 per cent of the questions answered correctly. Many have more questions than anyone can possibly answer. In such tests, speed is usually one of the important factors in your score.

To achieve a passing mark or grade on each of the examinations, it's *not* necessary for the candidate to be able to answer correctly as many questions as he would be required to answer on an ordinary examination. The mark or grade given the candidate is determined by comparing the results with the results attained by a very large group of high school seniors. *Consequently, candidates should do their best and not be discouraged by seeming difficulties of any of the examination items.* There is no way for a candidate to judge whether or not he is accomplishing a satisfactory mark. Attention is called to the fact that over 60% of the candidates pass the examination. This percentage demonstrates the ability of self-educated adults to receive a satisfactory score.

HOW TO BE A MASTER TEST TAKER

It's really quite simple. Do things right . . . right from the beginning. Make successful methods a habit by practicing them on all the exercises in this book. Before you're finished you will have invested a good deal of time. Make sure you get the largest dividends from this investment.

SCORING PAPERS BY MACHINE

A typical machine-scored answer sheet is shown below, reduced from the actual size of 8¼ x 11 inches. Since it's the only one that reaches the office where papers are scored, it's important that the blanks at the top be filled in completely and correctly.

The chances are very good that you'll have to mark your answers on one of these sheets. Consequently, we've made it possible for you to practice with them throughout this book.

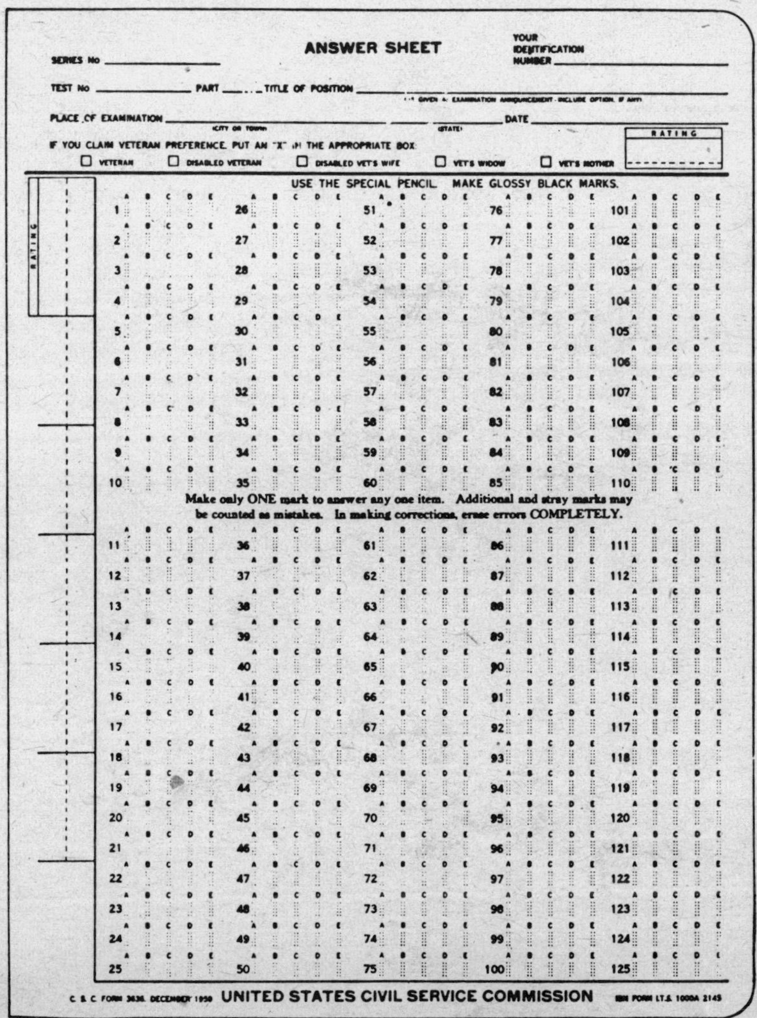

FOLLOW DIRECTIONS CAREFULLY

It's an obvious rule, but more people fail for breaching it than for any other cause. By actual count there are over a hundred types of directions given on tests. You'll familiarize yourself with all of them in the course of this book. And you'll also learn not to let your guard down in reading them, listening to them, and following them. Right now, before you plunge in, we want to be sure that you have nothing to fear from the answer sheet and the way in which you must mark it; from the most important question forms and the ways in which they are to be answered.

HERE'S HOW TO MARK YOUR ANSWERS ON MACHINE-SCORED ANSWER SHEETS:

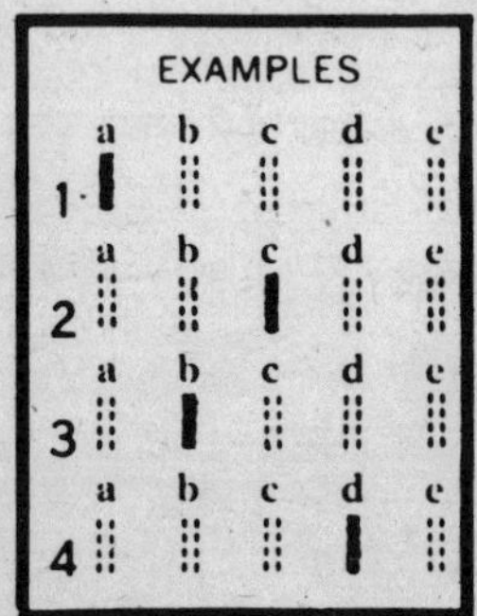

**Make only ONE mark for each answer. Additional and stray marks may be counted as mistakes.
In making corrections, erase errors COMPLETELY.
Make glossy black marks.**

(a) Each pencil mark must be heavy and black. Light marks should be retraced with the special pencil.

(b) Each mark must be in the space between the pair of dotted lines and entirely fill this space.

(c) All stray pencil marks on the paper, clearly not intended as answers, must be completely erased.

(d) Each question must have only one answer indicated. If multiple answers occur, all extraneous marks should be thoroughly erased. Otherwise, the machine will give you *no* credit for your correct answer.

MULTIPLE CHOICE METHODS

Multiple choice questions are very popular these days with examiners. The chances are good that you'll get this kind on your test. So we've arranged that you practice with them in the following pages. But first we want to give you a little help by explaining the best methods for handling this question form.

You know, of course, that these questions offer you four or five possible answers, that your job is to select *only* the *best* answer, and that even the incorrect answers are frequently *partly* correct. These partly-true choices are inserted to force you to think . . . and prove that you know the right answer.

USE THESE METHODS TO ANSWER MULTIPLE CHOICE QUESTIONS CORRECTLY:

1. Read the item closely to see what the examiner is after. Reread it if necessary.

2. Mentally reject answers that are clearly wrong.

3. Suspect as being wrong any of the choices which contain broad statements hinging on "cue" words like

absolute
absolutely
all
always
axiomatic
categorical
completely
doubtless
entirely
extravagantly
forever
immeasurably
inalienable
incontestable
incontrovertible
indefinitely
indisputable
indubitable
inevitable
inexorable
infallible
infinite
inflexible

inordinately
irrefutable
inviolable
never
only
peculiarly
positive
quite
self-evident
sole
totally
unchallenged
unchangeable
undeniable
undoubtedly
unequivocal
unexceptionable
unimpeachable
unqualified
unquestionable
wholly
without exception

If you're unsure of the meanings of any of these words, look them up in your dictionary.

4. A well-constructed multiple choice item will avoid obviously incorrect choices. The good examiner will try to write a cluster of answers, all of which are plausible. Use the clue words to help yourself pick the *most* correct answer.

5. In the case of items where you are doubtful of the answer, you might be able to bring to bear the information you have gained from previous study. This knowledge might be sufficient to indicate that some of the suggested answers are not so plausible. Eliminate such answers from further consideration.

6. Then concentrate on the remaining suggested answers. The more you eliminate in this way, the better your chances of getting the item right.

7. If the item is in the form of an incomplete statement, it sometimes helps to try to complete the statement before you look at the suggested answers. Then see whether the way you have completed the statement corresponds with any of the answers provided. If one is found, it is likely to be the correct one.

8. Use your head! Make shrewd inferences. Sometimes with a little thought, and the information that you have, you can reason out the answer. We're suggesting a method of intelligent guessing in which you can become quite expert with a little practice. It's a useful method that may help you with some debatable answers.

NOW, LET'S TRY THESE METHODS OUT ON A SAMPLE MULTIPLE-CHOICE QUESTION.

1. Leather is considered the best material for shoes chiefly because
   (A) it is waterproof
   (B) it is quite durable
   (C) it is easily procurable
   (D) it is flexible and durable
   (E) it can be easily manufactured in various styles.

Here we see that every one of the answer statements is plausible: leather is waterproof if treated properly; it is relatively durable; it is relatively easily procurable; it bends and is shaped easily, and is, again, durable; it constantly appears in various styles of shoes and boots.

However, we must examine the question with an eye toward identifying the key phrase which is: *best* for shoes *chiefly*.

Now we can see that (A) is incorrect because leather is probably not the *best* material for shoes, simply because it is waterproof. There are far better waterproof materials available, such as plastics and rubber. In fact, leather must be treated to make it waterproof. So by analyzing the key phrase of the question we can eliminate (A).

(B) seems plausible. Leather is durable, and durability is a good quality in shoes. But the word *quite* makes it a broad statement. And we become suspicious. The original meaning of *quite* is completely, wholly, entirely. Since such is the case we must reject this choice because leather is *not completely* durable. It does wear out.

(C) Leather is comparatively easy to procure; but would that make it *best* for shoes? And would that be the *chief* reason why it is used for making shoes? Although the statement in itself is quite true, it does not fit the key phrase of the question and we must, reluctantly, eliminate it.

(D) is a double-barreled statement. One part, the durability, has been suggested in (B) above. Leather is also quite flexible, so both parts of the statement would seem to fit the question.

(E) It is true that leather can be manufactured in various styles, but so can many other materials. Again, going back to the key phrase, this could be considered one, but not the *chief* reason why it is *best* for shoes.

So, by carefully analyzing the *key* phrase of the question we have narrowed our choices down to (D). Although we rejected (B) we did recognize that durability is a good quality in shoes, but only one of several. Since flexibility is also a good quality, we have no hesitation in choosing (D) as the correct answer.

The same question, by slightly altering the answer choices, can also call for a *negative* response. Here, even more so, the identification of the key phrase becomes vital in finding the correct answer. Suppose the question and its responses were worded thus:

2. Leather is considered the best material for shoes chiefly because
   (A) it is waterproof
   (B) it is easily colored
   (C) it is easily procurable
   (D) it can easily be manufactured in various styles
   (E) none of these.

We can see that the prior partially correct answer (B) has now been changed, and the doubly-correct answer eliminated. Instead we have a new response possibility (E), "none of these."

We have analyzed three of the choices previously and have seen the reason why none of them is the *chief* reason why leather is considered the *best* material for shoes. The two new elements are (B) "easily colored," and (E) "none of these."

If you think about it, leather *can* be easily colored and often is, but this would not be the chief reason why it is considered *best*. Many other materials are just as easily dyed. So we must come to the conclusion that *none* of the choices is *completely* correct—none fit the key phrase. Therefore, the question calls for a negative response (E).

We have now seen how important it is to identify the key phrase. Equally, or perhaps even more important, is the identifying and analyzing of the key *word*—the qualifying word—in a question. This is usually, though not always, an adjective or adverb. Some of the key words to watch for are: *most, best, least, highest, lowest, always, never, sometimes, most likely, greatest, smallest, tallest, average, easiest, most nearly, maximum, minimum, chiefly, mainly, only, but* and *or*. Identifying these key words is usually half the battle in understanding and, consequently, answering all types of exam questions.

Rephrasing the Question

It is obvious, then, that by carefully analyzing a question, by identifying the key phrase and its key words, you can usually find the correct answer by logical deduction and, often, by elimination. One other way of examining, or "dissecting," a question is to restate or rephrase it with each of the suggested answer choices integrated into the question.

For example, we can take the same question and rephrase it.
(A) The chief reason why leather is considered the best material for shoes is that it is waterproof.
or
(A) Because it is waterproof, leather is considered the best material for shoes.
or
(A) Chiefly because it is waterproof, leather is considered the best material for shoes.

It will be seen from the above three new versions of the original statement and answer that the question has become less obscure because it has been, so to speak, illuminated from different angles. It becomes quite obvious also in this rephrasing that the statement (A) is incorrect, although the *original* phrasing of the question left some doubt.

The rules for understanding and analyzing the key phrase and key words in a question, and the way to identify the *one* correct answer by means of intelligent analysis of the important question-answer elements, are basic to the solution of all the problems you will face on your test.

In fact, perhaps the *main* reason for failing an examination is failure to *understand the question*. In many cases, examinees *do* know the answer to a particular problem, but they cannot answer correctly because they do not understand it.

METHODS FOR MATCHING QUESTIONS

In this question form you are actually faced with multiple questions that require multiple answers. It's a difficult form in which you are asked to pair up one set of facts with another. It can be used with any type of material . . . vocabulary, spatial relations, numbers, facts, etc.

A typical matching question might appear in this form:

Directions: Below is a set of words containing ten words numbered 1 to 10, and twenty other words divided into five groups labeled Group A to Group E. For each of the numbered words select the word in one of the five groups which is most nearly the same in meaning. The letter of that group is the answer for that numbered item.

Although this arrangement is a relatively simple one for a "matching" question, the general principle is the same for all levels of difficulty. Basically, this type of question consists of two columns. The elements of one of the columns must be matched with some or all of the elements of the second column.

1. fiscal	**Group A**
2. deletion	indication ambiguous
	excruciating thin
3. equivocal	**Group B**
4. corroboration	confirmation financial
5. tortuous	phobia erasure
6. predilection	**Group C**
7. sallow	fiduciary similar
	yellowish skill
8. virtuosity	**Group D**
9. scion	theft winding
	receive procrastination
10. tenuous	**Group E**
	franchise heir
	hardy preference

Correct Answers

1. B	4. B	6. E	8. C
2. B	5. D	7. C	9. E
3. A			10. A

There are numerous ways in which these questions may be composed, from the simple one shown above to the most difficult type of arrangement. In many cases the arrangement of the question may be so complicated that more time may be spent upon the comprehension of the instructions than on the actual question. This again, points up the importance of fully and quickly understanding the instructions before attempting to solve any problem or answer any question.

Several general principles apply, however, when solving a matching question. Work with one column at a time and match each item of that column against all the items in the second column, skipping around that second column looking for a proper match. Put a thin pencil line through items that are matched so they won't interfere with your later selections. (This is particularly important in a test that tells you to choose any item only once. The test gets real tricky, however, when you are asked to choose an item more than once.)

Match each item very carefully—don't mark it unless you are certain—because if you have to change any one, it may mean changing three or four or more, and that may get you hopelessly confused. After you have marked all your *certain* choices, go over the unmarked items again and make a *good* guess at the remaining items, if you have time.

USE CONTROLLED ASSOCIATION when you come to an item which you are not able to match. Attempt to recall any and all facts you might have concerning this item. Through the process of association, a fact recalled might provide a clue to the answer.

TRUE-FALSE TACTICS

True-false questions may appear on your test. Because they are easier to answer they are used less frequently than multiple-choice questions. However, because examiners find that they are easier to prepare, here are some suggestions to help you answer them correctly.

I. Suspect the truth of broad statements hinging on those *all or nothing* "cue" words we listed for you in discussing multiple-choice questions.

II. Watch out for "spoilers" . . . the word or phrase which negates an otherwise true statement.
Vegetation is sparse on the Sahara desert where the climate is hot and humid.   T F

III. Statements containing such modifiers as *generally, usually, most,* and similar words are usually true.

IV. If the scoring formula is "Rights minus Wrongs", don't guess. If you know it's true, mark it T. If you don't know it's true, ask yourself "What have I learned that would make it false?" If you can think of nothing on either side, omit the answer. Of course, if the R-W formula is not being used it is advisable to guess if you're not sure of an answer.

V. Your first hunch is usually best. Unless you have very good reason to do so, don't change your first answer to true-false questions about which you are doubtful.

Single-Statement Question

The basic form of true-false question is the "single-statement" question; i.e., a sentence that contains a single thought, such as:

1. The Statue of Liberty is in New York
         T   F

The same statement becomes slightly more difficult by including a negative element

2. The Statue of Liberty is not in New York
         T   F

or, more subtly:
3. The Statue of Liberty is not in Chicago
         T   F

or, by adding other modifiers:
4. The Statue of Liberty is sometimes in New York   T   F

5. The Statue of Liberty is always in New York   T   F

Even from these very simple and basic examples of a "single-statement" true-false question it can be seen that a *complete understanding* of the subject area as well as of the phrasing of the question is essential before you attempt to answer it. Careless or hasty reading of the statment will often make you miss the *key* word, especially if the question appears to be a very simple one.

An important point to remember when answering this type of question is that the statement must be *entirely true* to be answered as "true"; if even just a *part* of it is false, the answer must be marked "false."

Composite-Statement Question

Sometimes a true-false question will be in the form of a "composite statement," a statement that contains more than one thought, such as:

6. The Statue of Liberty is in New York, and Chicago is in Illinois   T F

Some basic variations of this type of composite-statement question are these:

7. The Statue of Liberty is in New York, and Chicago is in Michigan   T F
8. The Statue of Liberty is not in New York and Chicago is in Illinois   T F
9. The Statue of Liberty is not in New York and Chicago is in Michigan   T F

Of the four questions above, only question 6 is true. Each of the other statements (7 , 8 , 9), is false because each contains at least *one* element that is false.

It can be seen from the above that in a composite statement *both* elements, or "substatements," must be true in order for the answer to be "true." Otherwise, the answer must be "false."

This principle goes for all composite statements that are, or can be, connected by the word "and," even if the various "thoughts" of the statement seem to be entirely unrelated.

We have seen how to handle a composite statement that consists of *unrelated* substatements. Finally, we will examine a composite true-false statement which consists of *related* elements:

10. The Golden Gate Bridge is in San Francisco, which is not the capital of California.   T F
11. The Golden Gate Bridge is in San Francisco, the capital of California.   T F
12. The Golden Gate Bridge is not in San Francisco, the capital of California.   T F
13. The Golden Gate Bridge is not in San Francisco, which is not the capital of California.   T F

Again, only the first composite statement (10) is true. All the rest are false because they contain at least one false substatement.

PART TWO

Practice With Model Tests

I. SAMPLE EXAM FOR PRACTICE

To begin your studies, test yourself now to see how you measure up. This examination is similar to the one you'll get, and is therefore a practical yardstick for charting your progress and planning your course. Adhere strictly to all test instructions. Mark yourself honestly and you'll find where your weaknesses are and where to concentrate your study.

The time allowed for the entire examination is 5 hours. In order to create the climate of the test to come, that's precisely what you should allow yourself . . . no more, no less. Use a watch and keep a record of your time, especially since you may find it convenient to take the test in several sittings.

In constructing this Examination we tried to visualize the questions you are *likely* to face on your actual exam. We included those subjects on which they are *probably* going to test you.

Although copies of past exams are not released, we were able to piece together a fairly complete picture of the forthcoming exam.

A principal source of information was our analysis of official announcements going back several years.

Critical comparison of these announcements, particularly the sample questions, revealed the testing trend; foretold the important subjects, and those that are likely to recur.

The questions on each Test are represented exactly on the special Answer Sheet provided. Mark your answers on this sheet. It's just about the way you'll have to do it on the real exam.

As a result you have an Examination which simulates the real one closely enough to provide you with important training.

Proceed through the entire exam without pausing after each Test. Remember that you are taking this Exam under actual battle conditions, and therefore you do not stop until told to do so by the proctor.

Certainly you should not lose time by trying to mark each Test as you complete it. You'll be able to score yourself fairly when time is up for the entire Exam.

Correct answers for all the questions in all the Tests of this Exam appear at the end of the Exam.

Don't cheat yourself by looking at these answers while taking the Exam. They are to be compared with your own answers *after* the time limit is up.

ANALYSIS AND FORECAST: SAMPLE EXAMS FOR PRACTICE

The timetable below is both an index to the practice tests and a preview of the actual exam. In constructing this examination, we have analyzed every available announcement and official statement about the exam and thus predict that this is what you may face.

It is well known that examiners like to experiment with various types of questions, so the test you take may be slightly different in form or content. However, we feel certain that if you have mastered each subject covered here, you will be well on your way to scoring high.

SUBJECT TESTED	Time Allowed
CORRECTNESS AND EFFECTIVENESS OF EXPRESSION ENGLISH USAGE SPELLING	1 hour
INTERPRETATION OF READING MATERIALS IN THE SOCIAL STUDIES SOCIAL STUDIES READINGS GRAPH AND TABLE INTERPRETATION	1 hour
INTERPRETATION OF READING MATERIALS IN THE NATURAL SCIENCES	1 hour
INTERPRETATION OF LITERARY MATERIALS	1 hour
GENERAL MATHEMATICAL ABILITY	1 hour

ANSWER SHEET FOR SAMPLE EXAMINATION I.

DIRECTIONS: For each question read all the choices carefully. Then select that answer which you consider correct or most nearly correct. Write the letter preceding your best choice next to the question. Should you want to answer on the kind of answer sheet used on machine-scored examinations, we have provided several such facsimiles. In machine-scored examinations, you should record all your answers on the answer sheet provided. Don't make the mistake of putting answers on the test booklet itself. On some machine-scored exams, you are instructed to "place no marks whatever on the test booklet." In other examinations you may be instructed to mark your answers in the test booklet. In such cases you should be careful that no other marks interfere with the legibility of your answers. Do NOT mark your booklet unless you are sure it is permitted. To help you understand multiple-choice procedure, the following sample item is given:

SAMPLE O: Columbus discovered America in

(A) 1066 (B) 1492 (C) 1509 (D) 1776 (E) 1942

Columbus discovered America in 1492, so the acceptable answer is shown on your answer sheet:

SAMPLE O   a   **b**   c   d   e

TEST I. CORRECTNESS AND EFFECTIVENESS OF EXPRESSION
PART A. ENGLISH USAGE

PART B. SPELLING

TEST II. INTERPRETATION OF READING MATERIALS IN THE SOCIAL STUDIES

PART A. SOCIAL STUDIES READINGS

PART B. GRAPH AND TABLE INTERPRETATION

1.____ 2.____ 3.____ 4.____ 5.____ 6.____ 7.____ 8.____
9.____ 10.____ 11.____ 12.____ 13.____ 14.____ 15.____ 16.____

TEST III. INTERPRETATION OF READING MATERIALS IN THE NATURAL SCIENCES

TEST IV. INTERPRETATION OF LITERARY MATERIALS

TEST V. GENERAL MATHEMATICAL ABILITY

TEST I. CORRECTNESS AND EFFECTIVENESS
OF EXPRESSION

TIME: 1 Hour

The emphasis in this test is upon ability to avoid errors in spelling, punctuation, capitalization, and grammatical usage. Consideration is also given to ability to choose the best words or phrases and to organize ideas in clear, well-balanced sentences.

PART A. ENGLISH USAGE

DIRECTIONS: Read each Theme through carefully to get the general meaning. Then go back and look at the underlined and numbered portions of the story. Some of the underlined words and phrases contain errors in grammar, punctuation or choice of words. Others are correct as written. Study the suggested corrections in the right-hand column and choose the one you think is best. All of the suggestions may be grammatically correct, but one is always more effective than the others.

THEME I.

Here is the story of a boy who <u>use to be</u> a clerk in a grocery store. One of the jobs <u>that come</u> his way <u>was</u> the arrangement of goods in the <u>store window</u>. The owner of the store <u>didn't hardly care</u> what the boy <u>done</u> as long as the window looked <u>neatly</u>. The boy realized that there was a chance

1. (A) NO CHANGE   (C) had used to be
    (B) used to be   (D) use to was

2. (A) NO CHANGE   (C) that came
    (B) which come   (D) which had came

3. (A) NO CHANGE   (C) we're
    (B) were   (D) was'

4. (A) NO CHANGE   (C) storewindow
    (B) store-window   (D) stores window

5. (A) NO CHANGE
    (B) didn't care hardly
    (C) hardly didn't care
    (D) hardly cared

6. (A) NO CHANGE   (C) did done
    (B) did   (D) had did

7. (A) NO CHANGE   (C) neat
    (B) neatlier   (D) neaty

to use what his <u>Art Teacher</u> <u>had learned</u> him in high school.

Instead of using paints and <u>brushes he</u> arranged fruits and vegetables, canned goods, and even bars of soap to make attractive displays. People <u>begun</u> to notice the <u>window, often</u> these same people entered the store to make <u>there</u> purchases. The manager <u>seen</u> that much of the new business was due to the fine windows and <u>give</u> the boy credit.

Now <u>many years</u> have gone by, and the boy <u>hisself</u> has became the manager of the store. He <u>don't</u> do any decorating <u>now, he</u> says, however, that he still needs his <u>art because</u> he must supervise the window displays and the counter arrangements.

THEME II.

Do you know <u>its not</u> necessary <u>to always travel</u> to <u>distant lands</u> to <u>bring back</u> things of scientific

8. (A) NO CHANGE   (C) Art teacher
   (B) art Teacher   (D) art teacher

9. (A) NO CHANGE   (C) teached
   (B) learned   (D) had taught

10. (A) NO CHANGE   (C) brushes; he
   (B) brushes, he   (D) brushes. He

11. (A) NO CHANGE   (C) had began
   (B) began   (D) begin

12. (A) NO CHANGE   (C) window. Often
   (B) window often   (D) window: often

13. (A) NO CHANGE   (C) they're
   (B) their   (D) the'ir

14. (A) NO CHANGE   (C) seed
   (B) was sawing   (D) saw

15. (A) NO CHANGE   (C) gived
   (B) gave   (D) had gived

16. (A) NO CHANGE   (C) many years'
   (B) much years   (D) years by the many

17. (A) NO CHANGE   (C) his own self
   (B) himself   (D) him self

18. (A) NO CHANGE   (C) dont
   (B) do not   (D) doesn't

19. (A) NO CHANGE   (C) now he says
   (B) now: he says   (D) now. He says

20. (A) NO CHANGE   (C) art. Because
   (B) art on account of   (D) art, because

21. (A) NO CHANGE   (C) it's not
   (B) it isnt   (D) it ain't

22. (A) NO CHANGE
   (B) to travel
   (C) always to travel
   (D) to always go traveling

23. (A) NO CHANGE   (C) distant land's
   (B) lands of distance   (D) distance lands

24. (A) NO CHANGE   (C) bring
   (B) take back   (D) take

value? Right here in the good old <u>USA</u> you can
25

find hidden treasures. Not every inch of space in

<u>our'</u> country has been <u>explored, there</u> are some
26   27

spots still unknown to <u>American's</u>. Consider the
28

Atlantic seaboard and the <u>Mississippi valley</u> where
29

there are beautiful <u>wild-birds</u> never before seen by
30

man.

25. (A) NO CHANGE
    (B) U.S.A.
    (C) US
    (D) United states of America

26. (A) NO CHANGE   (C) ourn
    (B) our   (D) ou'r

27. (A) NO CHANGE (C) explored there
    (B) explored; There (D) explored. There

28. (A) NO CHANGE (C) men of America
    (B) Americans   (D) American Citizens

29. (A) NO CHANGE
    (B) Mississippi-valley
    (C) Mississippi Valley
    (D) Mississippi's Valley

30. (A) NO CHANGE   (C) Wildbirds
    (B) wildbirds   (D) wild birds

END OF PART

*Go on to the next Test in the Examination, just as you would do
on the actual exam. Check your answers when you have completed
the entire Examination. The correct answers for this Test, and
all the other Tests, are assembled at the conclusion of this
Examination.*

TEST I. CORRECTNESS AND EFFECTIVENESS
OF EXPRESSION

PART B. SPELLING

DIRECTIONS: In this test all words but one of each group are spelled correctly. Indicate the misspelled word in each group.

	(A)	(B)	(C)	(D)
1.	afterwards	account	chocalate	machinery
2.	canal	generaly	obey	scenery
3.	tomatoe	seldom	pavement	oxygen
4.	fortunate	abscence	lowest	mailman
5.	bullet	fraction	marraige	kindness
6.	weave	strenghth	particular	thrifty
7.	umberella	tractor	tardy	parties
8.	apartment	discovary	industries	mystery
9.	grazing	fairyland	ninetey	Capitol
10.	fluffy	literature	intestines	acurate
11.	girraffe	empire	caterpillar	laboratory
12.	product	vapor	discription	precious
13.	snowey	schoolroom	trout	wreck
14.	surounded	unknown	wolves	stationery
15.	adjective	bakeing	independence	happiest
16.	investigate	lemon	mansion	apointment
17.	vitamins	traffic	prizoner	occupied
18.	sister's	penmenship	showing	weighed
19.	instrument	likely	fireworks	aquainted
20.	ambulence	gallon	colonist	advertisement

TEST II. INTERPRETATION OF READING MATERIALS
IN THE SOCIAL STUDIES

TIME: 1 Hour

PART A. SOCIAL STUDIES READINGS

This test measures ability to read with understanding and to evaluate critically reading selections concerning social, political, economic, and cultural problems and issues. Since ability to evaluate depends upon a person's background in a field, the test indirectly measures the individual's understanding of ideas and knowledge of the social studies.

DIRECTIONS: Below each of the following passages of social science reading material you will find one or more incomplete statements about the passage. Select the words or expressions that most satisfactorily complete each statement in accordance with the meaning of the paragraph.

Reading Passage I

It is only within the last twenty years that any sizable number of Latin-American children have been able to go to school. Education was reserved for the upper-income groups, and poverty and widespread disease hampered efforts to extend it to others. With the democratic movements of more recent years, however, Latin Americans have been giving more attention to education. In most of the nations, control and administration rest in the central government. All elementary education is free and supposedly compulsory. But rural schools usually have only two- or three-year courses and for the most part are one-room schools with only one teacher. Many regions have no schools at all. The city elementary schools have from five to seven grades and are often conducted in buildings rented from private owners. Mexico has made strenuous efforts to improve rural education, Colombia to extend adult education and Chile to improve normal schools. The secondary schools offer courses ranging from four to six years. Until recently they have acted as professional schools. Now, however, they are putting more emphasis on training for trade and industry. Education of the Indians, much neglected in Latin America, is being pushed in Mexico, Peru and Guatemala. In Bolivia the Indians in two provinces have financed schools themselves. Latin America has sixty-seven universities, of which only seventeen are privately controlled. The University of Mexico and that of San Marcos at Lima, Peru, are both older than Harvard by nearly a century.

1. The best of the following titles for this paragraph is:
   (A) Universities in Latin America
   (B) Education of Indians
   (C) Education in Latin America
   (D) Compulsory education
   (E) Stamping out illiteracy

2. Forty years ago Latin-American schools were reserved for children of
   (A) Indians   (C) laborers
   (B) peasants   (D) sailors
         (E) well-to-do people

3. The writer says that the spread of education has been hampered by
   (A) superstition
   (B) disease
   (C) government opposition
   (D) illiteracy
   (E) railroads

4. The total number of universities in Latin America is
   (A) 6   (C) 17
   (B) 2   (D) 20
         (E) 67

5. The University of Mexico was founded
   (A) 17 years ago   (C) 67 years ago
   (B) 20 years ago   (D) 100 years ago
         (E) centuries ago

Reading Passage II

Compared with the world's larger nations, Italy is very small. The whole land area could be tucked into the borders of California, with plenty of room to spare. And yet Italy has a population of 45,-000,000. Shaped like a boot, the country is 760 miles long and, at most points, only 100 to 150 miles wide.

Italy is practically cut off from the rest of Europe. In the north, she is separated from her neighbors—France, Switzerland, Germany, and Yugoslavia—by a towering arc of mountain chains. On the south, east, and west, she is surrounded by water.

Most of Italy—two thirds to be exact—is mountainous. In addition to the Alps in the north, there are the Apennines running almost the entire length of the peninsula. This chain is cut across by highly fertile river valleys.

Italy has only one region of plains, in the north, hemmed in between the Alps and the Apennines and watered by the Po and Adige rivers. This "Plain of Lombardy" is the richest farm region and is equal in size to Vermont and New Hampshire combined.

The climate of Italy is similar to that of Florida and California, except that the winter is likely to be colder in northern Italy than in the northern part of either of these states.

The tourist to Italy is surprised at the full use to which the Italians put their soil. Crowded as they are in a small area, they can not afford to let any land go to waste. They are good farmers. Along the silt-enriched banks of rivers, in the valleys and northern plains region, they have cultivated every inch of ground they can. They have cut terraces into the mountainsides. Nearly half the population lives on the soil.

6. The title that best expresses the main theme or subject of this selection is:
   (A) The climate of Italy
   (B) Italy and the rest of Europe
   (C) Good farmers
   (D) Agriculture and geography of Italy
   (E) Tourists in Italy

7. In shape Italy is
   (A) longer than she is wide
   (B) 760 miles across and 150 miles long
   (C) wider than she is long
   (D) wider and longer than California
   (E) almost square

8. A fact stated by the writer about Italy is that
   (A) there is no region of plains
   (B) natural boundaries separate her almost completely from her neighbors
   (C) very few of her citizens cultivate the soil
   (D) she is underpopulated
   (E) she is one of the larger nations

9. The Apennines are
   (A) river valleys   (C) mountains
   (B) peninsulas   (D) tourists
         (E) plains

10. Winter in northern Italy is
    (A) warmer than that of California
    (B) colder than that of Florida
    (C) similar to that of New Hampshire
    (D) comparable to that of Switzerland
    (E) longer than that of Vermont

11. The Italians show that they are good farmers by
    (A) surprising tourists
    (B) being isolated from Europe
    (C) cultivating the valleys only
    (D) living on mountains
    (E) making full use of their soil

Reading Passage III

On the population map of the world the tropical deserts are shown as great blank spaces; yet they have contributed many things to our lives. When you step into a store to buy a box of dates, you are buying the sunshine and the dryness of the oases of the Sahara, Arabia, Mesopotamia or the Coachella Valley. A lettuce salad or fresh peas for dinner in winter represent the work of an irrigation farmer in the Salt River Valley or the Imperial Valley. The fine broadcloth shirt or balloon-cloth dress which you received on your birthday was made of silky, long-fibered cotton either from the Imperial Valley or from Egypt. Your half-wool and half-cotton sweater may contain Australian wool and Peruvian cotton—both steppe and desert products.

These are only a few of the physical contributions which the tropical deserts make to our daily lives. In addition they have made important cultural contributions. Our number system is from Arabia. The desert people developed irrigation. The necessity of measuring water and noting land boundaries after the Nile floods led to surveying and the development of mathematics and engineering. The desert people studied the stars so that they could find their way at night across the limitless expanses of the desert; in this way they became our early astronomers.

12. The population of the deserts of the world is
    (A) scant   (C) starving
    (B) dense   (D) large
            (E) unfriendly

13. Some products of the Imperial Valley mentioned in the paragraph are
    (A) dates
    (B) wool and cotton
    (C) borax and wool
    (D) cotton and lettuce
    (E) nitrates

14. Balloon cloth is made
    (A) of silk
    (B) of cotton
    (C) of wool
    (D) partly of cotton
    (E) partly of wool

15. Surveying was developed because people needed to
    (A) determine land boundaries after floods
    (B) find their way across the desert at night
    (C) have some means of irrigation
    (D) learn a number system
    (E) study the stars

16. Culturally, the deserts have
    (A) been of no value
    (B) contributed several important sciences and processes
    (C) not influenced our lives
    (D) been retarded by the Nile floods
    (E) been blank spaces

17. The early astronomers used stars to guide them across
    (A) seas   (C) forests
    (B) rivers   (D) deserts
            (E) mountains

Reading Passage IV

The Mohawk Valley has not always been the same as it is now. Geologists say that some 10,000 or more years ago the region was covered with a huge glacier or river of ice flowing slowly south from Canada. This river was split by the Adirondacks into two main streams, one following the Champlain and Hudson Valleys and the other going westward toward the Great Lakes. The first of these main streams split again near Cohoes, sending one branch southward toward the sea and the other up the Mohawk Valley. The other main stream also divided, one branch going into the Great Lakes basin and the second swinging around to meet the Mohawk Valley branch near Little Falls. During the slow process of melting under a changing climate, perhaps over thousands of years, the ice deposited its trapped rocks and dirt and in some cases made dams, which in turn formed lakes. As the water rose, it cut its way through the earth deposits and linked up the lakes with rivers along the slopes. One of these glacial lakes was Lake Albany, which extended to north of the Hoosick River. The Mohawk River at that time had a delta at Schenectady, and the deposits of that delta remain in what is now known as the Sand Plains. As the level of Lake Albany fell, the route of the Mohawk, which once ran along the northern edge of the Helderberg cliffs, gradually changed to its present channel. The ice and water to the west hewed the pass through the southernmost spur of the Adirondacks at Little Falls deeper and deeper, until it became the lowest-level pass through the whole Allegheny mountain system. The fact that it *is* the lowest pass made the Erie Canal and the Barge Canal possible and also had a tremendous effect on railroading. Through the Western Gateway at Schenectady up through the gap at Little Falls to the great plains beyond the Great Lakes and the Mississippi have gone thousands and thousands of people to settle the great inland empire of America.

18. The title that best expresses the main theme or subject of this selection is:
    (A) How the Mohawk River changed its channel
    (B) Glacial lakes and rivers
    (C) The influence of the Mohawk Valley on history
    (D) The importance of New York State waterways
    (E) Geographic development of the Mohawk region

19. Changes in the geography of the Mohawk Valley were largely due to
    (A) the melting of the ice sheet
    (B) the snow in the Adirondacks
    (C) the overflow of Lake Albany
    (D) the number of lakes
    (E) the nearness of the Helderberg mountains

20. The Sand Plains owe their existence to deposits made by the
    (A) Mohawk River   (C) Hudson River
    (B) Great Lakes   (D) Erie Canal
           (E) Hoosick River

21. The Western Gateway is
    (A) in Canada   (D) at Little Falls
    (B) on the Great Lakes   (E) at Schenectady
    (C) at Albany

Reading Passage V

The rebirth of politics in Europe has brought two political terms prominently into the news—"Left" and "Right." Readers might be interested in knowing the source of those terms. At one time during the French Revolution, when the revolutionary assembly moved into new quarters, it happened quite by chance that those who thought the revolution had gone far enough occupied the seats which were at the right as they faced the chairman. Those who wanted to go further with the revolution sat over on the left, while moderates sat in the center. Since that time, it has been the custom in all of the parliaments on the continent of Europe for the more conservative forces to sit on the right, while the liberals or radicals or socialists, who want to modify the older forms of government, have occupied the seats on the left. This custom has given rise to the practice of calling conservative political parties "the Right" or "Rightist," and liberal or radical political parties "the Left," or "Leftist."

22. The title that best expresses the main theme or subject of this selection is:
    (A) Effect of the French Revolution
    (B) Modern politics
    (C) Origin of "Rightist" and "Leftist"
    (D) Parliamentary procedure
    (E) The type of government in Europe

23. The writer indicates that in Europe there is increased interest in
    (A) higher birth rates   (D) conservation
    (B) revolution   (E) socialism
    (C) politics

24. In the parliaments of Europe today the representatives who sit at the right are
    (A) conservatives   (D) radicals
    (B) moderates   (E) revolutionists
    (C) liberals

25. The present-day European representatives who occupy seats on the left are usually
    (A) wrong in their views
    (B) satisfied with conditions as they are
    (C) supporters of the head of the government
    (D) slow to change
    (E) in favor of change

END OF PART

Go on to the next Test in the Examination, just as you would do on the actual exam. Check your answers when you have completed the entire Examination. The correct answers for this Test, and all the other Tests, are assembled at the conclusion of this Examination.

TEST II. INTERPRETATION OF READING MATERIALS IN THE SOCIAL STUDIES

PART B. GRAPH AND TABLE INTERPRETATION

DIRECTIONS: All the questions in this test refer to the following chart. Read each question carefully and answer it on the basis of the chart. Select the best case and mark the correct letter on the answer sheet.

HOSPITAL CARE FOR PATIENTS

Case	Rent	Food	Shelter	Light	Fuel	Milk	Clothing	Household Supplies	Medical Care	Cod Liver Oil	Hospitalization	Fare	Cash Allowance
A	X	X	X		X		X				X		
B	X	X			X	X		X					
C		X		X		X		X	X	X			
D	X	X	X		X			X					
E			X	X			X		X			X	X
F		X			X		X		X				
G	X	X	X	X			X				X		
H	X		X				X					X	

Which case received:

1. Food, light, and hospitalization?

2. Medical service, shelter, clothing, and fuel?

3. Rent, food, shelter, fuel and household supplies?

4. Fuel, shelter, clothing, no hospitalization, but medical service?

5. Rent, shelter, no household supplies, no hospitalization, but fare?

6. Food, milk, household supplies, no fuel, but medical service?

7. Shelter, clothing, light, no cod liver oil, but medical service?

8. Shelter, clothing, no medical service, no cash allowance, but light?

9. Food, shelter, fuel, but no hospitalization?

10. Rent, fuel, milk, and household supplies?

TEST III. INTERPRETATION OF READING MATERIALS
IN THE NATURAL SCIENCES

TIME: 1 Hour

This test places a special emphasis on scientific vocabulary and ability to pay close attention to detail and logic. It consists of a selection of passages from the field of natural sciences at the high school level and a number of questions testing a persons's ability to comprehend and to interpret the content of each passage.

DIRECTIONS: Below each of the following passages of natural science reading material you will find one or more incomplete statements about the passage. Select the words or expressions that most satisfactorily complete each statement in accordance with the meaning of the paragraph.

Reading Passage I

Cyrus McCormick invented the first American reaper in 1831, but did not secure the patent on it until three years later. Meanwhile, in 1833, a Baltimore seaman named Obed Hussey was granted a patent for a reaping machine which was not so successful as McCormick's.

McCormick's work was aided greatly by the experiments of earlier inventors. In 1822, Henry Ogle invented a reaper in England; however, farm laborers feared that they would be thrown out of work, and public opinion prevented him from manufacturing it. Then, in 1826, the Reverend Patrick Bell, a Scotchman, combined the plans of earlier inventors and brought out a successful reaper. For this he was given a prize by the Scottish Agricultural Society. Some of the Bell reapers were brought to the United States, and it is quite probable that McCormick was acquainted with the machine. However, McCormick's invention was superior, and he deserves the credit he has received.

Others were working on models of reaping machines, and each one added new ideas. One of the first improvements was a device that raked the grain as the knives cut it. Another was a seat for the operator, and still another tied the grain into bundles. Throughout the 75 years which followed McCormick's invention, additional improvements made the reaping machine more efficient. Perhaps the most important was the gasoline tractor, which was attached to the reaper and propelled it, taking the place of the slower-moving horses.

1. The first American patent for a reaping machine was issued to
   (A) Obed Hussey
   (B) Henry Ogle
   (C) Reverend Patrick Bell
   (D) Cyrus McCormick
   (E) the Scottish Agricultural Society

2. Ogle's reaper was not manufactured because
   (A) people feared that it would cause unemployment
   (B) there was no seat for the operator
   (C) Ogle refused to join the Agricultural Society
   (D) McCormick's reaper was already on the market
   (E) the Reverend Patrick Bell copied his design

3. The author considers that the most important improvement added to a reaping machine was
   (A) a rake
   (B) knives
   (C) a driver's seat
   (D) a bundling machine
   (E) a tractor

4. Which statement is *true* according to this passage?
   (A) McCormick invented his first reaping machine while living in England.
   (B) McCormick's reaper was imitated by British inventors.
   (C) McCormick's reaper was better than those made by other inventors of his time.
   (D) McCormick's reaper was invented and patented the same year.
   (E) No improvements were added to reaping machines for 75 years after McCormick's invention.

Reading Passage II

Were all mosquitoes males, the human race would doubtless pay them small attention, for the male mosquito's food is vegetable juice. It is only the female mosquito that has an appetite for animal blood and an apparatus for procuring it. The female mosquito's proboscis (feeding organ) is a flexible tube with a groove on the upper side. Within this groove are sheathed six needle-keen stylets with points like lancets. It is these with which the tapping of the blood streams is done. When the mosquito has discovered a good feeding-side, she presses her proboscis against it until the external sheath is bent back and the stylets are allowed to plunge into the flesh. Upon the uppermost of these piercing organs there is a tiny trough or channel through which the blood of the victim is drawn up. So tiny and quick is the mosquito's puncture that in itself it would cause no distress to man or animal. The distress is caused by a different operation. As she draws in the blood, she pours out also the secretion of her salivary glands—a fiercely irritant spittle which she injects deep into the wound. The purpose of this is to delay the coagulation of the blood until her feeding is completed.

5. The title that best expresses the central idea of this paragraph is:
   (A) The mosquito appetite
   (B) Male *vs* female mosquitoes
   (C) The structure of a male mosquito
   (D) Why mosquitoes bite human beings
   (E) How a mosquito bites

6. The male mosquito lives on
   (A) dew   (C) blood
   (B) vegetable juice   (D) grass leaves
          (E) spittle

7. The female mosquito pierces the skin of her victim by means of her
   (A) lancets   (C) groove
   (B) stylets   (D) glands
          (E) sheath

Reading Passage III

Hatting was one of the first domestic industries to develop in the colonies. As early as 1640, American hats were one of the homemade articles used for barter and exchange. By the beginning of the eighteenth century, hatting had become one of New England's important industries; in the 1730's hats were being exported from the colonies in sufficient numbers to arouse uneasiness among hatters in the mother country and to cause them to exert successful pressure on Parliament for a law prohibiting the export of hats from one colony to another, and from any colony to Great Britain or any other country.

Wool was the principal raw material, but a considerable proportion of the hats were made of fur felt, using beaver fur as the base. The average price of wool hats during the eighteenth century ranged from 40 to 80 cents, and beaver hats ranged from $2.50 to $3.50.

8. The title that best expresses the main theme or subject of this selection is:
   (A) Raw materials for hats
   (B) Colonial exports
   (C) How hats were made
   (D) Kinds of hats in America
   (E) An early American industry

9. A law regarding the hat trade was enacted by Parliament in response to a complaint by
   (A) colonists
   (B) Indians
   (C) English noblemen
   (D) citizens of foreign countries
   (E) English hatmakers

10. This law made it illegal for
    (A) Great Britain to export hats
    (B) the colonies to import hats
    (C) the hatters to use beaver fur
    (D) the colonies to export hats
    (E) the colonies to change the price of hats

11. American hats
    (A) were made principally of wool
    (B) did not suit the customers in Great Britain
    (C) were an unimportant part of New England industry
    (D) were sent only to Great Britain
    (E) were not made until 1730

12. Beaver hats
    (A) were unpopular
    (B) were much cheaper than those of wool
    (C) were made mainly for barter with the Indians
    (D) cost more than wool hats
    (E) were not exported

Reading Passage IV

The people of Montana laughingly refer to the little wind-blown settlement of Ekalaka in the eastern badlands as "Skeleton Flats." Curious as it sounds, the name is well earned. So many fossils have been dug up in the vicinity of Ekalaka, an otherwise completely unremarkable little town, that it has become world-renowned for its vast fossil beds. So many dinosaur bones have been found nearby, that the ranchers use the bones for doorstops.

It all began 45 years ago when Walter H. Peck, whose hobby was geology, found the bones of a Stegosaurus, a huge plant-eating dinosaur. The entire community soon became infected with Peck's enthusiasm and everyone started digging for bones. On week ends, led by the science teacher from the local high school, young and old would go out looking for new finds. They never returned empty-handed. It seems that there is no end to the fossil riches around Ekalaka.

Among the rare finds were remains of a Brontosaurus, an 80-foot long monster which used to weigh 40 tons. They also found the skeleton of a Triceratops. Its head alone weighed 1,000 pounds. Careful search also yielded fossilized fishes, complete with stony scales, and remains of a sea reptile of tremendous size. The prize of them all, however, was a Pachycephalosaurus, a dinosaur with a peculiar bulging skull several inches thick. Local folk simply spoke of it as "the Bonehead." When descriptions of it were sent back to New York, scientific circles were immediately excited; the Ekalakans had dug up something completely unknown to science at that time.

Ekalaka now has its own fossil museum of which it is extremely proud. It is even toying with the idea of giving its "skeleton flats" national recognition by taking a touring exhibit of its rarest fossils on the road, to show all over the nation.

13. Ekalaka has been referred to as "Skeleton Flats" because
    (A) it is wind-blown
    (B) its people are underfed
    (C) its soil is poor
    (D) many fossils have been unearthed there
    (E) dinosaur bones decorate some of the homes

14. The first person to arouse interest in Ekalaka's fossils was
    (A) a high-school boy
    (B) a rancher
    (C) a teacher
    (D) a museum director
    (E) an amateur geologist

15. The supply of fossils near Ekalaka seems to be
    (A) of an inferior quality
    (B) without limit
    (C) of interest only to the town's inhabitants
    (D) near exhaustion
    (E) of no scientific value

16. The first fossil found in the vicinity of Ekalaka was that of a
    (A) fish
    (B) monster weighing 40 tons
    (C) dinosaur which lived on plants
    (D) sea reptile
    (E) giant beast of prey

17. The passage describes a possible future activity of the Ekalakans as
    (A) building a local museum
    (B) exhibiting their fossils in other cities
    (C) renaming their town
    (D) erecting a statue to Walter H. Peck
    (E) making doorstops out of fossilized bones

Reading Passage V

Paricutín is Mexico's newest volcano, a huge baby christened from the hamlet where it was born. One Dionisio Pulido and his son were plowing their field for the spring planting of corn, when their crude ox-drawn plow turned up a wisp of white smoke. The startling vision was accompanied by odd rumbling sounds in the earth. The place was two miles outside the Michoacán village called Paricutín and the date was February 20, 1943. The frightened Pulido hastened to tell the priest of his village and then the head man of Parangaricutiro, another village slightly more important and slightly farther away. Everyone thought the man crazy but he had only to lead them to the spot and let them see for themselves. Within a few hours the wisp was a column of ash-dust and within a day there was a true volcanic cone thirty or forty feet high. Now it is a mass of lava half a mile high, erupting from a crater in the midst of a desolate area of ash thirty-five miles in diameter. Despite the size and activity of Paricutín, however, its life expectancy is indeterminable. Other volcanic cones in the neighborhood have been short-lived.

18. The title that best expresses the main theme or subject of this selection is:
    (A) Mexico's largest volcano
    (B) How a volcano grows
    (C) The story of Paricutín
    (D) A sight to remember
    (E) Destruction brought about by Paricutín

19. Mexico's newest volcano was named for the
    (A) man who owned the field
    (B) parish priest
    (C) head man
    (D) nearest village
    (E) district

20. This volcano is now a
    (A) wisp of smoke
    (B) column of ash-dust
    (C) cone thirty feet high
    (D) huge erupting crater
    (E) dead heap of ash

21. The life period of Paricutín
    (A) will last only a few years
    (B) will cover many centuries
    (C) will continue forever
    (D) can not be calculated
    (E) is over

Reading Passage VI

Many people know that Ben Franklin's kite experiment helped to prove that lightning is electricity. Kites have been used for scientific purposes since the middle 1700's—for testing weather conditions, taking aerial photographs, etc. They have also been employed in many interesting ways during wartime. Centuries ago, a Korean general sent a kite, with line attached, to the opposite bank of a river. A cable followed the line, forming the nucleus from which a bridge was built. The Japanese developed a man-carrying kite, invaluable in scouting the enemy's position. Many armies used to employ kites for signaling purposes. Now some airplane lifeboats are equipped with kites carrying radio antennas which automatically signal S.O.S.

22. The title below that best expresses the main theme or subject of this selection is:
    (A) Kite making as a hobby
    (B) Methods of signaling
    (C) Uses of kites through the years
    (D) Our debt to Ben Franklin
    (E) Wartime use of kites

23. The author tells us that the Japanese used kites for

    (A) photography   (C) radio signaling
    (B) scouting   (D) scientific studies
              (E) weather predicting

24. The most recent use of kites mentioned is carrying
    (A) bridge cables   (C) photographers
    (B) soldiers   (D) electricity
              (E) radio antennas

END OF TEST

If you finish before the allotted time is up, work on this part only.
When time is up, proceed directly to the next part and do not
return to this part.

TEST IV. INTERPRETATION OF LITERARY MATERIALS

TIME: 1 Hour

This test is based on a selection of passages, both prose and verse. The questions emphasize knowledge and special abilities not frequently needed in ordinary reading. The abilities to interpret figures of speech, to cope with unusual sentence structure and word meaning, and to recognize mood and purpose are often tested, as is an understanding of literary forms.

DIRECTIONS: Below each of the literary passages you will find one or more incomplete statements about the passage of prose, po- etry, or drama. Each "stem" is followed by four or five "foils." Read each passage slowly, visualizing the plot, setting, action, characters, meaning, tone, and style. Re-read the passage before answering each question. From the emotions and attitudes expressed, choose the BEST "foil." Blacken the corresponding space on the answer sheet.

Dramatic Passage I.

Christy (looking at her with delight).   I'll have great times if I win the crowning prize I'm seeking now, and that's your promise that you'll wed me in a fortnight, when our banns is called.

Pegeen (backing away from him).   You've right daring to go ask me that, when all knows you'll be starting to some girl in your own townland, when your father's rotten in four months, or five.

Christy (indignantly).   Starting from you, is it? *(He follows her.)* I will not, then, and when the airs is warming in four months, or five, it's then yourself and me should be pacing Neifin in the dews of night, the times sweet smells do be rising, and you'd see a little shiny new moon, maybe, sinking on the hills.

Pegeen (looking at him playfully).   And it's that kind of a poacher's love you'd make, Christy Mahon, on the sides of Neifin, when the night is down?

Christy.   It's little you'll think if my love's a poacher's, or an earl's itself, when you'll feel my two hands stretched around you, and I squeezing kisses on your puckered lips, till I'd feel a kind of pity for the Lord God in all ages sitting lonesome in his golden chair.

Pegeen.   That'll be right fun, Christy Mahon, and any girl would walk her heart out before she'd meet a young man was your like for eloquence, or talk, at all.

Christy (encouraged).   Let you wait, to hear me talking, till we're astray in Erris, when Good Friday's by, drinking a sup from a well, and making mighty kisses with our wetted mouths, or gaming in a gap of sunshine, with yourself stretched back unto your necklace, in the flowers of the earth.

Pegeen (in a lower voice, moved by his tone).   I'd be nice so, is it?

Christy (with rapture).   If the mitered bishops seen you that time, they'd be the like of the holy prophets, I'm thinking, do be straining the bars of Paradise to lay eyes on the Lady Helen of Troy, and she abroad, pacing back and forward, with a nosegay in her golden shawl.

Pegeen (with real tenderness).   And what is it I have, Christy Mahon, to make me fitting entertainment for the like of you, that has such poet's talking, and such bravery of heart?

Christy (in a low voice).   Isn't there the light of seven heavens in your heart alone, the way you'll be an angel's lamp to me from this out, and I abroad in the darkness, spearing salmons in the Owen, or the Carrowmore?

Pegeen.   If I was your wife, I'd be along with you those nights, Christy Mahon, the way you'd see I was a great hand at coaxing bailiffs, or coining funny nicknames for the stars of night.

Christy.   You, is it? Taking your death in the hailstones, or in the fogs of dawn.

Pegeen.   Yourself and me would shelter easy in a narrow bush *(with a qualm of dread)*, but we're only talking, maybe, for this would be a poor, thatched place to hold a find lad is the like of you.

Christy (putting his arm around her).   If I wasn't a good Christian, it's on my naked knees I'd be saying my prayers and paters to every jackstraw you have roofing your head, and every stony pebble is paving the laneway to your door.

Pegeen (radiantly).   If that's the truth, I'll be burning candles from this out to the miracles of God that have brought you from the south today, and I, with my gowns bought ready, the way that I can wed you, and not wait at all.

Christy.   It's miracles, and that the truth. Me there toiling a long while, and walking a long while, not knowing at all I was drawing all times nearer to this holy day.

Pegeen.   And myself, a girl, was tempted often to go sailing the seas till 'd marry a man with ten kegs of gold, and I not knowing at all there was the like of you drawing nearer, like the stars of God.

Christy.   And to think I'm long years hearing women talking that talk, to all bloody fools, and this the first time I've heard the like of your voice talking sweetly for my own delight.

Pegeen.   And to think it's me is talking sweetly, Christy Mahon, and I the fright of seven townlands for my biting tongue. Well, the heary's a wonder; and, I'm thinking, there won't be our like in Mayo, for gallant lovers, from this hour, today. *(Drunken singing is heard outside.)* There's my father coming from the wake, and when he's had his sleep we'll tell him, for he's peaceful then. *(They separate.)*

Christy (taking up the loy).   Then I'll make you face the gallows or quit off from this.

(Shawn flies out of the door.)

Christy.   Well, fine weather be after him *(going to Michael, coaxingly)*, and I'm thinking you wouldn't wish to have that quaking blackguard in your house at all. Let you give us your blessing and hear her swear her faith to me, for I'm mounted on the springtide of the stars of luck, the way it'll be good for any to have me in the house.

Pegeen (at the other side of Michael).   Bless us now, for I swear to God I'll wed him, and I'll not renege.

Michael (standing up in the center, holding on to both of them).   It's the will of God, I'm thinking, that all should win an easy or a cruel end, and it's the will of God that all should rear up lengthy families for the nurture of the earth. What's a single man, I ask you, eating a bit in one house and drinking a sup in another, and he with no place of his own, like an old braying jackass strayed upon the rocks? *(To Christy)* It's many would be in dread to bring your like into their house for to end them, maybe, with a sudden end; but I'm a decent man of Ireland, and I liefer face the grave untimely and I seeing a score of grandsons growing up little gallant swearers by the name of God, then go peopling my bedside with puny weeds the like of what you'd breed, I'm thinking, out of Shaneen Keogh. *(He joins their hands.)* A daring fellow is the jewel of the world, and a man did split his father's middle with a single clout, should have the bravery of ten, so may God and Mary and St. Patrick bless you, and increase you from this mortal day.

Christy and Pegeen.   Amen, O Lord!

(Hubbub outside.)

(Old Mahon rushes in, followed by all the crowd, and Widow Quin. He makes a rush at Christy, knocks him down and begins to beat him.)

Pegeen (dragging back his arm).   Stop that, will you? Who are you at all?

Mahon.   His father, God forgive me!

Pegeen (drawing back).   Is it rose from the dead?

Mahon.   Do you think I look so easy quenched with the tap of a loy? *(Beats Christy again.)*

Pegeen (glaring at Christy).   And it's lies you told, letting on you had him slitted, and you nothing at all.

Christy (catching Mahon's stick).   He's not my father. He's a raving maniac would scare the world. *(Pointing to Widow Quin.)* Herself knows it is true.

Crowd.   You're fooling Pegeen! The Widow Quin seen him this day, and you likely knew! You're a liar!

Christy (dumbfounded).   It's himself was a liar, lying stretched out with an open head on him, letting on he was dead.

Mahon.   Weren't you off racing the hills before I got my breath with the start.I had seeing you turn on me at all?

Pegeen.   And to think of the coaxing glory we had given him, and he after doing nothing but hitting a soft blow and chasing northward in a sweat of fear. Quit off from this.

Christy (piteously).   You've seen my doings this day, and let you save me from the old man; for why would you be in such a scorch of haste to spur me to destruction now?

Pegeen.   It's there your treachery is spurring me, till I'm hard set to think you're the one I'm after lacing in my heartstrings half-an-hour gone by. *(To Mahon)* Take him on from this, for I think bad the world should see me raging for a Munster liar, and the fool of men.

—J.M. Synge, *The Playboy of the Western World*

DIRECTIONS: Read and answer each question carefully. Select the best answer and blacken the proper space on the answer sheet.

1. Both Pegeen and Michael seem to be

    (A) sad that Christy is leaving
    (B) proud that Christy apparently killed his father
    (C) sorry that Christy asked Pegeen to marry him
    (D) angry that Christy is still at large after his terrible crime

2. Pegeen and Christy

    (A) believe they will be married that very day
    (B) are fond of Shawn Keogh
    (C) have met for the first time that day
    (D) have known each other all their lives

3. When Christy says "You'll be an angel's lamp to me," he is using a

    (A) cliche
    (B) metaphor
    (C) simile
    (D) apostrophe

4. This story probably takes place in

    (A) England
    (B) an imaginary country
    (C) Ireland
    (D) the United States

5. What is obvious is that the author

    (A) does not want us to take the apparent murder of Christy's father seriously
    (B) looks upon Christy with horror
    (C) has written a tragedy
    (D) believes Christy is a fool

6. Pegeen becomes very angry at Christy because

    (A) he apparently did not kill his father
    (B) allows Mahon to beat him
    (C) lied about wishing to marry her
    (D) has to go to jail

Nonfiction Passage II.

In his lace-bedecked crib the little Dauphin, whiter than the cushions upon which he lies, is resting now with closed eyes. They think that he sleeps; but no. The little Dauphin is not asleep. He turns to his mother, and seeing that she is weeping, he says to her:

"Madame queen, why do you weep? Is it because you really believe that I am going to die?"

The queen tries to reply. Sobs prevent her from speaking.

"Pray do not weep, madame queen; you forget that I am the Dauphin, and that dauphins cannot die like this."

The queen sobs more bitterly than ever, and the little Dauphin begins to be alarmed.

"I say," he says, "I don't want Death to come and take me and I will find a way to prevent his coming here. Let them send at once forty very strong troopers to stand guard around our bed! Let a hundred big guns watch night and day with matches lighted, under our windows! And woe to Death if it dares approach us!"

To please the royal child the queen makes a sign. In a moment they hear the big guns rumbling through the courtyard; and forty tall troopers, halberds in hand, take their places about the room. They are all old soldiers with gray mustaches. The little Dauphin claps his hands when he sees them. He recognizes one of them and calls him:

"Lorrain! Lorrain!"

The soldier steps forward toward the bed.

"I love you dearly, my old Lorrain. Let me see your big sword. If Death tries to take me you must kill him, won't you?"

"Yes, Monseigneur," Lorrain replies. And two great tears roll down his bronzed cheeks.

At that moment the chaplain approaches the little Dauphin and talks with him for a long time in a low voice, showing him a crucifix. The little Dauphin listens with an expression of great surprise, then, abruptly interrupting him, he says:

"I understand what you say, monsieur l'abbé, but tell me, couldn't my little friend Beppo die in my place, if I gave him a lot of money?"

The chaplain continues to speak in a low voice, and the little Dauphin's expression becomes more and more astonished.

When the chaplain has finished, the little Dauphin replies with a deep sigh:

"All this that you tell me is very sad, monsieur l'abbé, but one thing consoles me, and that is that up yonder, in the paradise of the stars, I shall still be the Dauphin. I know that the good Lord is my cousin, and that He cannot fail to treat me according to my rank."

Then he adds, turning to his mother:

"Let them bring me my richest clothes, my doublet of white ermine, and my velvet slippers! I wish to make myself handsome for the angels, and to enter paradise in the costume of a Dauphin.''

A third time the chaplain leans toward the little Dauphin and talks to him for a long time in a low voice. In the midst of his harangue, the royal child angrily interrupts:

''Why, then, to be Dauphin is to be nothing at all!''

And refusing to listen to anything more, the little Dauphin turns toward the wall and weeps bitterly.

—Alphonse Daudet, ''The Death of the Dauphin''

DIRECTIONS: Read and answer each question carefully. Select the best answer and blacken the proper space on the answer sheet.

7. When the Dauphin says ''I don't want Death to come and take me,'' he is using

   (A) personification
   (B) a simile
   (C) a metaphor
   (D) a parallel

8. The Dauphin believes he can defeat Death by

   (A) having his mother take his place
   (B) praying for life
   (C) having soldiers protect him
   (D) dressing in fine clothes

9. The Dauphin accepts he will die when

   (A) his mother weeps
   (B) Lorrain says he cannot stop Death
   (C) the chaplain tells him it will happen
   (D) he sees the crucifix

10. The Dauphin is

    (A) humble
    (B) proud
    (C) pretending
    (D) happy

11. The Dauphin believes that

    (A) God is his cousin
    (B) Death is kind
    (C) he will return to earth
    (D) he will not go to heaven

12. When the chaplin spoke to the Dauphin for the last time, he probably told him that

    (A) there was no heaven
    (B) he couldn't make his friend Beppo take his place
    (C) paradise is not in the stars as the Dauphin thought
    (D) in the eyes of God he was only a human being like anyone else

Poetry Passage III.

1 She walks in beauty, like the night
2   Of cloudless climes and starry skies;
3 And all that's best of dark and bright
4   Meet in her aspect and her eyes:
5 Thus mellow'd to that tender light
6   Which heaven to gaudy day denies.

7 One shade the more, one ray the less,
8   Had half impair'd the nameless grace
9 Which waves in every raven tress,
10   Or softly lightens o'er her face;
11 Where thoughts serenely sweet express
12   How pure, how dear their dwelling-place.

13 And on that cheek, and o'er that brow,
14   So soft, so calm, yet eloquent,
15 The smiles that win, the tints that glow,
16   But tell of days in goodness spent,
17 A mind at peace with all below,
18   A heart whose love is innocent!

—Gordon Lord Byron, "She Walks In Beauty"

DIRECTIONS: Read and answer each question carefully. Select the best answer and blacken the proper space on the answer sheet.

13. The poet's comparison of his love to the night (lines 1–2) is

(A) a metaphor
(B) simile
(C) hyperbole
(D) oxymoron

14. In the first stanza which is personified?

(A) eyes
(B) aspect
(C) night
(D) beauty

15. What "tell of days in goodness spent"?

(A) "the night of cloudless climes"
(B) "a heart whose love is innocent"
(C) "a mind at peace with all below"
(D) "the smiles that win, the tints that glow"

16. "One shade the more, one ray the less" is

(A) iambic pentameter
(B) trochaic hexameter
(C) iambic tetrameter
(D) anapestic hexameter

17. The poet is

(A) worshipful
(B) cynical
(C) scornful
(D) arrogant

END OF TEST

TEST V. GENERAL MATHEMATICAL ABILITY

TIME: 1 Hour

This test covers topics taught at both the elementary and high school level. Some topics which may be covered are definitions, ratios, percent, decimals, fractions, mathematical symbols, indirect measurement, interpretation of graphs and tables, scale drawings, approximate computation, and units of measurement. Some questions are based on techniques taught in elementary algebra and plane geometry courses. Questions frequently test knowledge of mathematical principles and stress their applications through the performance of mathematical operations and manipulations. The ability to express practical problems in mathematical terms is frequently tested. The test may also include one or two questions based on the concepts of modern mathematics.

DIRECTIONS: In the following multiple choice questions, choose the correct answer from the choices offered.

1. Subtract \$94.78 from \$360.50
   (A) \$265.72   (C) \$391.24
   (B) \$455.28   (D) \$164.80

2. Add: $8\frac{3}{8}$, 12, $15\frac{5}{16}$
   (A) $22\frac{5}{8}$ (C) $32\frac{7}{8}$
   (B) $28\frac{3}{16}$ (D) $35\frac{11}{16}$

3. Divide 16 by $2\frac{2}{3}$
   (A) 2   (C) 6
   (B) 4   (D) 8

4. Multiply 956 by 507
   (A) 329,141   (C) 563,215
   (B) 484,692   (D) 613,218

5. Divide 1.672 by .08
   (A) 200.9   (C) 2.9
   (B) 20.9   (D) .29

6. By buying a coat during a sale, a girl received a 20% discount. The discount amounted to \$12. What was the original price of the coat?
   (A) \$30   (C) \$50
   (B) \$40   (D) \$60

7. A boy deposited in his school savings account the money he had saved during the summer. Find the amount of his deposit if he had 10 one-dollar bills, 9 half dollars, 8 quarters, 16 dimes, and 25 nickels.
   (A) \$16.20   (C) \$18.60
   (B) \$17.42   (D) \$19.35

8. At the annual rate of \$1.50 per \$100, how much does it cost for a \$1,000 fire insurance policy for one year?
   (A) \$15   (C) \$40
   (B) \$25   (D) \$50

9. If a car averages 18 miles to a gallon of gasoline, how many gallons of gasoline will be used on a trip of 810 miles?
   (A) 20   (C) 45
   (B) 35   (D) 60

10. In a recent year 120 pupils were enrolled in the seventh grade of a junior high school. The following year the seventh grade enrollment was 160 pupils. Find the per cent of increase in enrollment.
    (A) 25%   (C) 40%
    (B) $33\frac{1}{3}$%   (D) 50%

11. 5 is what per cent of 25?
    (A) 5   (C) 500
    (B) 50   (D) 20

12. Which fraction is closest in value to $\frac{3}{7}$?
    (A) $\frac{1}{2}$
    (B) $\frac{2}{3}$
    (C) $\frac{41}{100}$
    (D) $\frac{42}{100}$

13. If a man invests $1,000 at an annual rate of 5%, how much interest will the man have after one year?
    (A) $20
    (B) $50
    (C) $100
    (D) $120

14. If 3 apples cost 24¢, how many dozen apples can be bought for $1.92?
    (A) $1\frac{1}{2}$
    (B) 1
    (C) 2
    (D) $5\frac{1}{3}$

15. If Mary is "X" years old now and her sister is 3 years younger, then 5 years from now her sister will be what age?
    (A) X + 5 years
    (B) X + 3 years
    (C) X + 2 years
    (D) 8 years

16. Which number does *not* go into 10116 evenly (without a remainder)?
    (A) 2
    (B) 4
    (C) 3
    (D) 8

17. $\frac{1}{6}$ of what number is 8?
    (A) $\frac{3}{4}$
    (B) $\frac{4}{3}$
    (C) 48
    (D) 24

18. $\frac{3}{16} \div \frac{2}{3} =$
    (A) $\frac{1}{8}$
    (B) 8
    (C) $\frac{9}{32}$
    (D) $\frac{1}{4}$

19. How many pints are equal to 2 gallons?
    (A) 8
    (B) 16
    (C) 4
    (D) 2

20. .0033 =
    (A) $\frac{33}{100}$
    (B) $\frac{3}{10}$
    (C) $\frac{3}{100}$
    (D) $\frac{33}{10,000}$

21. At the rate of four peaches for a quarter, 20 peaches will cost
    (A) 80¢
    (B) $1.00
    (C) $1.20
    (D) $1.25

22. A pint of milk is what part of half a gallon?
    (A) $\frac{1}{8}$
    (B) $\frac{1}{4}$
    (C) $\frac{1}{2}$
    (D) one-sixteenth

23. When one fifth is added to one third the sum is
    (A) $\frac{1}{4}$
    (B) $\frac{1}{8}$
    (C) eight-fifteenths
    (D) one-fifteenth

24. If John works 15 hours at 90 cents an hour he will earn
    (A) $6
    (B) $10
    (C) $13.50
    (D) $12.35

25. When 81.3 is divided by 10 the quotient is
    (A) 0.0813
    (B) 0.813
    (C) 8.13
    (D) 813

END OF EXAMINATION

If you finish before the allotted time is up, check your work on this test only. Do not go back to earlier tests. When time runs out, compare your answers for this test and all the other tests in the examination with the correct key answers that follow.

CORRECT ANSWERS FOR SAMPLE EXAMINATION I.

(Please make every effort to answer the questions on your own before look-ing at these answers. You'll make faster progress by following this rule.)

TEST I. CORRECTNESS AND EFFECTIVENESS OF EXPRESSION

PART A. ENGLISH USAGE

1.B	6.B	11.B	16.A	21.C	26.B
2.C	7.C	12.C	17.B	22.C	27.D
3.A	8.D	13.B	18.D	23.A	28.B
4.A	9.D	14.D	19.D	24.A	29.C
5.D	10.B	15.B	20.A	25.B	30.D

PART B. SPELLING

1.C	5.C	9.C	13.A	17.C
2.B	6.B	10.D	14.A	18.B
3.A	7.A	11.A	15.B	19.D
4.B	8.B	12.C	16.D	20.A

TEST II. INTERPRETATION OF READING MATERIALS IN THE SOCIAL STUDIES

PART A. SOCIAL STUDIES READINGS

1.C	6.D	11.E	16.B	21.E
2.E	7.A	12.A	17.D	22.C
3.B	8.B	13.D	18.E	23.C
4.E	9.C	14.B	19.A	24.A
5.E	10.B	15.A	20.A	25.E

PART B. GRAPH AND TABLE INTERPRETATION

1.G	3.D	5.H	7.E	9.D
2.F	4.F	6.C	8.G	10.B

TEST III. INTERPRETATION OF READING MATERIALS
IN THE NATURAL SCIENCES

1.A	5.E	9.E	13.D	17.B	21.D
2.A	6.B	10.D	14.E	18.C	22.C
3.E	7.B	11.A	15.B	19.D	23.B
4.C	8.E	12.D	16.C	20.D	24.E

TEST IV. INTERPRETATION OF LITERARY MATERIALS

1.B	4.C	7.A	10.B	13.B	16.C
2.C	5.A	8.C	11.A	14.C	17.A
3.B	6.A	9.C	12.D	15.D	

TEST V. GENERAL MATHEMATICAL ABILITY

1.A	6.D	11.D	16.D	21.D
2.D	7.D	12.D	17.C	22.B
3.C	8.A	13.B	18.C	23.C
4.B	9.C	14.C	19.B	24.C
5.B	10.B	15.C	20.D	25.C

II. SAMPLE EXAM FOR PRACTICE

This Examination is very much like the one you'll take. It was constructed by professionals who utilized all the latest information available. They derived a series of Tests which neatly cover all the subjects you are likely to encounter on the actual examination. Stick to business; follow all instructions closely; and score yourself objectively. If you do poorly . . . review. If necessary, take this Examination again for comparison.

The time allowed for the entire examination is 5 hours.

TEST I. CORRECTNESS AND EFFECTIVENESS OF EXPRESSION

TIME: 1 Hour

PART A. ENGLISH USAGE

DIRECTIONS: Read each Theme through carefully to get the general meaning. Then go back and look at the underlined and numbered portions of the story. Some of the underlined words and phrases contain errors in grammar, punctuation or choice of words. Others are correct as written. Study the suggested corrections in the right-hand column and choose the one you think is best. All of the suggestions may be grammatically correct, but one is always more effective than the others.

THEME I.

Scientists are remodeling different kinds of plants. They have <u>all ready</u> changed 65 kinds of flowers, fruits, vegetables, and trees. <u>Because of</u> such alterations, we have tobacco that resists disease, cantaloupes that <u>can't not get</u> rotten, and

1. (A) NO CHANGE   (C) allready
   (B) already   (D) al ready

2. (A) NO CHANGE
   (B) Because there is
   (C) On account there is
   (D) On account there are

3. (A) NO CHANGE   (C) cant get
   (B) cant not get   (D) can't get

lettuce with crisplier leaves. The most important
4

thing that scientists are using is a poisonous drug

called colchicine (pronounced *koll-tshis-een*). This
5

here drug has unbelievable effects upon growths.
6   7

It very often creates new kinds of plant life where

nature can't do it. The Department of Agriculture
8

sends men all over the world to find plants that

grow in foreign soil and that can grow in our coun-

try, these plants are brought back here and are
9

crossed with those at home. The resulting plants
10

are often superior to our original plants.

4. (A) NO CHANGE   (C) crisp-like
    (B) crispier   (D) crisplike

5. (A) NO CHANGE   (C) That there
    (B) That here   (D) This

6. (A) NO CHANGE   (C) defects
    (B) affects   (D) affections

7. (A) NO CHANGE   (C) growth
    (B) growings   (D) growing

8. (A) NO CHANGE   (C) done
    (B) did   (D) doed

9. (A) NO CHANGE
    (B) country these
    (C) country, while these
    (D) country. These

10. (A) NO CHANGE   (C) result
    (B) resulted   (D) resulter

THEME II.

Just because a person cannot read or write, it
11   12

does not mean that he is stupid. Very often there

is no connection on knowing how to read and write
13

and intelligence. Take the Chinese for example.
14

I have lived in China for many years and have
15

many friends their who cannot read and cannot
16

write—yet they are wise. Here in America, there

are people who, although they read newspapers
17

and books, do not learn much that is worthwhile

upon what they read. Knowing how to read don't
18   19

mean knowing how to think. Wisdom is an im-
20

portant part of civilization—the Chinese have wis-

dom.

11. (A) NO CHANGE   (C) as
     (B) since   (D) on account of

12. (A) NO CHANGE   (C) nor
     (B) and   (D) and not

13. (A) NO CHANGE   (C) among
     (B) between   (D) by

14. (A) NO CHANGE   (C) Chinese; for
     (B) Chinese. For   (D) Chinese, for

15. (A) NO CHANGE   (C) many year
     (B) many a year   (D) much years

16. (A) NO CHANGE   (C) they're
     (B) their   (D) there

17. (A) NO CHANGE   (C) who. Although
     (B) who although   (D) who; although

18. (A) NO CHANGE   (C) at
     (B) on   (D) from

19. (A) NO CHANGE   (C) does not
     (B) do not   (D) doesnt

20. (A) NO CHANGE   (C) in knowing
     (B) to know   (D) knowledge

ANSWER SHEET FOR SAMPLE EXAMINATION II.

Make only ONE mark for each answer. Additional and stray marks may be counted as mistakes.

TEST I. CORRECTNESS AND EFFECTIVENESS OF EXPRESSION

PART A. ENGLISH USAGE

PART B. SPELLING

TEST II. INTERPRETATION OF READING MATERIALS IN THE SOCIAL STUDIES

PART A. SOCIAL STUDIES READINGS

PART B. GRAPH AND TABLE INTERPRETATION

1. ____   2. ____   3. ____   4. ____   5. ____   6. ____   7. ____   8. ____
9. ____   10. ____   11. ____   12. ____   13. ____   14. ____   15. ____   16. ____

TEST III. INTERPRETATION OF READING MATERIALS IN THE NATURAL SCIENCES

TEST IV. INTERPRETATION OF LITERARY MATERIALS

TEST V. GENERAL MATHEMATICAL ABILITY

THEME III.

Everyone has at one time or <u>another</u> felt the need
₂₁
to express himself. What must you do in order to
learn to say exactly what you want to <u>say</u>. You will
₂₂
have to study <u>very careful</u> the English language
₂₃

and especially <u>it's</u> grammar. Some people think
₂₄
that <u>Good english</u> is fancy English, but that <u>isnt</u>
₂₅   ₂₆

true. Just because a person uses long words it <u>does</u>
₂₇

<u>not</u> mean that he speaks <u>good</u>. The person <u>whom</u>
                ₂₈   ₂₉
uses simple words and phrases which say exactly

what he means is using better English <u>than</u> the
₃₀
individual who shows off with hard-to-understand
expressions.

21. (A) NO CHANGE   (C) an other
    (B) the other   (D) t'other

22. (A) NO CHANGE   (C) say:
    (B) say!   (D) say?

23. (A) NO CHANGE
    (B) very careful-like
    (C) with carefulness
    (D) very carefully

24. (A) NO CHANGE   (C) its'
    (B) its   (D) it is

25. (A) NO CHANGE   (C) good english
    (B) good English   (D) Good English

26. (A) NO CHANGE   (C) aren't
    (B) isn't   (D) aint

27. (A) NO CHANGE   (C) don't
    (B) do not   (D) did not

28. (A) NO CHANGE   (C) well
    (B) fine   (D) correct

29. (A) NO CHANGE   (C) which
    (B) who   (D) what

30. (A) NO CHANGE   (C) to
    (B) from   (D) instead of

END OF PART

*Go on to the next Test in the Examination, just as you would do
on the actual exam. Check your answers when you have completed
the entire Examination. The correct answers for this Test, and
all the other Tests, are assembled at the conclusion of this
Examination.*

TEST I. CORRECTNESS AND EFFECTIVENESS
OF EXPRESSION

PART B. SPELLING

DIRECTIONS: In this test all words but one of each group are spelled correctly. Indicate the misspelled word in each group.

1. (A) winner	(B) expiriment	(C) parrot	(D) scrubbing
2. (A) forehead	(B) dungarees	(C) improved	(D) lisence
3. (A) respect	(B) zeroe	(C) watermelon	(D) verses
4. (A) parlor	(B) league	(C) prepareing	(D) thirsty
5. (A) bench	(B) groceries	(C) lenth	(D) naughty
6. (A) lately	(B) kindergarden	(C) nephew	(D) caravan
7. (A) amendment	(B) bacon	(C) importence	(D) furnished
8. (A) dreaming	(B) instance	(C) younger	(D) mountinous
9. (A) anntenna	(B) lowest	(C) legislature	(D) daylight
10. (A) meantime	(B) daintyness	(C) gentlemen	(D) dentist
11. (A) defence	(B) guitar	(C) issued	(D) marshmallows
12. (A) somewhere	(B) strawberies	(C) partner	(D) thoughts
13. (A) occupation	(B) printing	(C) smokeing	(D) varnish
14. (A) permision	(B) silence	(C) division	(D) lantern
15. (A) project	(B) walrus	(C) section	(D) transpertation
16. (A) training	(B) territory	(C) wedding	(D) sissors
17. (A) visiters	(B) palace	(C) plantation	(D) whale
18. (A) bacteria	(B) agraculture	(C) attacked	(D) beaver
19. (A) greater	(B) knight	(C) excelent	(D) difficult
20. (A) freight	(B) dictionery	(C) mirror	(D) gentle

TEST II. INTERPRETATION OF READING MATERIALS
IN THE SOCIAL STUDIES

TIME: 1 Hour

PART A. SOCIAL STUDIES READINGS

DIRECTIONS: Below each of the following passages of social science reading material you will find one or more incomplete statements about the passage. Select the words or expressions that most satisfactorily complete each statement in accordance with the meaning of the paragraph.

Reading Passage I

While Europeans were still creeping cautiously along their coasts, Polynesians in frail canoes were fearlessly making trips between Hawaii and New Zealand three thousand eight hundred miles apart. Without chart, compass or sextant, the Vikings of the Pacific explored every island in their vast domain. During the daytime they guided themselves by the sun, trend of waves, wind and the flight of the seabirds; but in long voyages between island groups, stars were used as guides. A youth studying navigation was taught to view the heavens as a cylinder on which were marked the highways of navigation. An invisible line bisected the sky from the North Star to the Southern Cross. For trans-Pacific voyages large twin canoes were often used, fastened together by canopied platforms which shielded the voyagers from sun and rain. Such craft were remarkably seaworthy and could accommodate as many as sixty or eighty persons, in addition to water, food, domestic animals and other supplies necessary for a long voyage. Some of the vessels had as many as three masts. As the Vikings of the Atlantic were equipped with oars, so the mariners of the Pacific were provided with paddles. A steering paddle took the place of a rudder and was so important that it aways had a personal name. Polynesian legends of old-time voyages give not only the name of the canoe and the hero who discovered a new island, but also the name of the steering paddle he used.

S1675

1. The best of the following titles for this paragraph is:
   (A) European sailors
   (B) History of the Pacific Ocean
   (C) Study of navigation
   (D) The Polynesian canoe
   (E) Early Polynesian sailors

2. The Polynesian mariners of early times guided their boats by
   (A) chart   (C) stars
   (B) compass   (D) sextant
          (E) lighthouses

3. The Polynesian sailor evidently considered the most important part of the ship to be the
   (A) mast   (C) canopy
   (B) sail   (D) oar
          (E) steering paddle

4. The Polynesians made trips to
   (A) the Atlantic   (C) Europe
   (B) New Zealand   (D) the North Star
          (E) the Southern Cross

5. The Polynesans made their voyages for
   (A) trade   (C) exploration
   (B) conquest   (D) culture
          (E) colonization

Reading Passage II

Like the United States today, Athens had courts where a wrong might be righted. Since any citizen might accuse another of a crime, the Athenian courts of law were very busy. In fact, unless a citizen was unusually peaceful or very unimportant, he would be sure to find himself in the courts at least once in every few years.

At a trial both the accuser and the person accused were allowed a certain time to speak. The length of time was marked by a water clock. Free men testified under oath as they do today, but the oath of a slave was counted as worthless.

To judge a trial, a jury was chosen from the members of the assembly who had reached 30 years of age. The Athenian juries were very large, often consisting of 201, 401, 501, 1,001, or more men, depending upon the importance of the case being tried. The juryman swore by the gods to listen carefully to both sides of the question and to give his honest opinion of the case. Each juryman gave his decision by depositing a white or black stone in a box. To keep citizens from being too careless in accusing each other, there was a rule that if the person accused did not receive a certain number of votes, the accuser was condemned instead.

6. The title that best expresses the main idea of this selection is:
   (A) Athens and the United States
   (B) Justice in ancient Athens
   (C) Testifying under oath
   (D) Accusing the accused
   (E) The duties of juries

7. People in Athens were frequently on trial in a law court because
   (A) they liked to serve on juries
   (B) a juryman agreed to listen to both sides of a question
   (C) the people of Athens were unusually peace-loving
   (D) the slaves were troublesome
   (E) any person might accuse another of a crime

8. An Athenian was likely to avoid accusing another without a good reason because
   (A) the jury might condemn the accuser instead of the accused man
   (B) the jury might be very large
   (C) cases were judged by men over 30 years old
   (D) there was a limit on the time a trial could take
   (E) a juryman gave his decision by putting a stone in a box

9. Which statement is *true* according to this selection?
   (A) An accused person was denied the privilege of telling his side of the case.
   (B) The importance of the case determined the number of jurors.
   (C) A jury's decision was handed down in writing.
   (D) A citizen had to appear in court every few years.
   (E) Older jurors were used for the most important cases.

Reading Passage III

"All roads lead to Rome," according to an old saying. One of these roads, which goes from Naples to Rome, is the ancient Appian Way, famed in legend and story. The Appian Way is a marvel of road building. It was begun more than 22 centuries ago by a Roman magistrate named Appius Claudius Caecus, for whom it is named. It was designed as a military highway and was laid as straight as possible, like a railroad. The paving consisted of large hexagonal blocks of lava, fitted tightly together and held with cement. Under these blocks were layers of rubble and thick stones, with a foundation below. The surface of the highway was rounded to let the water drain away. There were cuts through hills, and fillings in hollows; embankments across swamps, and bridges across ravines. So careful was the construction that some of the original blocks remain.

10. The Appian Way was built for
    (A) army use
    (B) pleasure driving
    (C) the first railway train
    (D) bringing food to market
    (E) a race course

11. The Way was paved with pieces of
    (A) cement   (D) gravel
    (B) wood   (E) lava
    (C) metal

12. The surface of this road was
    (A) flat   (D) rough
    (B) rounded   (E) hollow
    (C) winding

13. One of the most remarkable features of this noted road has been its
    (A) length   (D) beauty
    (B) straightness (E) location
    (C) durability

Reading Passage IV

The peopling of this Northwest Territory by companies from the eastern states, such as the Ohio Company, under the leadership of Rev. Manasseh Cutler, of Ipswich, Massachusetts, furnishes many interesting historic incidents. The first towns to be established were Marietta, Zanesville, Chillicothe, and Cincinnati. After the Ohio Company, came the Connecticut Company which secured all the territory bordering Lake Erie, save a small portion known as fire lands and another portion known as Congress lands. The land taken up by the Connecticut people was called the Western Reserve, and was settled almost entirely by New England people. The remainder of the state of Ohio was settled by Virginians and Pennsylvanians. On account of the British having control of the lakes Ontario and Erie, the Massachusetts and Connecticut people made their journey into the Western Reserve through the southern part of the state. General Moses Cleaveland, the agent for the Connecticut Land Company, led a body of surveyors to the tract, venturing by way of Lake Ontario. He quieted the Indian claims to the eastern portion of the reserve by giving them five hundred dollars, two head of cattle and one hundred gallons of whisky. Landing at the mouth of the Conneaut River, General Moses Cleaveland and his party of fifty, including two women, celebrated Independence Day, 1796, by a feast of pork and beans with bread. A little later a village was established at the mouth of the Cuyahoga River, which was given the name of Cleaveland, in honor of the agent of the company. It is related that the name was afterward shortened to Cleveland by one of the early editors because he could not get so many letters into the heading of his newspaper.

14. The Northwest Territory mentioned in the first sentence covers the area now known as
    (A) Connecticut
    (B) Ohio
    (C) Pennsylvania
    (D) Virginia
    (E) Massachusetts

15. The Connecticut Company secured all the territory bordering Lake Erie except
    (A) the Western Reserve
    (B) Marietta, Zanesville, Chillicothe, and Cincinnati
    (C) land near the mouth of the Cuyahoga River
    (D) portions known as fire lands and Congress lands
    (E) Ipswich

16. In making their way into the Western Reserve, New England people avoided the northern areas because
    (A) the British controlled lakes Ontario and Erie
    (B) peace had not been made with the Indians
    (C) the Connecticut Company would not let them go through the Western Reserve
    (D) the Ohio Company was not friendly
    (E) Virginians and Pennsylvanians settled the remainder of the state

17. General Moses Cleaveland quieted Indian claims to the eastern portion of the reserve by
    (A) giving the Indians a feast of pork and beans with bread
    (B) surveying the tract of land
    (C) giving a party for fifty Indians
    (D) giving the Indians money, cattle and whisky
    (E) celebrating their Independence Day, 1796

18. The city of Cleveland was named in honor of
    (A) an editor
    (B) a surveyor
    (C) a land agent
    (D) a minister
    (E) an Indian

Reading Passage V

An advertising agency in Shanghai placed the first lipstick and vanishing cream advertising in Chinese papers about 50 years ago, and since that time the advertising and sale of cosmetics have been important businesses there. It must not be assumed, however, that such advertisements started Chinese girls on the cosmetic road to beauty. Five thousand years ago, according to authentic Chinese history, Chinese girls were plucking useless hairs from their eyebrows and putting rouge on their cheeks. The oldest retail shop in China is an establishment in Hangchow, which was the Chinese equivalent of a beauty shop centuries ago and still does a thriving business in rouge, talcum and other aids to daintiness and beauty. The best Chinese customers for cosmetics, though, are the married women and not the debutantes. Chinese women discovered many centuries ago that, if they would make themselves attractive enough, their husbands would willingly employ servants to do the cooking and scrubbing. The result is that Chinese women are the most perfectly groomed in the world and, everything considered, enjoy the greatest measure of luxury. Every woman, rich or poor, has a beauty kit. Only aged widows deny themselves such vanities, because the use of cosmetics might imply a desire to remarry, which would be looked upon as wantonness.

19. The title that best expresses the main theme or subject of this selection is:
    (A) Advertising cosmetics
    (B) Why Chinese girls always find husbands
    (C) The oldest retail shop in the world
    (D) The use of cosmetics in China
    (E) A beauty kit for every woman

20. Chinese women
    (A) never use any cosmetics
    (B) have just begun to use cosmetics
    (C) have used cosmetics only during the past 35 years
    (D) have used some form of cosmetics for 5000 years past
    (E) have used cosmetics for five centuries only

21. The best customers for cosmetics in China are
    (A) young girls   (C) servants
    (B) wives   (D) middle-aged spinsters
          (E) old widows

22. Chinese women as a whole
    (A) are unattractive
    (B) are overworked
    (C) are careless about their appearance
    (D) are better groomed than most women
    (E) do not like to have servants

Reading Passage VI

The Tuaregs, wanderers of the Sahara Desert, are born fighters. Tall, muscular, capable of almost superhuman resistance and patience when stalking a human prey, the Tuareg prince hides his light complexion and fine, intelligent features under the litham. This dark cloth, which entirely covers his face except for the eyes, he is supposed to wear even during sleep and barely to raise while eating. Like the Bedouin of Central Arabia, he firmly believes that a man is surrounded by malignant spirits constantly endeavoring to penetrate into him by way of his lips and nostrils, in order to take possession of his soul—a superstition that is probably only a poetic way of describing the whirling, all-pervading sands of the desert.

23. The complexion of the Tuaregs is
    (A) light   (C) black
    (B) brown   (D) yellow
              (E) red

24. The litham worn by the Tuareg man is a
    (A) turban   (C) veil
    (B) sash   (D) robe
              (E) neck scarf

25. The litham is supposedly worn for protection from
    (A) the glare of the sun   (C) evil spirits
    (B) sandstorms   (D) cold
              (E) tribal enemies

END OF TEST
If you finish before the allotted time is up, work on this part only.
When time is up, proceed directly to the next part and do not
return to this part.

TEST II. INTERPRETATION OF READING MATERIALS IN THE SOCIAL STUDIES

PART B. GRAPH AND TABLE INTERPRETATION

DIRECTIONS: Read each question in this test carefully. Answer each one on the basis of the following table. Select the best answer and write it in the proper space on the answer sheet.

Comparison of Petroleum Production in Four Different Countries for 1928-1932 (in thousands of barrels)

YEAR	U.S.	MEXICO	RUSSIA	PERSIA
1928	901,474	50,151	87,800	43,806
1929	1,007,323	44,689	103,000	42,489
1930	898,001	39,530	135,200	44,450
1931	851,081	33,039	162,800	40,638
1932	785,159	32,802	154,000	45,517

1. Which country led in the production of petroleum in 1932?

2. The smallest total amount of petroleum produced by any country in all years was produced by___________.

3. Which country shows the most consistent decline in the production of petroleum?

4. What per cent of the total production of petroleum in 1931 was produced by Russia?

5. During what year did all the countries combined produce the least amount of petroleum?

6. The amount of petroleum produced by Persia in 1930 was 7/34 of its total petroleum production between 1928-1932. Express this fraction as a decimal. Carry your answer to 2 decimal places only.

7. In which year was the average petroleum output of all countries nearest the total production of Persia for 1928 to 1932 inclusive?

8. Which group of countries produced the least amount of petroleum during 1930? (A) Russia and Persia (B) Mexico and Russia. Write either A or B for answer.

9. During which single year did both Mexico and Persia show the greatest per cent decrease over the previous year in the production of petroleum?

10. In which year did Mexico show the greatest numerical decrease (in thousands of barrels) in its production of petroleum?

11. Compute the per cent increase in production of petroleum for the United States from 1928 to 1929. Express as a decimal carrying your answer to two places. Do not use the word or sign "per cent" after your answer.

TEST III. INTERPRETATION OF READING MATERIALS
IN THE NATURAL SCIENCES

TIME: 1 Hour

DIRECTIONS: Below each of the following passages of natural science reading material you will find one or more incomplete statements about the passage. Select the words or expressions that most satisfactorily complete each statement in accordance with the meaning of the paragraph.

Reading Passage I

The use of wood as a material from which to make paper was first suggested in the Western world in a treatise dated November 15, 1719, by René de Réaumur (1683–1757), a celebrated naturalist residing in France. Réaumur had observed the habits of certain wasps and concluded that the wood filaments used by these insects to construct their paperlike nests could also be used in the actual process of papermaking. Human invention in the making of paper had been anticipated by the wasp, which may be considered as a professional papermaker, devoting most of her time and energies to the making of this material which she uses in the construction of nests. For this purpose the wasp seeks dry wood, which she saws or rasps by mastication. She mixes the material with a glucy substance exuded for the purpose, and, working the whole into a paste, spreads the paper substance in a manner truly remarkable. The nest is usually a prolonged irregular spheroid, exceptionally light in weight, of a dark color, and bound with repeated bands of paper to the bough from which it is suspended. The nest is water-resistant to a high degree, partly because of the rounded top but more because of the fact that the paper strips overlap like the shingles of a house.

1. The title that best expresses the main theme or subject of this selection is:
   (A) What a French naturalist decided
   (B) The habits of wasps
   (C) Wasp nests
   (D) The papermaking industry
   (E) The contribution of the wasp to paper-making

2. The man who first suggested the making of paper from wood was a specialist in
   (A) farming
   (B) papermaking
   (C) printing
   (D) trade
   (E) nature study

3. The primary source of the material used in the nests of papermaking wasps is
   (A) dirt
   (B) water
   (C) paste
   (D) wood
   (E) glue

4. The shape of the nest of the papermaking wasp is usually
   (A) oblong
   (B) regular
   (C) flat
   (D) spherical
   (E) square

5. The papermaking wasp makes its nest highly waterproof by
   (A) constructing it of heavy material
   (B) putting bands around it
   (C) overlapping the strips of material
   (D) hanging it on a bough
   (E) turning it upside down

Reading Passage II

How can we know that the birds we see in the South in the winter are the same ones that come north in the spring? One time John J. Audubon, a bird lover, wondered about this. Every year he watched a pair of little phoebes nesting in the same place. He wondered if they were the same birds. He decided to put tiny silver bands on their legs. The next spring back came the birds with the bands to the very same place. Back came the young birds to build their nests on the walls of farm buildings in the neighborhood. The phoebe, it was learned, wintered wherever it was warm enough to find flies. In summer, phoebes could be seen from Georgia to Canada; in winter, anywhere from Georgia to Florida and Mexico. The phoebe was the first kind of bird to be banded, and Mr. Audubon was the first birdbander. Today there are hundreds of birdbanders all over America. These peoples band all kinds of birds.

The government of the United States has a special birdbanding department which makes all the birdbands. The bands do not hurt the birds, as they are made of aluminum and are very light. They come in different sizes for different size birds. Each band has a special number. On each band are these words: "Notify Fish and Wildlife Service, Washington, D.C." Anyone who finds a dead bird with a band on its legs is asked to send the band to Washington with a note telling where and when the bird was found. In this way naturalists add to their knowledge of the habits and needs of birds.

6. The title below that best expresses the main theme or subject of this selection is:
   (A) The migration of birds
   (B) The work of John Audubon
   (C) The habits and needs of birds
   (D) The Fish and Wildlife Service
   (E) Studying birdlife through birdbanding

7. According to the selection, Audubon proved his theory that
   (A) birds prefer a diet of flies
   (B) birds return to the same nesting place each spring
   (C) silver is the best material for birdbands
   (D) phoebes are the most interesting birds to study
   (E) the government should make a scientific study of birds

8. Audubon's purpose in banding the phoebes was to

   (A) satisfy his curiosity
   (B) notify the government
   (C) start a birdbanding department
   (D) gain fame as the first birdbander
   (E) prevent the birds from flying too far south

9. The migration habits of phoebes depend upon
   (A) nesting places
   (B) the help of bird lovers
   (C) the available food supply
   (D) the number of young birds
   (E) protection by the Fish and Wildlife Service

10. Which statement is *true* according to the selection?
   (A) Residents of Georgia may expect to see phoebes all year long.
   (B) The weight of a band causes a bird considerable discomfort.
   (C) The government offers a reward for information about dead birds.
   (D) All young birds build their nests on the walls of farm buildings.
   (E) Phoebes are more plentiful in the East than any other kind of bird.

Reading Passage III

One day recently a man in a ten-gallon hat knocked quietly on the gate of New York's famous Bronx Zoo. "Just stopped on my way through town," he told Zoo officials. "I've got an animal outside I think you might like to see."

The Zoo officials raised their eyebrows to new heights and looked at each other meaningfully. If there was ever a case of bringing coals to Newcastle, this was it. But the man in the hat did not seem to notice. He introduced himself as Gene Holter and went on talking. "I call it a zonkey," he said mildly, "because it's a cross between a donkey and a zebra. I've got his parents out there too."

The Zoo officials didn't wait to hear about the parents. They had already left their desks and started for the gate. Outside, Mr. Holter opened the side door of a huge truck and reached inside. Calmly, he pulled out a gibbon, a kind of ape, and hung it on a tree. Then he walked past five ostriches (he uses them for sulky racing) and carried out the baby zonkey.

Just three weeks old, the only zonkey in the world had long ears, a face and legs that were candy-striped and a body covered with brown baby fuzz. The parents were on hand, too. The father was no ordinary zebra either. He was broken to ride, and one of the Zoo officials realized a dream of a lifetime when he jumped on the zebra's back and cantered around.

When last seen, Mr. Holter and his caravan were on their way to Dayton. You might catch them there, or you might go on to Anaheim, California, where they live the year round.

11. Mr. Holter's manner was
    (A) sulky   (D) commanding
    (B) boastful   (E) matter-of-fact
    (C) excitable

12. When Mr. Holter first talked to the Zoo officials, they
    (A) acted as though they doubted him
    (B) seemed to have bad dispositions
    (C) stopped to put coal on the fire
    (D) pretended to be busy
    (E) laughed at him

13. The Zoo officials were interested in seeing the zonkey chiefly because it was
    (A) so young
    (B) with its parents
    (C) comical to look at
    (D) trained to carry riders
    (E) the only one in the world

14. A person would be most likely to have an opportunity to see a zonkey by visiting
    (A) Africa
    (B) Dayton
    (C) Anaheim
    (D) Newcastle
    (E) the Bronx Zoo

Reading Passage IV

Few animals are as descriptively named as the varying hare (Lepus americanus), also commonly known as the snowshoe hare, white rabbit, or snowshoe rabbit. The species derives its various names from its interesting adaptations to the seasonal changes affecting its habitat.

The color changes are affected by means of a molt, and are timed (although the hares have no voluntary control over them) to coincide with the changing appearances of the background. The periods of transition, from white to brown in the spring, and from brown to white in the fall, each require more than two months from start to completion, during which time the hares are a mottled brown and white. In addition to the changes in color, in the fall the soles of the feet develop a very heavy growth of hair which functions as snowshoes.

In New York State, hares are most abundant in and around the Adirondack and Catskill mountains. Thriving populations, with less extensive ranges, are found in Allegany, Cattaraugus, Rensselaer, and Chenango counties. Smaller colonies of limited range are found in scattered islands.

15. The title that best expresses the main theme or subject of this selection is:
    (A) Seasonal changes in birds
    (B) The varying hare
    (C) An American animal
    (D) The abundance of hares
    (E) The effect of color changes

16. Terms used to name these rabbits are related to their
    (A) abundance in many parts of New York State
    (B) sensitiveness to weather conditions throughout the state
    (C) ability to adapt to the change of seasons
    (D) thick white coats
    (E) particularly shaped feet

17. These rabbits have both brown and white markings in
    (A) summer and winter
    (B) spring and fall
    (C) spring and summer
    (D) fall and winter
    (E) winter and spring

18. The parts of New York State where rabbit populations are most plentiful are
    (A) Allegany, Cattaraugus, Rensselaer, and Chenango counties
    (B) Adirondack and Catskill mountain regions
    (C) islands within the state
    (D) snowy areas in the hills
    (E) extensive ranges

Reading Passage V

Whales today are sought for food and fat substitutes, and to make glycerin, high explosives and soap. In early days the average whaling ship was of three hundred tons' burden; the average catch, three thousand barrels of oil. To get this amount of oil took from three to four years. The so-called mother ships of today are in reality great factories. Their average tonnage is thirty thousand, their season averages no more than four months, and they catch five hundred thousand tons a year. These mother ships have every improvement. The crew consists of two hundred and forty men, who receive a salary and a percentage. The mother ships have a number of killer boats which use guns firing a one-hundred-fifty-pound bomb or explosive harpoon. The whale is towed back to the mother ship and is hoisted to the vessel, which opens a vast door in its side to admit the entire whale. Eighty per cent of the whales are taken in the Antarctic. Today's whalers can not capture the sperm, right and bowhead whales, which were the standby of the old whalers, because these mammals can hear a powerboat twelve miles away.

19. The title that best expresses the main theme or subject of this selection is:
    (A) The dangers of whale fishing
    (B) Whale fishing today
    (C) The importance of whale fishing
    (D) Whaling boats
    (E) Whale fishing as an occupation

20. The season for whaling in modern times is about
    (A) 120 days   (D) 3 years
    (B) 240 days   (E) 4 years
    (C) 300 days

21. The average tonnage of whaling ships at the present time is about
    (A) 150   (D) 30,000
    (B) 300   (E) 500,000
    (C) 3000

22. Sperm whales are no longer captured, because they
    (A) have become extinct
    (B) have changed the place where they live
    (C) are warned by the noise of the boats
    (D) are too small to be profitable
    (E) are dangerous fighters

Reading Passage VI

Our ancestors made soap at home by boiling left-over fats with lye, which in the early days they made out of wood ashes. The soap of our great-grandmother's day was likely to contain a liberal amount of free alkali—a great contrast to the soap made by modern commercial methods, which is not considered satisfactory for use if it contains more than one-tenth of one per cent free alkali. Free alkali is harmful to hands and fabrics, just as lye is. Even when it is diluted with water, alkali makes the skin rough and red.

Modern soap, produced from commercially prepared fat and lye, is made in various forms, of which bars, flakes and granules are the most commonly used. The bar form is, of course, the oldest. To make bars, the soap is poured, while still warm and soft, into large molds. Flakes are not made by chipping up bars of soap. Instead the soft warm soap is poured over chilled metal to form a thin film, which hardens immediately and can be scraped off in the form of ribbons. These ribbons of soap are dried and then easily break up into flakes. Granulated soap is made by blowing hot liquid soap through nozzles with fine holes, into a heated tower. The particles of soap that are formed harden into tiny drops or bubbles. The three forms of soap, bars, flakes and granules, may all be made from the same basic soap mixture.

23. The title that best expresses the main theme or subject of this selection is:
    (A) Machines for making soap
    (B) The necessity for soap
    (C) Brands of toilet soap
    (D) The production of soap
    (E) Why soap should not contain free alkali

24. Our great-grandmothers made their own soap by using lye that was obtained from
    (A) grease   (D) grain
    (B) chips   (E) fats
    (C) ashes

25. Soap flakes are produced by
    (A) pouring hot liquid into molds
    (B) blowing the hot liquid through nozzles
    (C) chipping off bars
    (D) stamping granules
    (E) drying ribbons formed on chilled metal

END OF TEST

If you finish before the allotted time is up, work on this part only.
When time is up, proceed directly to the next part and do not
return to this part.

TEST IV. INTERPRETATION OF LITERARY MATERIALS

TIME: 1 Hour

> *DIRECTIONS: Below each of the literary passages you will find one or more incomplete statements about the passage of prose, poetry, or drama. Each "stem" is followed by four or five "foils." Read each passage slowly, visualizing the plot, setting, action, characters, meaning, tone, and style. Re-read the passage before answering each question. From the emotions and attitudes expressed, choose the BEST "foil." Blacken the corresponding space on the answer sheet.*

Fiction Passage I.

The officer's heart was plunging. He poured himself a glass of wine, part of which spilled on the floor, and gulped the remainder, leaning against the cool, green stove. He heard his man collecting the dishes from the stairs. Pale, as if intoxicated, he waited. The servant entered again. The Captain's heart gave a pang, as of pleasure, seeing the young fellow bewildered and uncertain on his feet, with pain.

"Schoner!" he said.

The soldier was a little slower in coming to attention.

"Yes, sir!"

The youth stood before him, with pathetic young mustache, and fine eyebrows very distinct on his forehead of dark marble.

"I asked you a question."

"Yes, sir."

The officer's tone bit like acid.

"Why had you a pencil in your ear?"

Again the servant's heart ran hot, and he could not breathe. With dark, strained eyes, he looked at the officer, as if fascinated. And he stood there sturdily planted, unconscious. The withering smile came into the Captain's eyes, and he lifted his foot.

"I—I forgot it—sir," panted the soldier, his dark eyes fixed on the other man's dancing blue ones.

"What was it doing there?"

He saw the young man's breast heaving as he made an effort for words.

"I had been writing."

"Writing what?"

Again the soldier looked him up and down. The officer could hear him panting. The smile came into the blue eyes. The soldier worked his dry throat, but could not speak. Suddenly the smile lit like a flame on the officer's face, and a kick came heavily against the orderly's thigh. The youth moved a pace sideways. His face went dead, with two black staring eyes.

"Well?" said the officer.

The orderly's mouth had gone dry, and his tongue rubbed in it as on dry brown-paper. He worked his throat. The officer raised his foot. The servant went stiff.

"Some poetry, sir," came the crackling, unrecognizable sound of his voice.

"Poetry, what poetry?" asked the Captain with a sickly smile.

Again there was the working in the throat. The Captain's heart had suddenly gone down heavily, and stood sick and tired.

"For my girl, sir," he heard the dry, inhuman sound.

"Oh!" he said, turning away. "Clear the table."

"Click!" went the soldier's throat; then again, "click!" and then half-articulate:

"Yes, sir."

The young soldier was gone, looking old, and walking heavily.

—D.H.Lawrence, "The Prussian Officer"

1. The two men in the story are

    (A) in the army
    (B) brothers
    (C) in the navy
    (D) old friends

2. The phrase, "pale, as if intoxicated . . ." means the officer

    (A) pretends he is drunk
    (B) is drunk
    (C) looks as if he is drunk
    (D) acts as if he was drunk

3. The officer kicked the orderly because

    (A) the servant had broken dishes
    (B) Schoner had attacked him
    (C) the young man acted sullenly
    (D) Schoner didn't answer a question

4. The soldier confessed with great difficulty that he

    (A) had been collecting dishes from the stairs
    (B) he had cleared the table
    (C) he had been writing poetry for his girl
    (D) he hated the Captain

5. The Captain's character and his actions might be said to be

    (A) courageous
    (B) benevolent
    (C) indifferent
    (D) sadistic

6. When Schoner leaves the room, it is obvious that he is

    (A) ill
    (B) humiliated
    (C) angry
    (D) cheerful

Nonfiction Passage II.

One night I went with an organizer named Scott to a mining town in the Fairmont district where the miners had asked me to hold a meeting. When we got off the car I asked Scott where I was to speak and he pointed to a frame building. We walked in. There were lighted candles on an altar. I looked around in the dim light. We were in a church and the benches were filled with miners.

Outside the railing of the altar was a table. At one end sat the priest with the money of the union in his hands. The president of the local union sat at the other end of the table. I marched down the aisle.

"What's going on?" I asked.

"Holding a meeting," said the president.

"What for?"

"For the union, Mother. We rented the church for our meeting."

I reached over and took the money from the priest. Then I turned to the miners.

"Boys," I said, "this is a praying institution. You should not commercialize it. Get up, every one of you and go out in the open fields."

They got up and went out and sat around in a field while I spoke to them. The sheriff was there and he did not allow any traffic to go along the road while I was speaking. In front of us was a school house. I pointed to it and I said, "Your ancestors fought for you to have a share in that institution over there. It's yours. See the school board, and every Friday night hold your meetings there. Have your wives clean it up Saturday morning for the children to enter Monday. Your organization is not a praying institution. It's a fighting institution. It's an educational institution along industrial lines. Pray for the dead and fight like hell for the living!"

—Mary Harris Jones, *The Autobiography of Mother Jones*

7. The title that best expresses the idea of this selection is

(A) the real meaning of a union
(B) a union meeting in a church
(C) organizing miners
(D) the meaning of a school building

8. The reason the writer wouldn't allow the meeting to go on in a church was that

(A) the light was too dim
(B) she didn't trust the priest
(C) she didn't want the church to be used used for anything else but religion
(D) few miners would come to it

9. When the writer told the miners to "Pray for the dead and fight like hell for the living," she meant

(A) they weren't religious enough
(B) for them to use the church for prayer and the school for organizing the union
(C) they should pity their dead friends, but get ready to go on strike
(D) that it was time they remembered the people who had sacrificed their lives for them

Dramatic Passage III.

Alquist (seated at table, turning pages of book). Oh, God, shall I never find it? Gall, Hallemeier, Fabry, how were the Robots made? Why did you leave not a trace of the secret? Lord, if there are no human beings left, at least let there be Robots. At least the shadow of man. *(Turning pages)* If I could only sleep. Dare I sleep before life has been renewed? Night again. Are the stars still there? Of what use are the stars? When there are no human beings. *(Examining a test tube.)* Nothing. No. No. I must find it. I must search. I must never stop, never stop—search—search—*(knock at door)* Who is it?

   (Enter a Robot servant.)

Servant. Master, the committee of Robots is waiting to see you.

Alquist. I can see no one.

Servant. It is the Central Committee, Master, just arrived from abroad.

Alquist. Well, well, send them in. *(Exit servant.)* No time—so little done. *(Re-enter Servant with Radius and group of Robots. They stand in group silently waiting.)* What do you want? Be quick; I have no time.

Radius. Master, the machines will not do the work. We cannot manufacture Robots.

  (Other Robots remain two abreast, right foot forward.)

First Robot. We have striven with all our might. We have obtained a billion tons of coal from the earth. Nine million spindles are running by day and by night. There is no longer room for all we have made. This we have accomplished in one year.

Alquist. For whom?

Radius. For future generations—so we thought. But we cannot make Robots to follow us. The machines produce only shapeless clods. The skin will not adhere to the flesh, nor the flesh to the bones.

Second Robot. Eight million Robots have died this year. Within twenty years there will be none left.

First Robot. Tell us the secret of life.

Radius. Silence is punishable with death.

Alquist. Kill me then.

Radius. Through me, the governments of the Robots of the world command you to deliver up Rossum's formula. *(Gesture of despair from Alquist)* Name your price. *(Silence)* We will give you the earth. We will give you endless possessions of the earth. *(Silence)* Make your own conditions.

Alquist. I have told you to find human beings.

Radius. There are none left.

Alquist. I told you to search in the wilderness, upon the mountains.

Radius.   We have sent ships and expeditions without number. They have been everywhere in the world. There is not a single human left.

Alquist.   Not even one? Why did you destroy them?

Radius.   We had learnt everything and could do everything. It had to be.

Second Robot.   We had to become the masters.

Radius.   Slaughter and domination are necessary if you would be human beings. Read history.

First Robot.   Teach us to multiply or we perish.

Alquist.   If you desire to live, you must breed like animals.

First Robot.   You made us sterile. We cannot beget children. Therefore, teach us how to make Robots.

Radius.   Why do you keep from us the secret of our own increase?

Alquist.   It is lost.

Radius.   It was written down.

Alquist.   It was—*(rising)* burnt. *(All draw back one step in consternation.)* I am the last human being, Robots, and I do not know what the others knew *(Sits.)*

Radius.   Then make experiments. Evolve the formula again.

Alquist.   I tell you I cannot. I am only a builder. I work with my hands. I have never been a learned man. I cannot create life.

Radius.   Try, try.

Alquist.   If you only knew how many experiments I have made already.

First Robot.   Then show us what we must do. The robots can do anything that human beings show them.

Alquist.   I can show you nothing. Nothing I do will make life proceed from these test tubes.

Radius.   Experiment, then, on live Robots. Experiment, then, on us.

Alquist.   It would kill you.

Radius.   You shall have all you need. A hundred of us. A thousand of us.

—Karel Capek, *R.U.R.*

10. This play is
    (A) set in the past
    (B) a comedy
    (C) set in the future
    (D) supposed to be happening today

11. Alquist is
    (A) a scientist   (C) the last man on earth
    (B) ruler of all robots   (D) a robot

12. Radius has to admit that
    (A) robots did not want to be masters
    (B) robots do not wish to live
    (C) robots do not create robots
    (D) the humans robots capture do not know how to create robots

13. Alquist cannot be threatened by the robots because
    (A) they are afraid of him
    (B) he does not worry about being killed
    (C) he really knows the secret of making robots
    (D) he can destroy all of them

14. Radius states that Alquist
    (A) should continue experimenting
    (B) must stop all experiments
    (C) will fail but robots will discover how to reproduce themselves
    (D) should experiment on robots

TEST V. GENERAL MATHEMATICAL ABILITY

TIME: 1 Hour

DIRECTIONS: In the following multiple choice questions, choose the correct answer from the choices offered.

Do not make any marks on the test itself. It is best to work out the solution to each question on a sheet of blank paper before looking at the suggested answers. This will help prevent you from being misled by answers that at first glance may look correct.

1. Which of the following has the same value as $1\frac{1}{2}\%$?
   (A) 1.5
   (B) .15
   (C) .015
   (D) .0015

2. What is 3,021 minus 447 minus 386?
   (A) 1,829
   (B) 1,940
   (C) 2,084
   (D) 2,188

3. What is 87,648 divided by 12?
   (A) 7,304
   (B) 8,269
   (C) 8,943
   (D) 9,212

4. What is 12 times 19 times 43?
   (A) 8,432
   (B) 8,864
   (C) 9,804
   (D) 9,962

5. What is 923 plus 18 plus 407?
   (A) 1,348
   (B) 2,420
   (C) 3,192
   (D) 4,642

6. The drawing at the right is part of a bar graph showing the population of a small village. How many people lived in the village in 1950?
   (A) 250
   (B) 2,500
   (C) 25,000
   (D) 250,000

7. A group left on a trip at 8:50 A.M. and reached their destination at 3:30 P.M. How long, in hours and minutes, did the trip take?
   (A) 3 hr. 10 min.
   (B) 4 hr. 40 min.
   (C) 5 hr. 10 min.
   (D) 6 hr. 40 min.

8. Find the amount of a 2% tax on a purchase amounting to $24.50.
   (A) 49¢
   (B) 65¢
   (C) $4.80
   (D) $5.60

9. On a scale drawing, a line $\frac{1}{4}$ inch long represents a length of 1 foot. On the same drawing, what length represents 4 feet?
   (A) 1 inch
   (B) 2 inches
   (C) 3 inches
   (D) 4 inches

10. One year the postage rate for sending 1 ounce of mail first class was increased from 3 cents to 4 cents. What was the per cent of increase in the postage rate?
    (A) $12\frac{1}{2}\%$
    (B) 15%
    (C) $33\frac{1}{3}\%$
    (D) 40%

11. $33\frac{1}{3}\%$ of 99 =
    (A) 33
    (B) 66
    (C) 27
    (D) 30

12. How many squares of 1 ft. by 1 ft. can be cut out of a square 1 yd. by 1 yd. so that there is no material remaining?
    (A) 3
    (B) 9
    (C) 4
    (D) 6

13. The volume of a cube whose side is 3 inches is
    (A) 9 cubic inches
    (B) 3 cubic inches
    (C) $\frac{1}{64}$ cubic feet
    (D) 27 cubic feet

14. Mr. Arnold gets $5 an hour for 8 hours and $6 an hour overtime (after 8 hours per day). How much will he receive if he works for 12 hours straight?
    (A) $60
    (B) $66
    (C) $84
    (D) $64

15. At 12:30 P.M. what is the smaller angle between the minute hand and the hour hand?
    (A) 180°
    (B) 175°
    (C) 165°
    (D) 150°

16. If a plane travels 1,000 miles in 5 hours, 30 minutes, what is its average speed in miles per hour?
    (A) $181\frac{9}{11}$ (C) 215
    (B) 200 (D) $192\frac{1}{2}$

17. What is the sum of 15.36, 16.64, 17.41, 18.59?
    (A) 58.01 (C) 59.20
    (B) 59.10 (D) 68.00

18. What is the value of $\frac{3}{4} \times \frac{1}{2} \div \frac{4}{7}$?
    (A) $\frac{3}{14}$ (C) $\frac{6}{7}$
    (B) $21\frac{1}{32}$ (D) $\frac{7}{9}$

19. $2\frac{7}{8} =$
    (A) 2.875 (C) 2.88
    (B) 2.935 (D) 2.75

20. 60 is what per cent of 2,500?
    (A) 2.2 (C) 24
    (B) 2.4 (D) .24

21. Choose the largest fraction
    (A) $\frac{3}{4}$ (C) $\frac{7}{10}$
    (B) $\frac{3}{5}$ (D) $\frac{5}{8}$

22. When 13 is divided by .02, the quotient is
    (A) 6,500 (C) 65
    (B) 650 (D) 6.5

23. What is the remainder when 593 is divided by 8?
    (A) 1 (C) 3
    (B) 2 (D) 4

24. A kitten now weighs $1\frac{1}{2}$ pounds more than it did eight weeks ago. Its average gain per week was
    (A) less than 2 ounces
    (B) 3 ounces
    (C) $3\frac{1}{2}$ ounces
    (D) more than 4 ounces

25. A recipe for 6 quarts of punch calls for $\frac{3}{4}$ cup of sugar. How much sugar is needed for 9 quarts of punch?
    (A) five-eighths of a cup
    (B) seven-eighths of a cup
    (C) $1\frac{1}{8}$ cups
    (D) $2\frac{1}{4}$ cups

END OF EXAMINATION

If you finish before the allotted time is up, check your work on this test only. Do not go back to earlier tests. When time runs out, compare your answers for this test and all the other tests in the examination with the correct key answers that follow.

CORRECT ANSWERS FOR SAMPLE EXAMINATION II.

(Please make every effort to answer the questions on your own before look-ing at these answers. You'll make faster progress by following this rule.)

TEST I. CORRECTNESS AND EFFECTIVENESS OF EXPRESSION

PART A. ENGLISH USAGE

1.B	6.A	11.A	16.D	21.A	26.B
2.A	7.C	12.C	17.A	22.D	27.A
3.D	8.A	13.B	18.D	23.D	28.C
4.B	9.D	14.D	19.C	24.B	29.B
5.D	10.A	15.A	20.A	25.B	30.A

PART B. SPELLING

1.B	5.C	9.A	13.C	17.A
2.D	6.B	10.B	14.A	18.B
3.B	7.C	11.A	15.D	19.C
4.C	8.D	12.B	16.D	20.B

TEST II. INTERPRETATION OF READING MATERIALS IN THE SOCIAL STUDIES

PART A. SOCIAL STUDIES READINGS

1.E	6.B	11.E	16.A	21.B
2.C	7.E	12.B	17.D	22.D
3.E	8.A	13.C	18.C	23.A
4.B	9.B	14.B	19.D	24.C
5.C	10.A	15.D	20.D	25.C

PART B. GRAPH AND TABLE INTERPRETATION

1. U.S.	4. 15%	7. 1932	10. 1931
2. Mexico	5. 1932	8. B	11. .11
3. Mexico	6. .21	9. 1931	

TEST III. INTERPRETATION OF READING MATERIALS IN THE NATURAL SCIENCES

1.E	6.E	11.E	16.C	21.D
2.E	7.B	12.A	17.B	22.C
3.D	8.A	13.E	18.B	23.D
4.D	9.C	14.C	19.B	24.C
5.C	10.A	15.B	20.A	25.E

TEST IV. INTERPRETATION OF LITERARY MATERIALS

1.A	3.D	5.D	7.A	9.B	11.C	13.B
2.C	4.C	6.B	8.C	10.C	12.C	14.D

TEST V. GENERAL MATHEMATICAL ABILITY

1.C	6.B	11.A	16.A	21.A
2.D	7.D	12.B	17.D	22.B
3.A	8.A	13.C	18.B	23.A
4.C	9.A	14.D	19.A	24.B
5.A	10.C	15.C	20.B	25.C

III. SAMPLE EXAM FOR PRACTICE

This professionally-written Examination enables you to display and exercise the important test-taking abilities leading to high scores . . . judgment, coolness, and flexibility. The various Tests fairly represent the actual exam. They should help in jogging your memory for all kinds of useful and relevant information which might otherwise be lost to you in achieving the highest exam rating possible.

The time allowed for the entire examination is 5 hours. In order to create the climate of the test to come, that's precisely what you should allow yourself . . . no more, no less. Use a watch and keep a record of your time, especially since you may find it convenient to take the test in several sittings.

TEST I. CORRECTNESS AND EFFECTIVENESS OF EXPRESSION

TIME: 1 Hour

PART A. ENGLISH USAGE

DIRECTIONS: Read each Theme through carefully to get the general meaning. Then go back and look at the underlined and numbered portions of the story. Some of the underlined words and phrases contain errors in grammar, punctuation or choice of words. Others are correct as written. Study the suggested corrections in the right-hand column and choose the one you think is best. All of the suggestions may be grammatically correct, but one is always more effective than the others.

THEME I.

Some people choose one way of solving their personal <u>problems. While</u> others choose other ways.
₁

1. (A) NO CHANGE
   (B) problems while
   (C) problems the while
   (D) problems, while

You can <u>get</u> a good idea of a <u>persons</u> character by
₂   ₃

2. (A) NO CHANGE   (C) arrive in
   (B) cop   (D) get up

3. (A) NO CHANGE   (C) persons'
   (B) person's   (D) persons's

the way he tries <u>to solve</u> his problems. If a <u>individ-</u>
             4   5

<u>ual</u> gets very <u>mad</u> and gives all kinds of nonsensical
         6

excuses, you may conclude that he is living in an

unreal world. He needs help to get back to the real

world—the world of <u>thinkers' and scientists'</u>. He
               7

may need encouragement to work hard in order to

be part <u>of</u> reality. Maybe he is trying to accomplish
       8

the impossible and needs a task that is possible

<u>to be performed</u>. That person is <u>wise</u> if he can learn
     9   10

what the world expects from him in order to get

along in the world.

4. (A) NO CHANGE
   (B) in solving
   (C) in the solution of
   (D) for the solution of

5. (A) NO CHANGE   (C) a guy
   (B) an individual   (D) a fella

6. (A) NO CHANGE   (C) angry
   (B) angered   (D) much angry

7. (A) NO CHANGE
   (B) thinker's and scientist's
   (C) thinkers' and scientists
   (D) thinkers and scientists

8. (A) NO CHANGE   (C) in
   (B) from   (D) with

9. (A) NO CHANGE   (C) to perform
   (B) for performing   (D) for performance

10. (A) NO CHANGE   (C) hep
   (B) smart   (D) knowledged

THEME II.

The coast of <u>north Africa</u> is <u>allmost</u> as pleasant
             11   12

as <u>southern California</u>, with hot, dry summer and
     13

heavy rains in winter. The mountains of <u>Morocco's</u>

<u>and Algeria's</u> have a heavy winter snowfall and
   14

excellent <u>ski grounds.</u> Temperatures in the coast
     15

land's higher altitudes <u>are falling below</u> freezing
                  16

11. (A) NO CHANGE   (C) North Africa
   (B) north africa   (D) Northafrica

12. (A) NO CHANGE   (C) all most
   (B) almost   (D) al most

13. (A) NO CHANGE
   (B) southern california
   (C) Southern California
   (D) South California

14. (A) NO CHANGE
   (B) Morocco and Algeria's
   (C) Morocco's and Algeria
   (D) Morocco and Algeria

15. (A) NO CHANGE   (C) skiing grounds
   (B) skier grounds   (D) grounds to ski

16. (A) NO CHANGE
   (B) is falling below
   (C) fall below
   (D) has been falling below

ANSWER SHEET FOR SAMPLE EXAMINATION III.

Make only ONE mark for each answer. Additional and stray marks may be counted as mistakes.

TEST I. CORRECTNESS AND EFFECTIVENESS OF EXPRESSION

PART A. ENGLISH USAGE

PART B. SPELLING

TEST II. INTERPRETATION OF READING MATERIALS IN THE SOCIAL STUDIES

PART A. SOCIAL STUDIES READINGS

PART B. GRAPH AND TABLE INTERPRETATION

1. ____   2. ____   3. ____   4. ____   5. ____   6. ____   7. ____   8. ____

TEST III. INTERPRETATION OF READING MATERIALS IN THE NATURAL SCIENCES

TEST IV. INTERPRETATION OF LITERARY MATERIALS

TEST V. GENERAL MATHEMATICAL ABILITY

on <u>winter's nights.</u> South of the mountains the true
17

desert begins. It is not a continuous sea of <u>land,</u>
18

<u>some</u> parts are great stretches of sand, but <u>others</u>
19

are rock and gravel. One may travel for days and

<u>not see scarcely any</u> sand.
20

THEME III.

If you want to see a <u>collection of junk</u> from all
21

over the world, go to the Caledonian Market in

London. Here rubbish is something which is sold

and looking for rubbish is a <u>pass time.</u> You learn
22

here what unbelievable human needs and desires

there are. People hunt about, with open-mouthed

curiosity, <u>at</u> the leftovers from thousands of attic
23

rooms and basements. The Market is the <u>next to last</u>
24

resting place of unwanted vases, musical instru-

ments that will not play, sewing machines that will

not sew, baby carriages that will not roll, bicycles

<u>whose</u> wheels will not turn. There are other articles
25

from which all hope has long <u>flied.</u> There are stories
26

of fortunes being picked up in the Market. Once

<u>seven-hundred</u> gold sovereigns worth about $3000
27

<u>was found</u> in a secret drawer of a <u>crazy old bureau.</u>
28   29

And book buyers have discovered valuable editions

of Milton and Dickens and Carlyle. There <u>ain't</u>
30

<u>nothing</u> one can not buy in the Market.

17. (A) NO CHANGE   (C) Winter's nights
    (B) winter nights   (D) Winter nights

18. (A) NO CHANGE   (C) land; some
    (B) land some   (D) land and some

19. (A) NO CHANGE   (C) others'
    (B) other's   (D) other ones

20. (A) NO CHANGE
    (B) not see scarcely no
    (C) see scarcely no
    (D) see scarcely any

21. (A) NO CHANGE
    (B) collection in junk
    (C) junky collection
    (D) collection with junk

22. (A) NO CHANGE   (C) pastime
    (B) passtime   (D) past time

23. (A) NO CHANGE   (C) between
    (B) upon   (D) among

24. (A) NO CHANGE   (C) next to a last
    (B) next-to-last   (D) next from last

25. (A) NO CHANGE   (C) who'se
    (B) who's   (D) whos'e

26. (A) NO CHANGE   (C) fleed
    (B) flowed   (D) fled

27. (A) NO CHANGE
    (B) seven hundred
    (C) sevenhundred
    (D) 7 hundred

28. (A) NO CHANGE   (C) were found
    (B) was finded   (D) has been

29. (A) NO CHANGE
    (B) old crazy bureau
    (C) bureau that was old and crazy
    (D) crazy and old bureau

30. (A) NO CHANGE   (C) isn't anything
    (B) aren't nothing   (D) isn't nothing

TEST I. CORRECTNESS AND EFFECTIVENESS OF EXPRESSION

PART B. SPELLING

DIRECTIONS: In this test all words but one of each group are spelled correctly. Indicate the misspelled word in each group.

1. (A) chalk   (B) agreament   (C) navy   (D) magazine

2. (A) enemy   (B) enjoying   (C) whistleing   (D) letting

3. (A) neighber   (B) gasoline   (C) liberty   (D) neighborhood

4. (A) noticed   (B) musical   (C) motive   (D) seperate

5. (A) backwards   (B) advantege   (C) bacon   (D) measure

6. (A) embroidery   (B) furnace   (C) memery   (D) marked

7. (A) justice   (B) kettle   (C) gobble   (D) dificult

8. (A) metal   (B) miner   (C) cammera   (D) fountain

9. (A) aprentice   (B) increased   (C) grave   (D) goodness

10. (A) downtown   (B) convention   (C) express   (D) garbege

11. (A) seventy   (B) labratory   (C) knowledge   (D) lemonade

12. (A) petroleum   (B) alcohol   (C) cough   (D) atempt

13. (A) practiceing   (B) astonished   (C) mittens   (D) drawer

14. (A) tarriff   (B) barefooted   (C) activity   (D) catalogue

15. (A) cradle   (B) sanwiches   (C) dreadful   (D) dough

16. (A) measles   (B) scooter   (C) orchard   (D) sailer

17. (A) ticket   (B) worshipped   (C) buldog   (D) we've

18. (A) various   (B) timber   (C) usual   (D) aviater

19. (A) pitcher   (B) stable   (C) militery   (D) vegetable

20. (A) cramberries   (B) ringing   (C) peaches   (D) September

TEST II. INTERPRETATION OF READING MATERIALS
IN THE SOCIAL STUDIES

TIME: 1 Hour

PART A. SOCIAL STUDIES READINGS

DIRECTIONS: Below each of the following passages of social science reading material you will find one or more incomplete statements about the passage. Select the words or expressions that most satisfactorily complete each statement in accordance with the meaning of the paragraph.

Reading Passage I

In the year 1799, an officer of the French army was stationed in a little fortress near Alexandria on the Rosetta· River, one of the mouths of the Nile in Egypt. He was interested in the ruins of the ancient civilization of Egypt; he had seen the Sphinx and the Pyramids, those mysterious structures erected by men of another age. One day, when a trench was being dug, he found to his surprise a stone of black slate on which were cut letters he could read. He had studied Greek in school and knew that this was an inscription written in that language. Along with the Greek letters there ran an inscription in the same kind of Egyptian letters which he had seen carved on other ruins. There were three kinds of writing on the stone: one set of lines in Greek, and the other two sets in characters which, while both unknown, were plainly unlike each other.

The young officer had his wits about him. As soon as he saw the lines of Greek letters below the other two inscriptions, he said to himself, "If each line should be telling the same fact in a different language, the Greek letters would give the key to what the other letter meant." So he took good care of the stone and turned it over to scholars who were puzzling over Egyptian carvings.

In 1802 a French professor by the name of Champollion began to work on the inscriptions, trying to study out by the Greek key how the Egyptian characters told the same story. Champollion worked for twenty years on that stone. Other scholars began, worked a year or two, found out

one or two letters, and gave it up. But Champollion kept right on until finally he made out the stone's secret. In 1823 he announced to the world of scholars that he had found out what fourteen of the signs meant. Twenty years to find out what the fourteen signs meant! But in finding out those fourteen puzzle signs, he had discovered the secret of Egyptian writing. He had unlocked the secret of the Rosetta Stone; this let all the written records of Egypt be known to the world some five thousand years after an unknown person had inscribed the same information in three different tongues!

1. The title below that best expresses the main idea of this passage is:
   (A) A French officer's courage
   (B) The work of Champollion
   (C) Values in the study of Greek
   (D) The story of the Rosetta Stone
   (E) Ancient Egyptian writings

2. The Rosetta Stone derived its name from
   (A) the man who found it
   (B) its size and shape
   (C) the place near which it was found
   (D) the person who translated the inscriptions
   (E) its color

3. The discoverer of the stone apparently
   (A) spent more than twenty years in Egypt
   (B) liked to dig trenches
   (C) was fond of puzzles
   (D) was familiar with more than one language
   (E) could speak Egyptian

S1675

4. The author suggests that Champollion discovered the meaning of the inscriptions because he
    (A) knew more Greek than the other scholars
    (B) used the work of other students of language to gain fame for himself
    (C) was more interested in ancient civilization than the other scholars
    (D) did not give up easily as the other scholars
    (E) had more time to spare than anyone else

5. The carvings on the stone were considered very important because they
    (A) explained the reasons for building the Sphinx and the Pyramids
    (B) provided work for Champollion for twenty years
    (C) proved the value of learning Greek
    (D) gave a clue to the meaning of ancient inscriptions
    (E) proved that, even in digging trenches, there is glory

6. The inscriptions on the stone were
    (A) all in the same language
    (B) all in unknown languages
    (C) in Greek, French, and an unknown language
    (D) in French and two unknown languages
    (E) in Greek and two unknown languages

Reading Passage II

For generations, historians and boat lovers have been trying to learn more about the brave ship which brought the Pilgrims to America. The task was a difficult one because the *Mayflower* was such a common name for ships back in early seventeenth century England that there were at least twenty of them when the Pilgrims left for the new world.

An exact duplicate of the *Mayflower* has been built in England and given to the people of the United States as a symbol of the good will and common ancestry linking Britons and Americans. The Pilgrims' *Mayflower* apparently was built originally as a fishing vessel. It seems to have been 90 feet long by 22 feet wide, displacing 180 tons of water. The duplicate measures 90 feet by 26 feet, displaces 183 tons, and has a crew of 21, as did the original vessel. The new *Mayflower* has no motor but travels faster than the old boat.

What happened to the historic boat? So far as can be told, the *Mayflower* went back to less colorful jobs and, not too many years later, was scrapped. What happened to the beams, masts, and planking is questionable. In the English city of Abingdon, there is a Congregational church which contains two heavy wooden pillars. Some say these pillars are masts from the *Mayflower*. A barn in the English town of Jordans seemed to be built of old ship timbers. Marine experts said these timbers were impregnated with salt and, if put together, would form a vessel 90 feet by 22 feet. The man who owned the farm when the peculiar barn was built was a relative of the man who appraised the *Mayflower* when it was scrapped.

So the original *Mayflower* may still be doing service ashore while her duplicate sails the seas again.

7. The title that best expresses the main theme or subject of this selection is:
    (A) the fate of the *Mayflower*
    (B) a symbol of good will
    (C) the scrapping of the *Mayflower*
    (D) the *Mayflower*—old and new
    (E) the search for the Pilgrims' boat

8. A long search was made for the Pilgrims' boat because it
    (A) contained valuable materials
    (B) might still do sea service
    (C) has historical importance
    (D) would link Great Britain and America
    (E) could serve as a model for other boats

9. It has been difficult to discover what happened to the original *Mayflower* because
    (A) it has become impregnated with salt
    (B) it was such a small vessel
    (C) the search was begun too late
    (D) records of fishing boats were not carefully kept
    (E) many ships bore the same name

10. The British recently had a duplicate of the *Mayflower* built because
    (A) the original could not be located
    (B) they wanted to make a gesture of friendship
    (C) parts of the original could be used
    (D) historians recommended such a step
    (E) England is a nation of boat lovers

11. Compared with the original *Mayflower*, the modern duplicate
    (A) is longer
    (B) displaces less water
    (C) carries a larger crew
    (D) is somewhat wider
    (E) is less speedy

12. When the author says that the original boat
    may still be doing service ashore, he means
    that
    (A) it may be whole and entire somewhere
    (B) present-day buildings may include parts
        of it
    (C) it may be in a boat lover's private collec-
        tion
    (D) its memory creates good will
    (E) historians still discuss it

Reading Passage III

About the year 1812 two steam ferryboats were
built under the direction of Robert Fulton for cross-
ing the Hudson River, and one of the same description was built for service on the East River. These
boats were what are known as twin boats, each of
them having two complete hulls united by a deck
or bridge. Because these boats were pointed at both
ends and moved equally well with either end fore-
most, they crossed and recrossed the river without
losing any time in turning about. Fulton also con-
trived, with great ingenuity, floating docks for the
reception of the ferryboats, and a means by which
they were brought to the docks without a shock.
These boats were the first of a fleet which has since
carried hundreds of millions of passengers to and
from New York.

13. The title below that best expresses the main
    theme or subject of this selection is:
    (A) Crossing the Hudson River by boat
    (B) Transportation of passengers
    (C) The invention of floating docks
    (D) The beginning of steam ferryboat service
    (E) Twin boats on the East River

14. The steam ferryboats were known as twin boats
    because
    (A) they had two distinct hulls
    (B) they could move as easily forward as
        backward
    (C) each ferryboat had two captains
    (D) two boats were put into service at the
        same time
    (E) two sides of the river could be served at
        once

15. Which statement is *true* according to the se-
    lection?
    (A) Boats built under Fulton's direction are
        still in use.

    (B) Fulton planned a reception to celebrate
        the first ferryboat trip.
    (C) Fulton piloted the first steam ferryboats
        across the Hudson.
    (D) Fulton developed a satisfactory way of
        docking the ferryboats.
    (E) Because of their design, the steam ferry-
        boats had to be turned around in mid-
        stream.

16. Robert Fulton lived in the
    (A) seventeenth century
    (B) eighteenth century
    (C) nineteenth century
    (D) twentieth century
    (E) twenty-first century

Reading Passage IV

On the whole the Eskimos are a coastal people.
Their total number is not more than 35,000. Of
these about 14.500 live along the coast of Greenland. Eskimo settlements are scattered along the
northern coast of North America from Labrador
to Alaska's panhandle. On Baffin Island and on
other large islands there are Eskimo villages. The
Eskimos spend most of their time near the sea and
get much of their living from the sea. However, one
tribe, the Caribou Eskimos, live inland west of
Hudson Bay. Some of them have never seen the
sea.

Although life in one village is in many ways very
much like life in another, there are some differences. The reason is that the Eskimos must use
what they find in the particular district where they
live. The Copper Eskimos who live beside Coro-
nation Gulf build thick-walled winter houses of
snow blocks. Alaskan Eskimos do not use such
houses and most of them have never even seen one.
Their winter homes are made of turf and mud. The
Eskimos of southern Greenland are expert in
handling a kayak, or Eskimo canoe. They fish in the
open water of the sea. The Eskimos of northern
Greenland have little chance to use kayaks because
the water along the coast is frozen almost all the
year. All tribes, however, have one thing in common. They are primarily fishermen and hunters.

17. The title below that best expresses the main
    theme or subject of this selection is:
    (A) The Caribou Eskimos
    (B) The Eskimos
    (C) Eskimo fishing
    (D) Eskimo homes
    (E) The Copper Eskimos

18. Most Eskimos live
    - (A) near the water
    - (B) on the plains
    - (C) in the forests
    - (D) inland
    - (E) on islands

19. The Caribou Eskimos are
    - (A) from the coast of Greenland
    - (B) not hunters and fishermen
    - (C) scattered along the coast of North America
    - (D) not coastal people
    - (E) skilled at gaining their living from the sea

20. A comparison of different Eskimo villages shows that the way of life in each
    - (A) is quite similar to that in the others
    - (B) is very unlike that in the others
    - (C) has nothing to do with the location
    - (D) is very civilized
    - (E) is much like our own way of life

21. Alaskan Eskimos make their winter homes of
    - (A) snow blocks
    - (B) skins and furs
    - (C) wood
    - (D) turf and mud
    - (E) stones

22. A kayak is a kind of
    - (A) sled
    - (B) house
    - (C) boat
    - (D) animal
    - (E) spear

23. All Eskimo tribes
    - (A) are skilled in the use of the kayak
    - (B) hunt and fish for a living
    - (C) make homes of snow blocks
    - (D) live in Greenland
    - (E) depend on the ocean for a living

Reading Passage V

The pack horse and the trail were the means for acquiring the products of the East. In the beginning every family collected all the furs they could, by hunting and trapping or by trading with the Indians, to send over the mountains for barter. Later they also collected quantities of wood ashes for the potash. Still later they raised cattle and horses for sale on the Atlantic coast. In the fall of the year each family went into a sort of association with some of their neighbors to make up a pack train. They went to Baltimore to do their bartering for salt and for iron and steel. The common price for a bushel of alum salt was a good cow and calf.

24. The settlers brought supplies from the East by
    - (A) canoe
    - (B) stagecoach
    - (C) pack train
    - (D) railroad
    - (E) stone boat

25. They paid for what they bought by
    - (A) check
    - (B) coins
    - (C) gold
    - (D) greenbacks
    - (E) barter

END OF PART

Go on to the next Test in the Examination, just as you would do on the actual exam. Check your answers when you have completed the entire Examination. The correct answers for this Test, and all the other Tests, are assembled at the conclusion of this Examination.

TEST II. INTERPRETATION OF READING MATERIALS IN THE SOCIAL STUDIES

PART B. GRAPH AND TABLE INTERPRETATION

DIRECTIONS: Read each question in this test carefully. Answer each one on the basis of the following table. Select the best answer and write it in the proper space on the answer sheet.

CHILDREN REMAINING AS PUBLIC CHARGES IN INSTITUTIONS, 1929-1935

End of year	Dependent or Neglected	Delinquent	Blind	Deaf	Total number of children remaining as public charges at end of year
1929	15,594	1,079	59	218	16,950
1930	18,042	1,109	57	192	19,400
1931	20,526	1,437	56	268	22,287
1932	21,515	1,335	53	311	23,314
1933	21,929	1,292	37	377	23,635
1934	20,992	1,236	37	394	22,659
1935	21,045	1,175	36	424	22,680

1. At the end of what year did the largest number of children remain public charges?

2. What percentage of the total number of children who were public charges at the end of 1929 were classed as dependent or neglected?

3. Of the total number of children remaining at the end of the year 1930, what percentage were not classed as dependent or neglected?

4. How many more deaf and blind children were cared for in 1934 than were cared for in those two groups in 1929?

5. Has the number of children in any one of the four groups shown a continuous and uninterrupted increase beginning with 1929 through 1935? Yes or No?

6. There is an arithmetical error in the Column "Total No. of Children remaining as Public Charges at the end of the Year." Write the year in which the error occurs.

7. The number of blind children cared for in 1935 is 9/14th of the number of blind children cared for in 1931. Express this fraction as a decimal. Carry your answer to three places only.

8. How many delinquent and blind children remained under care at the end of 1931?

TEST III. INTERPRETATION OF READING MATERIALS
IN THE NATURAL SCIENCES

TIME: 1 Hour

DIRECTIONS: Below each of the following passages of natural science reading material you will find one or more incomplete statements about the passage. Select the words or expressions that most satisfactorily complete each statement in accordance with the meaning of the paragraph.

Reading Passage I

The Nile is the second longest river in the world and in spite of rapids and cataracts is navigable for a distance equal to that from New York to San Francisco. Every year from August to January, the Nile is in flood, reaching its highest level during September. The floods of the Nile are caused by the heavy summer rains in Ethiopia. When the waters recede, they leave behind a deposit of alluvial mud. This fertile deposit year after year has so enriched the soil that the Egyptians are able to grow abundant crops without using fertilizers. Even though the Nile valley is so productive, no agriculture can be carried on without irrigation. The reason for this is that most of the winds are from the northeast. As these winds blow from a cooler to a warmer region, the air is warmed and so takes up moisture instead of depositing it.

1. The floods of the Nile are caused by
   (A) melting snow   (C) large springs
   (B) summer rains   (D) high mountains
       (E) overflow of lakes

2. The soil of Egypt is very
   (A) stony   (C) sandy
   (B) thin   (D) fertile
       (E) unproductive

3. In Egypt the winds
   (A) deposit rain
   (B) come from the southern mountains
   (C) interfere with navigation
   (D) are made cooler
   (E) take up moisture

Reading Passage II

The kangaroo is found nowhere in the world but in Australasia. Ages ago, when that part of our earth was cut off from the Asian mainland, this fantastic animal from nature's long-ago was also isolated. There are about two dozen species distributed through Australia, southward to Tasmania and northward to New Guinea and neighboring islands. Some are no bigger than rabbits; some can climb trees. They are known by a variety of picturesque names; wallabies, wallaroos, potoroos, boongaries and paddymelons. But *the* kangaroo— the one that is Australia's national symbol—is the great gray kangaroo of the plains, admiringly known throughout the island continent as the Old Man, and also as Boomer, Forester, and Man of the Woods. His smaller mate, in Australian talk, is a flyer. Their baby is known as Joey.

A full-grown kangaroo stands taller than a man, and commonly weighs 200 pounds. Even when he sits in his favorite position, reposing on his haunches and tilting back on the propping support of his "third leg"—his tail—his head is five feet or more above the ground. His huge hind legs, with steel-spring power, can send him sailing over a ten-foot fence with ease, or in a fight can beat off a dozen dogs. A twitch of his tail can break a man's leg like a match stick.

Kangaroos provide an endless supply of tall tales to which wide-eyed visitors are treated in the land Down Under. The beauty of tall tales about the kangaroo is that they can be almost as tall as you please and still be close to fact.

4. Kangaroos are found only
   (A) in Australia
   (B) in Australasia
   (C) on the Asian mainland
   (D) in Tasmania
   (E) on New Guinea

5. A female kangaroo is called
   (A) a wallaby   (C) a Joey
   (B) a potoroo   (D) a flyer
             (E) the Old Man

6. The amazing jumping power of the kangaroo
   is chiefly due to
   (A) the power of his hind legs
   (B) the support of his tail
   (C) his size
   (D) his weight
   (E) his tilted sitting position

7. Which statement is *true* according to the passage?
   (A) The name "Old Man" shows the people's
       dislike of kangaroos.
   (B) Visitors to Australia hear very little about
       kangaroos.
   (C) A kangaroo's tail is a powerful weapon.
   (D) The most widely known species of kangaroo is no larger than a rabbit.
   (E) Kangaroos have three legs.

8. The author believes that the stories told about
   kangaroos are generally
   (A) harmful   (C) suspicious
   (B) true   (D) beautiful
             (E) ancient

Reading Passage III

While it is pleasant to recognize birds, wherever one may be, and while thousands of bird lovers the world over eagerly compete in the effort to acquire the largest possible day, year and life lists, birds warrant far more attention. Few fields have benefited more from amateur effort than natural history. Everyone interested in birds may, by a constructive use of his time, contribute materially to the advance of the science. In the process, the bird watcher will find birds fascinating and will thoroughly enjoy his hobby. To anyone who has spent a few hours in close observation of birds at their nests or during their courtship periods, these creatures provide unending delight. To make significant studies requires no equipment beyond notebooks and knowledge of what has already been published. To the beginner, there is one further suggestion: make the acquaintance of fellow hobbyists and join the local bird-study group, if possible. Much bird study is carried on as a social avocation, and one of its finest rewards is the memory of days afield with co-workers.

9. The best of the following titles for this paragraph is:
   (A) Pleasant outdoor hobbies
   (B) Bird-study clubs
   (C) How bird study benefits science
   (D) Bird study as a hobby
   (E) Learning to identify birds

10. The writer suggests that the beginner in bird
    study should
    (A) learn to identify birds
    (B) compete with other bird lovers
    (C) join a bird-study club
    (D) acquire bird lists
    (E) buy good equipment

11. Besides enjoying a pleasant hobby, the amateur bird lover can make an especially significant contribution to
    (A) the pleasure of fellow hobbyists
    (B) natural science
    (C) the identification of birds
    (D) day, year and life lists
    (E) local bird-study clubs

Reading Passage IV

Europe's longest river is the Volga, which winds its way for 2,325 miles through the heart of European Russia. Apart from draining a vast region equal to the combined area of France, Italy and Germany, the Volga has served for hundreds of years as the principal highway in the Russian interior, where roads and highways are even now few and far between. On the numerous small river boats that ply the Volga are shipped wheat and other grains from the Ukraine to the northern cities of Russia, oil from Caucasus, and northern timber to the ports of the Caspian and Black seas. The Volga, however, offers two drawbacks to shipping. The first is the period during which the river is frozen, sometimes lasting as long as five and a half months. The second difficulty is that the river is shallow in spots, so that even in summer only certain types of vessels can navigate it.

12. Shipments to the northern cities on the Volga
    are carried on
    (A) small boats   (C) canoes
    (B) large steamers   (D) ocean-going ships
             (E) rafts

13. The Volga is difficult to navigate because it is
    (A) winding (C) narrow
    (B) full of boats (D) long
        (E) shallow in some places

14. Ships traveling southward on the Volga carry
    (A) wheat (C) wood
    (B) furs (D) oil
        (E) ice

Reading Passage V

A sloth rolls a perfect ball of itself in a lofty swaying crotch, with head and feet and legs all gathered close inside. The crotch is unusually high up or far out among the lesser branches where the eagle or the jaguar find but precarious hold. No man can seize a sloth by the long hair of the back and pull it off. So strong are its muscles, so viselike the grip of its dozen talons, that either the crotch must be broken off or the long claws unfastened one by one. The sloth may have twenty ribs, broad and flat slats. Its skin is so thick and tough that many an Indian's arrow falls back without even scratching the hide. Finally, it has two coats of fur, the under one short and matted and the outer one long, harsh and coarse.

15. When grasped, the sloth
    (A) fights bravely
    (B) dives into the river
    (C) runs and hides
    (D) holds fast
    (E) ejects an odorous secretion

16. The sloth is notable for its
    (A) huge mass of fat (C) tough skin
    (B) beautiful plumage (D) small size
        (E) long silky hair

17. The sloth's favorite place of refuge is
    (A) a pile of stones
    (B) a hollow log
    (C) a cave
    (D) a swamp
    (E) the top of a tree

Reading Passage VI

The chuckwalla stands at the head of all animals of the desert in rhyme, story and legend. It is a big vegetarian, which eats by preference the blossoms of desert plants. When hard put to it, though, the chuckwalla has been known to eat such plebeian food as the leaves of the creosote bush. Like all the other vegetarians of the desert, the chuckwalla leaves its winter home among the rocks much later than do the insect eaters. When the warmth of the desert finally calls, the chuckwalla comes forth with his hide made up of folds and wrinkles and ascends the blistering hot rocks or clambers up the shrubs for the meal of blossoms. When eagle or falcon or human being appears, the chuckwalla slips into a rock crevice and waits. If the enemy attacks, the chuckwalla fills itself so full of air that it wedges itself tightly in the niche. Not even the strongest tug will dislodge it. If left alone, the chuckwalla loses the air naturally after a little.

White men who have tasted the cooked lizard write that it is excellent, and desert Indians consider it one of their greatest delicacies. On their chuckwalla forays, the Indians carry a pointed wire. With this they puncture and deflate the chuckwalla

In addition to the inflation method of defense, the chuckwalla has another surprise for its enemies. in order to withdraw it from the niche to which it has retreated.

It uses its big muscular tail as a club. The thwack it can deliver is a big surprise to him who feels it for the first time.

The chuckwalla has many color variations. Mostly the big lizard is mottled black and white, a color pattern matching faithfully the granite rocks among which it lives. A male that we found had extensive mottling of brick red. The chuckwalla lives among rocks on lower slopes of mountains in the Mohave and Colorado deserts, in southern Nevada, western Arizona and Lower California.

18. The best of the following titles for this selection is:
    (A) Animals of the desert
    (B) How the chuckwalla protects itself
    (C) The appearance of the chuckwalla
    (D) Interesting facts about the chuckwalla
    (E) A desert vegetarian

19. The chuckwalla prefers to eat
    (A) leaves (C) flesh
    (B) roots (D) insects
        (E) blossoms

20. The chuckwalla is valuable as
    (A) a pet
    (B) an article of food
    (C) a destroyer of birds
    (D) a source of leather
    (E) an ornament

21. The part of the United States frequented by the chuckwalla is the
    - (A) Southwest
    - (B) Atlantic coast
    - (C) North
    - (D) Northeast
    - (E) Mississippi valley

22. The chuckwalla helps to protect itself by
    - (A) flying
    - (B) inflation
    - (C) boldly attacking its enemy
    - (D) wrinkling its skin
    - (E) deflation

23. The Indians hunt the chuckwalla with a
    - (A) gun
    - (B) bow and arrow
    - (C) club
    - (D) sharp wire
    - (E) falcon

24. The chuckwalla likes
    - (A) cold
    - (B) heat
    - (C) rain
    - (D) eagles
    - (E) human beings

25. The color of the chuckwalla is
    - (A) usually black and white
    - (B) chiefly red
    - (C) a dull gray
    - (D) always the same
    - (E) arranged in stripes

END OF TEST

If you finish before the allotted time is up, work on this part only.
When time is up, proceed directly to the next part and do not
return to this part.

TEST IV. INTERPRETATION OF LITERARY MATERIALS

TIME: 1 Hour

DIRECTIONS: Below each of the following passages of literature you will find one or more incomplete statements about the passage. Each statement is followed by five words or expressions. Select the word or expression that most satisfactorily completes each statement in accordance with the direct or implied meaning of each passage.

Reading Passage I

High in the Swiss Alps long years ago, there lived a lonely shepherd boy who longed for a friend to share his vigils. One night, he beheld three wrinkled old men, each holding a glass. The first said: "Drink this liquid and you shall be victorious in battle."

The second said: "Drink this liquid and you shall have countless riches."

The last man said: "I offer you the happiness of music—the alphorn."

The boy chose the third glass. Next day, he came upon a great horn, ten feet in length. When he put his lips to it, a beautiful melody floated across the valley. He had found a friend. . . .

So goes the legend of the alphorn's origin. Known in the ninth century, the alphorn was used by herdsmen to call cattle, for the deep tones echoed across the mountainsides. And even today, on a quiet summer evening, its music can be heard floating among the peaks.

1. The story tells us that of the three old men, the one whose glass the boy chose was the
   (A) smallest in size   (D) oldest
   (B) most wrinkled   (E) last to speak
   (C) first to speak

2. One liquid offered to the boy would have brought him
   (A) defeat in battle
   (B) great wealth
   (C) lonely vigils
   (D) another boy to help him
   (E) three wishes

3. To the boy, the alphorn
   (A) seemed too heavy to play
   (B) seemed like a real friend
   (C) brought unhappiness
   (D) sounded unpleasant
   (E) brought great riches

4. The practical use of the alphorn is to
   (A) summon the three old men
   (B) make friends
   (C) call cattle
   (D) give summer concerts
   (E) tell the legends of the Alps

Reading Passage II

The famous Pony Express started at St. Joseph, Missouri, and followed the Oregon and California Trail for the most part, with many short cuts because mountain-bred horses, sure-footed as goats, could travel where no stagecoach could go. It ended at Sacramento, California, where a river steamer carried the mail on to San Francisco. Post stations were built along the trail at intervals of about 70 miles in open country, or 35 miles in the mountains. Each station was provided with food, shelter, a corral of horses, and two keepers. Between post stations, at intervals of about ten miles (which is as far as they wished their horses to run at high speed) were several relay stations, each with a keeper and a few extra horses, one of which was always saddled and ready to run.

Coming with a rush into the relay station, the post rider would swing down from his lathered mount, swing up on a fresh horse with his precious *mochila* (saddle bag), and be off without a moment's delay. He was expected to reach the next post station on time, and he did it or died trying. More than one rider came at dawn or dusk to find the post station burned, its keepers killed, its horses run off by Indians; and in that case he had to keep on to the next station without food or rest. The longest continuous run, 384 miles, was made by "Buffalo Bill," then a boy of 18; the fastest by Jim Moore, another youngster, who rode 280 miles in 22 hours.

Ninety riders were running the long trail at all hours of the day or night, often taking their lives in their hands to get the mail through within the time limit set for the run. Ten days was the time set, but the job was regularly done in eight. The average speed was eleven miles an hour, which was fast in a region where at one hour a horse might run his best and the next hour be swimming a river or cat-footing along a trail where a misstep meant death for horse and rider.

This daring Pony Express ran for less than two years; it ended in 1861, when a telegraph line offered a swifter means of communication.

5. The Pony Express ran between
   (A) St. Joseph and San Francisco
   (B) Oregon and California
   (C) St. Joseph and Sacramento
   (D) Sacramento and San Francisco
   (E) St. Joseph and Oregon

6. The greatest distance between post stations along the Pony Express run was about
   (A) 10 miles   (C) 50 miles
   (B) 35 miles   (D) 70 miles
       (E) 105 miles

7. The principal duty of a keeper of a relay station was to
   (A) guard the mail pouches
   (B) prepare meals
   (C) hunt Indians
   (D) plan short cuts for riders
   (E) have a horse ready for an incoming rider

8. The Pony Express riders waited at relay stations only long enough to
   (A) allow a stagecoach to pass
   (B) get a fresh mount
   (C) catch a few hours' sleep
   (D) escape thieving Indians
   (E) sort the mail

9. From this passage it would seem that most of the riders were
   (A) sure-footed   (C) middle-aged
   (B) faithful to duty   (D) mountain-bred
       (E) carefree

10. A Californian sending mail by Pony Express could expect his mail to reach the eastern end of the run
    (A) within 22 hours
    (B) between dawn and dusk
    (C) within 10 days
    (D) in about a month
    (E) in about 90 days

11. The Pony Express ended in 1861 because
    (A) messages could be sent more quickly by wire
    (B) fast horses had become scarce
    (C) riders would not work under such conditions
    (D) river boats had come into wider use
    (E) so many stations had been attacked by Indians

Reading Passage III

Members of one of the finest detective forces in the world wear no badges and carry no revolvers. Their only weapons are their strength and courage and a diploma from an intensive school—the Police Service Dog Center near Ottawa, Canada. Yes, these tough, intelligent sleuths are *dogs*—German Shepherds and Dobermans—trained by the Canadian Mounted Police to track down criminals and aid those in trouble.

From the time he enters school, each dog recruit is instilled with severe military discipline. First he is taught to heel, sit, and lie down. Next comes field training where he learns how to track down clues, guard prisoners, and rescue a drowning man or a victim pinned under a fallen tree. Another difficult lesson the dog detective must master is to accept food only once a day—and from no one but his trainer. This lesson is his best insurance against the jaws of a baited trap or a painful death from poisoned meat. In his final lessons the Police Service Dog learns to jump through windows, to climb up and down ladders, to scramble across narrow logs, and to fell an armed man without getting shot. Not only must he be tough—the four-footed Mountie must be a gentleman, too, because many of his missions are retrieving lost children and snowbound campers.

Trotting beside his Mountie master, the dog detective shares the blizzards and loneliness of Canada's bush country and knows no other code than the Mounted Police motto: "Maintain the Right."

12. Three qualities that the dogs must possess to a high degree are strength, courage, and
    (A) curiosity
    (B) intelligence
    (C) loneliness
    (D) sympathy
    (E) unselfishness

13. At the Police Service Dog Center, the dog is first taught to
    (A) avoid traps
    (B) obey simple directions
    (C) rescue drowning persons
    (D) guard prisoners
    (E) climb ladders

14. A dog must be trained in gentleness because he
    (A) may be given poisoned meat
    (B) may have to endure great loneliness
    (C) carries no weapons
    (D) shares the life of a Mountie
    (E) must often rescue helpless persons

15. The writer of this passage believes that Police Service Dogs
    (A) should be treated more kindly
    (B) should be insured against poisoning
    (C) should wear badges
    (D) perform valuable service
    (E) have a code of their own

Reading Passage IV

One hundred and fifty years ago, nine American families out of ten lived on farms. They raised their own corn in their own fields, built their houses from the trees in the wood lot and wove their own clothes with wool from sheep in the pasture. Nine-tenths of the things consumed in a typical New England village were grown and made right in the village. Less than one-tenth came in from other villages or towns. Only a tiny fraction came from other countries. The harder the family worked—and that meant the children too—the more they produced and the better they lived. The standard of living was a direct result of the energy exerted by the father, mother, sons and daughters.

Today, like my great-great-great-grandfather, I live on a New England farm. But I produce on my own place less than ten per cent of what I consume. I raise vegetables and apples, I cut firewood, and I bang my thumb with a hammer making a few rough benches and bookshelves. That is all. My wife spins no thread and weaves no cloth. Not ten per cent of our supplies originate in our town.

My great-great-great-grandfather was ninety per cent self-sufficient; that is, he was able to produce ninety per cent of the goods he needed. I am, you are, nearly every American is, at most, ten per cent self-sufficient. We can not live unless millions of people we have never seen keep sending us goods.

16. The title that best expresses the main theme or subject of this selection is:
    (A) Supplies from all over the world
    (B) An old-fashioned New England farm
    (C) Changes in self-sufficiency
    (D) My great-great-great-grandfather
    (E) Family labor

17. In the 1790's most American families
    (A) imported many articles
    (B) lived in cities
    (C) produced their own supplies
    (D) carried on a large trade
    (E) worked for someone else

18. The standard of living in former times depended directly on
    (A) the amount of money in circulation
    (B) the work of all members of the family
    (C) factory production
    (D) weaving cloth
    (E) the neighboring towns

Reading Passage V

Tom Sawyer said to himself that it was not such a hollow world after all. He had discovered a great law of human action without knowing it—namely, that in order to make a man or boy desire a thing it is only necessary to make the thing difficult to attain. If he had been a great and wise philosopher, he would now have understood that work consists of whatever a body is obliged to do, and that play consists of whatever a body is not obliged to do. And this would help him to understand why constructing artificial flowers or performing on a treadmill is work, while rolling tenpins or climbing Mont Blanc is only amusement. There are wealthy men in England who drive four-horse passenger coaches 20 or 30 miles on a daily line in the summer, because the privilege costs them considerable money; but if they were offered wages for the service, that would turn it into work, and then they would resign.

19. The "law of human action" discovered by Tom could be stated as follows: A man wants most that which
    (A) he already has
    (B) he is obliged to do
    (C) he can not easily attain
    (D) no one else likes
    (E) he can get for nothing

20. According to the author, play consists of
    (A) the things a person does of his own free will
    (B) the things a person has to do
    (C) jobs such as working a treadmill
    (D) the things that make this a hollow world
    (E) tasks done for wages

21. A man who does such a thing as drive a coach for amusement would resign if offered wages for the activity because
    (A) he doesn't want to earn money
    (B) it is a dangerous activity
    (C) he would lose money
    (D) he doesn't have time
    (E) the activity would then become work

Reading Passage VI

Each year, in May, the shade of Mark Twain hovers over Angel's Camp, California, when this colorful old mining town has all eyes on tailless, leaping amphibians of the genus Rana in the sort of contest Twain made famous in his early humorous story "The Celebrated Jumping Frog of Calaveras County."

Here, thousands of spectators gather each year to watch the country's finest jumpers leap their way to fame—and compete for a $500 first prize. And just to keep tradition straight, every frog must undergo a rigid inspection before the main event to make sure there is no foul play like loading the other fellow's frog with buckshot, as happened in Twain's merry tale.

As for record leaps, back in 1944, Alfred Jermy, of Calaveras County, was proud owner of Flash, a frog which held the world's championship with a leap of fifteen feet ten inches. In 1950, a seven-year-old boy's pet, X—100, stole top honors with three leaps averaging fourteen feet nine inches. But, as amazing as these records might seem to the novice, be assured they are mere "puddle-jumps."

Half the fun in visiting this famous Calaveras County jubilee is to hear the old prospectors talk about jumping contests in their day: a leap of 600 feet in a favorable wind—well, why not?

22. The amphibians mentioned in the first paragraph are
    (A) storytellers　　　(C) miners
    (B) frogs　　　　　(D) race officials
    　　　(E) people of Angel's Camp

23. Nowadays rigid inspection is made of the frogs before the contest because
    (A) there is a desire to carry on a tradition
    (B) there is a state law requiring such an inspection
    (C) so many spectators attend the contests
    (D) the finest jumping frogs are present
    (E) the stories of the prospectors need to be checked

24. The author suggests that
    (A) a first prize of $500 is too high
    (B) a small boy cannot properly train a champion
    (C) Mark Twain would disapprove of the modern contests
    (D) a frog cannot jump more than fifteen feet ten inches
    (E) old timers' stories of earlier contests stretch the truth

25. Calaveras County is
    (A) a fictitious place　　　(C) in Ireland
    (B) on some other planet　(D) in Australia
    　　　(E) in the United States

END OF TEST

If you finish before the allotted time is up, work on this part only.
When time is up, proceed directly to the next part and do not return to this part.

TEST V. GENERAL MATHEMATICAL ABILITY

TIME: 1 Hour

DIRECTIONS: In the following multiple choice questions, choose the correct answer from the choices offered.

Do not make any marks on the test itself. It is best to work out the solution to each question on a sheet of blank paper before looking at the suggested answers. This will help prevent you from being misled by answers that at first glance may look correct.

1. Find the value of $1\frac{1}{2} \times 1\frac{3}{4} \times \frac{2}{3}$
   (A) $1\frac{1}{3}$
   (B) $1\frac{3}{4}$
   (C) $2\frac{1}{2}$
   (D) $2\frac{3}{4}$

2. Change $\frac{3}{7}$ to a decimal correct to the *nearest hundredth*
   (A) .043
   (B) .43
   (C) 4.3
   (D) 43

3. Multiply $.86 by $5\frac{1}{2}$
   (A) $4.73
   (B) $5.16
   (C) $6.27
   (D) $7.14

4. Divide 20.25 by .045
   (A) .45
   (B) 4.5
   (C) 45
   (D) 450

5. Which of the following numbers when multiplied by 100 results in 10?
   (A) .01
   (B) .1
   (C) 1
   (D) 10

6. A porch lounge regularly sells for $29.50. How much money is saved if the lounge is bought at a 20% discount?
   (A) $4.80
   (B) $5.90
   (C) $6.20
   (D) $7.40

7. A man has an $8,000 life-insurance policy on which he pays a premium of $21.75 per $1,000 each year. Find his annual premium.
   (A) $108
   (B) $174
   (C) $200
   (D) $240

8. What is the largest number of half-pint bottles which can be filled from a 10-gallon can of milk?
   (A) 160
   (B) 170
   (C) 16
   (D) 17

9. What number multiplied by itself equals 144?
   (A) 12
   (B) 13
   (C) 14
   (D) 15

10. A boy received 25% commission for selling magazine subscriptions. One week he earned $12. How many dollars worth of magazine subscriptions did he sell that week?
    (A) $40
    (B) $43
    (C) $45
    (D) $48

11. 75% of 4 is the same as what per cent of 9?
    (A) 36
    (B) 25
    (C) 40
    (D) $33\frac{1}{3}$

12. Which is the fraction closest in value to $\frac{7}{9}$?
    (A) $\frac{6}{7}$
    (B) $\frac{8}{9}$
    (C) $\frac{9}{10}$
    (D) $\frac{3}{4}$

13. Which is the greatest fraction?
    (A) $\frac{2}{3}$
    (B) $\frac{3}{4}$
    (C) $\frac{5}{7}$
    (D) $\frac{8}{9}$

14. How many minutes are there in 1 day?
    (A) 60
    (B) 1,440
    (C) 24
    (D) $1,440 \times 60$

15. Where 1 mile = 5,280 ft., 60 miles per hour is equal to how many feet per minute?
    (A) 316,800
    (B) 3,168
    (C) 5,280
    (D) 600

16. How many inches are there in 3 yards?
    (A) 72
    (B) 36
    (C) 108
    (D) 24

17. $\frac{1}{5} = 5\%$ of what?
    (A) $\frac{4}{25}$
    (B) $6\frac{1}{4}$
    (C) 5
    (D) 16

18. $2.2 \times .00001 =$
    (A) .0022
    (B) .00022
    (C) .000022
    (D) .0000022

19. Which of the following numbers is *not* exactly divisible (without remainder) by 9?
    (A) 1,125
    (B) 2,151
    (C) 4,122
    (D) 3,179

20. Which is not equal to $\frac{1}{7}$?
    (A) $\frac{15}{56} - \frac{1}{8}$
    (B) $\frac{17}{21} - \frac{2}{3}$
    (C) $\frac{9}{14} - \frac{1}{2}$
    (D) $\frac{15}{31} - \frac{1}{9}$

21. For a charity sale a club bought 10 dozen doughnuts at 25 cents a dozen and sold them all at 5 cents each. Their profit was
    (A) less than $1
    (B) between $1 and $2
    (C) between $2 and $3
    (D) more than $3

22. If one-half gallon of ice cream will serve 10 children, how many quarts are needed for a party of 25 children?
    (A) $1\frac{1}{4}$
    (B) 3
    (C) 5
    (D) 10

23. A pile of magazines is 4 feet high. If each magazine is $\frac{3}{4}$ of an inch thick, the number of magazines is
    (A) 36
    (B) 48
    (C) 64
    (D) 96

24. An inch on a map represents 200 miles. On the same map a distance of 375 is represented by
    (A) $1\frac{1}{2}$ inches
    (B) $1\frac{7}{8}$
    (C) $2\frac{1}{4}$
    (D) $2\frac{3}{4}$ inches

25. Five girls each ate 3 cookies from a box containing 2 dozen. When part of a dozen was left?
    (A) $\frac{1}{8}$
    (B) $\frac{1}{4}$
    (C) $\frac{3}{4}$
    (D) $\frac{7}{8}$

END OF EXAMINATION

If you finish before the allotted time is up, check your work on this test only. Do not go back to earlier tests. When time runs out, compare your answers for this test and all the other tests in the examination with the correct key answers that follow.

CORRECT ANSWERS FOR SAMPLE EXAMINATION III.

(Please try to answer the questions on your own before looking at our answers. You'll do much better on your test if you follow this rule.)

TEST I. CORRECTNESS AND EFFECTIVENESS OF EXPRESSION

PART A. ENGLISH USAGE

1.D	6.C	11.C	16.C	21.A	26.D
2.A	7.D	12.B	17.B	22.C	27.B
3.B	8.A	13.A	18.C	23.D	28.C
4.A	9.C	14.D	19.A	24.B	29.A
5.B	10.A	15.C	20.D	25.A	30.C

PART B. SPELLING

1.B	5.B	9.A	13.A	17.C
2.C	6.C	10.D	14.A	18.D
3.A	7.D	11.B	15.B	19.C
4.D	8.C	12.D	16.D	20.A

TEST II. INTERPRETATION OF READING MATERIALS IN THE SOCIAL STUDIES

PART A. SOCIAL STUDIES READINGS

1.D	6.E	11.D	16.C	21.D
2.C	7.D	12.B	17.B	22.C
3.D	8.C	13.D	18.A	23.B
4.D	9.E	14.A	19.D	24.C
5.D	10.B	15.D	20.A	25.E

PART B. GRAPH AND TABLE INTERPRETATION

1. 1933	4. 154	7. 642,643
2. 92%	5. no	8. 1493
3. 7%	6. 1932	

TEST III. INTERPRETATION OF READING MATERIALS IN THE NATURAL SCIENCES

1.B	6.A	11.B	16.C	21.A
2.D	7.C	12.A	17.E	22.B
3.E	8.B	13.E	18.D	23.D
4.B	9.D	14.C,D	19.E	24.B
5.D	10.C	15.D	20.B	25.A

TEST IV. INTERPRETATION OF LITERARY MATERIALS

1.E	6.D	11.A	16.C	21.E
2.B	7.E	12.B	17.C	22.B
3.B	8.B	13.B	18.B	23.A
4.C	9.B	14.E	19.C	24.E
5.C	10.C	15.D	20.A	25.E

TEST V. GENERAL MATHEMATICAL ABILITY

1.B	6.B	11.D	16.C	21.D
2.B	7.B	12.D	17.D	22.C
3.A	8.A	13.D	18.C	23.C
4.D	9.A	14.B	19.D	24.B
5.B	10.D	15.C	20.D	25.C

IV. SAMPLE EXAM FOR PRACTICE

Plan on taking this Examination after you have done the testing, probing, and concentrated study which the earlier Examinations showed to be needed. If you have availed yourself of the Pinpoint Practice provided, you should find this Exam an excellent review and summary of all that you have learned. Your score here will give you a fair statement of where you stand. Certainly, it should be higher than your previous scores. If you're not satisfied, there's still time. Go back and review your weaker subjects. Then test yourself again. If you show improvement, you may congratulate yourself on having picked up a few more points on the actual exam.

The time allowed for the entire examination is 5   hours.

TEST I. CORRECTNESS AND EFFECTIVENESS OF EXPRESSION

TIME: 1 Hour

PART A. ENGLISH USAGE

DIRECTIONS: A sentence is given in which one part is under-lined.   If you think that the underlined part is correct as it stands, write the answer A. If you believe that the underlined part is incorrect, select from among the other choices (B or C or D) the one you think is correct.   Grammar, sentence structure, word usage, and punctuation are to be considered in your decision, and the original meaning of the sentence must be retained.

1. <u>Whoever</u> the gods wish to destroy, they first make mad.
   (A) NO CHANGE   (C) Whomever
   (B) Whoever,   (D) Whomever,

2. She is one of those girls <u>who are</u> always com-plaining.
   (A) NO CHANGE
   (B) who is
   (C) whom are
   (D) whom is

3. We buy only cherry plums, since we like <u>those kind</u> best.
   (A) NO CHANGE   (C) that kind
   (B) these kind   (D) that kinds

4. Making friends is more rewarding than <u>to be antisocial</u>.
   (A) NO CHANGE
   (B) being antisocial
   (C) being anti social
   (D) to be anti-social

ANSWER SHEET FOR SAMPLE EXAMINATION IV.

Make only ONE mark for each answer. Additional and stray marks may be counted as mistakes.

TEST I. CORRECTNESS AND EFFECTIVENESS OF EXPRESSION

PART A. ENGLISH USAGE

PART B. SPELLING

TEST II. INTERPRETATION OF READING MATERIALS IN THE SOCIAL STUDIES

PART A. SOCIAL STUDIES READINGS

PART B. GRAPH AND TABLE INTERPRETATION

TEST III. INTERPRETATION OF READING MATERIALS
IN THE NATURAL SCIENCES

TEST IV. INTERPRETATION OF LITERARY MATERIALS

TEST V. GENERAL MATHEMATICAL ABILITY

5. Jerry Cruncher was <u>very aggravated</u> by his wife's praying.
   (A) NO CHANGE
   (B) quite aggravated
   (C) much annoyed
   (D) very much aggravated

6. They invited my whole family to the cookout—my father, my mother, <u>my sister and I.</u>
   (A) NO CHANGE
   (B) my sister and me.
   (C) I and my sister.
   (D) me and my sister.

7. <u>Having raked the beach</u> for hours, the search for the lost ring was abandoned.
   (A) NO CHANGE
   (B) Having the beach raked
   (C) After we **had** raked the beach
   (D) Having raked, the beach

8. Her brother <u>never has</u> and never will be dependable.
   (A) NO CHANGE
   (B) hardly never has
   (C) never has been
   (D) not ever has

9. My mother is making chicken for dinner tonight, and I don't want to <u>miss it.</u>
   (A) NO CHANGE
   (B) miss tonight.
   (C) miss the chicken.
   (D) miss the dinner.

10. His tone <u>clearly implied</u> that he was bitterly disappointed.
    (A) NO CHANGE
    (B) clearly inferred
    (C) inferred clearly
    (D) implied a clear inference

11. Now kick your feet in the water <u>like Gregory just did.</u>
    (A) NO CHANGE
    (B) as Gregory just did.
    (C) like Gregory just done.
    (D) like Gregory did just.

12. Macy's sells merchandise of equal quality and <u>having a lower price.</u>
    (A) NO CHANGE
    (B) having lower prices.
    (C) having lower price.
    (D) has a lower price.

13. After I had sucked the lemon, the apple <u>tasted sweetly.</u>
    (A) NO CHANGE
    (B) tasted sweet.
    (C) tasted sweetened.
    (D) tastes sweetly.

14. The reason Frank is going to Arizona <u>is because he needs</u> a dry climate.
    (A) NO CHANGE
    (B) is that he needs
    (C) is because he needed
    (D) is on account of he needs

15. We can't assist <u>but one</u> of you at a time, so try to be patient.
    (A) NO CHANGE
    (B) We can assist but one
    (C) We can't assist only one
    (D) We can't only assist one

16. <u>If you would have been</u> prompt, we might have arrived in time for the first act.
    (A) NO CHANGE
    (B) If you were to have been prompt,
    (C) If you would've been prompt,
    (D) If you had been prompt,

17. <u>After he graduated high school</u>, he went to Dartmouth.
    (A) NO CHANGE
    (B) When he graduated high school,
    (C) After he was graduated from high school,
    (D) After he graduated in high school,

18. The recurrence of identical sounds, <u>help to awaken</u> the emotions.
    (A) NO CHANGE
    (B) help to wake up
    (C) helps to awaken
    (D) assist in awakening

19. Oliver Wendell Holmes decided to become a writer <u>being that</u> his father was a successful author.
    (A) NO CHANGE
    (B) on account of
    (C) since
    (D) in view of

20. Nothing would satisfy him <u>but that</u> I bow to his wishes.
    (A) NO CHANGE   (C) when that
    (B) although that   (D) that

21. <u>Let's you and me</u> settle the matter between ourselves.
    (A) NO CHANGE
    (B) Let's you and I
    (C) Let's
    (D) Let's me and you

22. <u>If you would have considered</u> all the alternatives, you would have chosen another course of action.
    (A) NO CHANGE
    (B) If you would've considered
    (C) If you considered
    (D) If you had considered

23. <u>Due to</u> the mechanic's carelessness, forty lives were lost.
    (A) NO CHANGE
    (B) As to
    (C) Because of
    (D) In view to

24. The language in Faulkner is somewhat <u>like Proust</u>.
    (A) NO CHANGE
    (B) like Proust's.
    (C) as Proust.
    (D) as Proust's.

25. By tomorrow, the book <u>will have lain</u> on the shelf for two full weeks.
    (A) NO CHANGE
    (B) will have lied
    (C) will have laid
    (D) will have lay

26. Asia is <u>as valuable</u> and more fully developed than Africa.
    (A) NO CHANGE
    (B) so valuable
    (C) as valued
    (D) as valuable as

27. Neither the diplomats nor our president <u>were to blame</u> for the fiasco.
    (A) NO CHANGE
    (B) was to blame
    (C) were in blame
    (D) were blamable

28. Rather than ignore the rules, <u>it would be advisable for you</u> to consider all aspects.
    (A) NO CHANGE
    (B) it would be smart for you
    (C) you are advised
    (D) one would advise you

29. The secret of happiness lies not in doing what you like, but <u>to like what you do</u>.
    (A) NO CHANGE
    (B) in liking what you do.
    (C) to like what you're doing.
    (D) to like which you do.

30. The orchestra <u>has risen as one man</u> to applaud the conductor.
    (A) NO CHANGE
    (B) has risen like one man
    (C) has rose as one man
    (D) has arose as one man

END OF PART

Go on to the next Test in the Examination, just as you would do on the actual exam. Check your answers when you have completed the entire Examination. The correct answers for this Test, and all the other Tests, are assembled at the conclusion of this Examination.

TEST I. CORRECTNESS AND EFFECTIVENESS OF EXPRESSION

TIME: 1 Hour

PART B. SPELLING

DIRECTIONS: In this test all words but one of each group are spelled correctly. Indicate the misspelled word in each group.

1. (A) afford   (B) closeing   (C) latter   (D) headache

2. (A) gravel   (B) artifishal   (C) lodge   (D) lilies

3. (A) document   (B) handsome   (C) frighten   (D) incorect

4. (A) atached   (B) flakes   (C) distributed   (D) continue

5. (A) conducter   (B) choice   (C) particular   (D) streamline

6. (A) thunder   (B) speaking   (C) recreation   (D) rockey

7. (A) provided   (B) runner   (C) sugested   (D) principle

8. (A) throughout   (B) silense   (C) political   (D) operation

9. (A) truth   (B) organized   (C) potatoe   (D) production

10. (A) worried   (B) spinach   (C) guilt   (D) suceeded

11. (A) throat   (B) within   (C) sheets   (D) twentyfive

12. (A) scarf   (B) settlement   (C) sweep   (D) wondring

13. (A) propertey   (B) pennies   (C) gathering   (D) eastern

14. (A) copper   (B) ribben   (C) considered   (D) further

15. (A) character   (B) oasis   (C) governer   (D) lonely

16. (A) anounce   (B) local   (C) grasshopper   (D) farmer's

17. (A) historical   (B) dustey   (C) kindly   (D) humbug

18. (A) current   (B) comunity   (C) cement   (D) calves

19. (A) changeing   (B) explained   (C) diameter   (D) consent

20. (A) sword   (B) reckord   (C) signed   (D) taste

TEST II. INTERPRETATION OF READING MATERIALS
IN THE SOCIAL STUDIES

TIME: 1 Hour

PART A. SOCIAL STUDIES READINGS

DIRECTIONS: Below each of the following passages of social science reading material you will find one or more incomplete statements about the passage. Select the words or expressions that most satisfactorily complete each statement in accordance with the meaning of the paragraph.

Reading Passage I

About 1200 B.C. there appeared along the shores of the northeastern Mediterranean a people known as the Phoenicians. Because the land where they settled was unfertile, farming was a difficult task, but there were forests of fine cedar near by, so these people became the world's first real shipbuilders and the first great seafaring traders and colonizers. From Tyre and Sidon on the east their vessels ranged the full length of the Mediterranean past the Straits of Gibraltar. They left settlements on Malta and Sicily; they founded Tripoli and Cadiz; but, most important of all, they founded Carthage.

Carthage was established about 850 B.C. at a sheltered point on the Gulf of Tunis. Because of its strategic location and its fine harbor, the colony grew to be the center of Phoenician trade. The city-state was nominally a republic, but in actual practice it was a plutocracy controlled by the wealthy aristocrats who owned great estates along the coast. There was, in fact, a popular assembly, but final control over all public affairs was held by the senate composed of 300 members, all of whom came from the ranks of the aristocrats. This government seems to have been successful, for under its guidance Carthage became one of the largest and richest cities of ancient times, with a population estimated at more than 1,000,000.

In time the ambitions of Carthage collided with those of other nations. Serious trouble began with the Greeks over the island of Sicily, but it was with Rome that the great struggle came in a series of three long and bitter wars extending intermittently

from 264 B.C. to 146 B.C. In this contest for supremacy in the Mediterranean, the Romans were finally victorious. In compliance with the plea of one of their leaders who insisted that Carthage must be destroyed if the Romans were ever to have peace, they killed or enslaved the Carthaginians, burned their city and plowed the site.

It has been said that in the long run only religion, art and wisdom insure immortality. The Carthaginians apparently were more successful at trade than at any of these, for there are today few traces of their civilization.

1. The title that best expresses the main theme or subject of this selection is:
   (A) What the Phoenicians accomplished
   (B) The first navy
   (C) The Carthaginian republic
   (D) The history of Carthage
   (E) Carthage versus Rome

2. The chief settlement made by the Phoenicians was
   (A) Tyre   (C) Malta
   (B) Sidon   (D) Tripoli
            (E) Carthage

3. According to the writer, one reason why the Phoenicians became shipbuilders was that they
   (A) wanted to travel
   (B) could not make a good living on their farms
   (C) had hostile neighbors
   (D) liked to be on the water
   (E) wanted to wage war

4. In the Carthaginian government final authority was held by the
   (A) people   (C) army
   (B) senate   (D) assembly
            (E) sailors

5. Carthage became noted for its
   (A) art   (C) trade
   (B) religion   (D) history
            (E) location

6. The Carthaginians and the Romans were engaged in war at intervals over a period of
   (A) 3 years   (C) 118 years
   (B) 100 years   (D) 410 years
            (E) 850 years

7. The final victor in the ancient Mediterranean wars was
   (A) Spain   (C) Sicily
   (B) Greece   (D) Rome
            (E) Carthage

8. The Carthaginian civilization
   (A) was permanently restored
   (B) greatly influenced modern civilization
   (C) was adopted by the Turks
   (D) ceased to exist
   (E) survives in Greece

Reading Passage II

The Caribbean Sea is to the Americans what the Mediterranean is to Europe—a central sea. The American body of water is not entirely landbound. Double strings of islands—the Cuba group and the Bahamas—form an arc at the Atlantic entrance. This arc is now firmly fortified. This Mediterranean of the West is the water passage between the Americas, and consequently it must be controlled by them if trade is carried on. The sea is as necessary to the Caribbean countries as the Mediterranean is to Italy.

The surrounding lands produce more oil than any other region of the same size in the world. They are rich in minerals, and the fertile soil produces great quantities of tropical fruits and vegetables. They are capable of supplying much of the goods formerly imported into the United States from Asia and Africa. In exchange, they need manufactured goods. Living standards, particularly in the beautiful but undeveloped islands, are low, and tropical diseases still exact a deadly toll.

9. The Caribbean Sea and the Mediterranean are alike in their
   (A) variety of exports
   (B) epidemics of serious diseases
   (C) undeveloped islands
   (D) geographical importance to surrounding areas
   (E) living standards

10. The Americas must control the Caribbean Sea in order to
    (A) carry on trade
    (B) prevent disease
    (C) compete with Italy
    (D) supply goods to Asia
    (E) form a land-bound arc

11. Lands bordering on the Caribbean are outstanding for their
    (A) manufacturing centers
    (B) production of oil
    (C) healthful living conditions
    (D) exports to Africa
    (E) lack of mineral supplies

Reading Passage III

In the British Museum a little glass case contains the mummies of two Egyptian kings who lived beside the Nile. With them are a few farm utensils used in the day when the two kings walked the earth—a broken plow, a rusted sickle, two sticks tied together with a leather strap. Those were the "bread tools" used in the Egyptian civilization 4,000 years ago. In the 1700's in America the same kinds of crude instruments were still the "bread tools" of most American farmers. In George Washington's Virginia home, Mount Vernon, some early American sickles are still preserved. They are very much like the reaping tools of farmers 4,000 years ago when the Egyptian kings were buried.

12. From this selection we may conclude that ancient Egyptians
    (A) kept their tools in glass cases
    (B) expected their rulers to walk long distances
    (C) engaged in farming
    (D) had only two wise kings
    (E) neglected their equipment

13. The "bread tools" mentioned in this selection were used in
    (A) preserving food   (C) constructing tombs
    (B) baking bread   (D) growing grain
             (E) helping walkers

14. A visitor to Mount Vernon may see on exhibition farm utensils that
    (A) were found in Egyptian tombs
    (B) are tied together with leather straps
    (C) have been lent by the British Museum
    (D) were invented by George Washington
    (E) are similar to ones used long ago in Egypt

Reading Passage IV

The Alaska Highway, which runs 1,523 miles from Dawson Creek, British Columbia, to Fairbanks, Alaska, was built by U. S. Army Engineers to counter a threatened Japanese invasion of Alaska. Rushed through in an incredible nine months, it was never properly surveyed. Some of the territory it passes through has not even been explored.

The story that the builders followed the trail of a wandering moose is probably not true, but the effect is much the same. The leading bulldozer simply crashed through the brush wherever the going was easiest, avoiding big trees, swampy hollows and rocks. Their problem was complicated by the necessity of following not the shortest or easiest route but one that would serve the string of United States-Canadian airfields that stretches from Montana to Alaska. Even on flat land the road twists into hairpin curves. In rough terrain it goes up and down like a roller coaster. In the mountains—sometimes clinging to the sides of cliffs 400 feet high—it turns sharply, without warning, giving rear-seat passengers the stomach-gripping sensation of taking off into space. There is not a guard-rail in its entire 1,500-mile length. Dust kicks up in giant plumes behind every car, and on windless days this dust hovers in the air like thick fog.

Both the Canadian Army and the Alaska Road Commission, who took over from the United States Army Engineers in 1946, do a commendable but heartbreaking job of maintenance. Where the road is built on eternally frozen ground, it buckles and heaves; on the jelly-like muskeg it is continually sinking and must be graveled afresh every month. Bridges thrown across rivers "a mile wide and a foot deep" are swept away in flash floods. Torrential thaws wash out miles of highways every spring. On mountainsides you can tell the age of the road by counting the remains of earlier roads that have slipped down the slope.

15. The title below that best expresses the main theme or subject of this selection is:
    (A) The job of the Alaska Road Commission
    (B) Surveying in the Far North
    (C) The Alaska Highway
    (D) A heartbreaking project
    (E) Exploring Alaska

16. The Alaska Highway was built originally to
    (A) make the route between Alaska and the United States shorter
    (B) promote trade with Alaska
    (C) meet a wartime emergency
    (D) help in exploration
    (E) attract settlers

17. The job of maintaining the road is complicated by the
    (A) threat of invasion
    (B) absence of United States Army Engineers
    (C) age of the road
    (D) lack of surveying
    (E) forces of nature

18. Which statement is *true* according to the passage?
    (A) The Alaska Highway has been closed since 1946.
    (B) The Alaska Highway was built in an unusually short period of time.
    (C) The Alaska Highway Commission should be criticized for its job of maintaining the highway.
    (D) The Alaska Highway stretches from Montana to Alaska.
    (E) Fog is a continual menace along the Alaska Highway.

Reading Passage V

The early settlers of Greenland brought with them from Iceland horses, cattle, sheep, goats and the domestic hen. The most important animal, on the whole, was the sheep. Sheep were able to feed out all winter, as in our own Wyoming and Montana, though it was advisable to lay up some hay for them in case of a spell of particularly bad weather. The sheep provided wool for most of the clothing of Greenland and meat as part of the flesh food of the country. Their milk was used for ordinary dairy purposes. Like the Norwegians and Icelanders of today, the Greenlanders used to drive their herds of sheep for considerable distances into the mountains for summer grazing. This was to reserve the home pasture for milk cows and to give the meadows a chance to produce hay. From the home field, if it was of any size, and from the wild meadow, the hay was brought home in pairs of huge bundles carried by the horses. Horses were important in Greenland, then, as pack animals and as steeds rather than for drawing sledges or wagons. Cattle were chiefly dairy animals. The Greenlanders produced a lot of butter and some cheese. The chief exports, however, were derived from the walrus. Ivory may have ranked highest as a source of revenue but ropes of walrus hide were a close second. Greenland falcons and polar bears were esteemed as gifts among European royalty.

19. The title that best expresses the central idea of this paragraph is:
    (A) The importance of the sheep
    (B) The economic life of colonial Greenland
    (C) Dairying in the Far North
    (D) Interesting animals
    (E) Exports from Greenland

20. The early Greenland colonist derived the greater part of his living from the
    (A) horse   (C) sheep
    (B) cow   (D) goat
                (E) hen

21. Apparently the winters in Greenland were
    (A) warm
    (B) extremely cold
    (C) characterized by heavy snowfall
    (D) similar to those in some of our northern states
    (E) very damp

22. In the summer, the Greenlanders drove their sheep to the mountains
    (A) for the healthful air
    (B) because the mountain grass was better
    (C) to harden them for the winter
    (D) to protect them from wild meadow grasses
    (E) to save hay

23. An important source of dairy products among the early settlers in Greenland was
    (A) horses   (C) reindeer
    (B) polar bears   (D) walruses
                (E) sheep

24. A considerable part of Greenland's export income came from
    (A) ivory   (C) beef
    (B) butter   (D) wool
                (E) hay

25. The royal families of Europe highly prized Greenland's
    (A) horses   (C) cattle
    (B) goats   (D) poultry
                (E) falcons

END OF PART

Go on to the next Test in the Examination, just as you would do on the actual exam. Check your answers when you have completed the entire Examination. The correct answers for this Test, and all the other Tests, are assembled at the conclusion of this Examination.

TEST II. INTERPRETATION OF READING MATERIALS IN THE SOCIAL STUDIES

PART B. GRAPH AND TABLE INTERPRETATION

DIRECTIONS: Read each question in this test carefully. Answer each one on the basis of the following table. Select the best answer among the given choices and blacken the proper space on the answer sheet.

BUREAU X
WEEKLY PAYROLL RECORD *

UNIT IN WHICH EMPLOYED	EMPLOYEE	TITLE	GROSS WEEKLY SALARY (BEFORE DEDUCTIONS)	WEEKLY DEDUCTIONS FROM GROSS SALARY		
				MEDICAL INSURANCE	INCOME TAX	PENSION SYSTEM
Accounting	Amoroso	Accountant	$95	$1.45	$12.50	$5.32
"	Knight	Bookkeeper	72	1.90	6.20	4.07
"	Rubin	Clerk	58	.65	8.20	3.31
"	Steurm	Typist	56	.65	7.90	3.53
"	Heller	Stenographer	61	1.45	6.40	3.78
Information	Reynolds	Clerk	56	1.30	5.60	4.22
"	Appel	Clerk	59	1.45	6.10	5.84
"	Wayne	Typist	58	1.30	5.90	6.26
"	Bustard	Stenographer	62	1.90	4.40	6.94
Mail	Horen	Clerk	66	1.30	7.40	5.54
"	Clift	Typist	54	.65	7.50	3.40
"	Maynard	Stenographer	58	1.90	3.60	3.71
Records	Balish	Clerk	64	.65	9.40	5.82
"	Meyers	Clerk	54	1.90	2.90	5.02
"	Warren	Typist	62	1.45	6.70	6.01
"	Stevens	Stenographer	69	.65	10.10	7.56

NOTE: Gross weekly salary is the salary before deductions have been made; take-home pay is the amount remaining after all indicated weekly deductions have been made. In answering questions involving annual amounts, compute on the basis of 52 weeks per year.

1. Balish's annual take-home pay is most nearly
   (A) $2500   (B) $2700
   (C) $3100   (D) $3300.

2. The difference between Wayne's gross annual salary and his annual take-home pay is most nearly
   (A) $300   (B) $500
   (C) $700   (D) $900.

3. Of the following, the employee whose weekly take-home pay is closest to that of Rubin's is
   (A) Steurm   (B) Reynolds
   (C) Appel   (D) Wayne.

4. The average gross annual salary of the typists is
   (A) less than $2750
   (B) more than $2750 but less than $3000
   (C) more than $3000 but less than $3250
   (D) more than $3250.

5. The average gross weekly salary of the stenographers exceeds the average gross weekly salary of the clerks by
   (A) $2   (B) $3
   (C) $4   (D) $5.

6. Of the following employees in the Accounting Unit, the one who pays the highest percentage of his gross weekly salary for the Pension System is
   (A) Knight   (B) Rubin
   (C) Steurm   (D) Heller.

7. For all of the Accounting Unit employees, the total annual deductions for Medical Insurance are less than the total annual deductions for the Pension System by most nearly
   (A) $600   (B) $700
   (C) $800   (D) $900.

8. Of the following, the employee whose total weekly deductions are most nearly 27% of his gross weekly salary is
   (A) Knight   (B) Reynolds
   (C) Meyers   (D) Stevens.

9. The total amount of the gross weekly salaries of all the employees in the Records Unit is most nearly
   (A) 95% of the total amount of the gross weekly salaries of all the employees in the Information Unit
   (B) 10% greater than the total amount of the gross weekly salaries of all the employees in the Mail Unit
   (C) 75% of the total amount of the gross weekly salaries of all the employees in the Accounting Unit
   (D) four times as great as the total amount deducted weekly for income tax for all the employees in the Records Unit.

10. For the employees in the Information Unit, the average weekly deduction for Income Tax
    (A) exceeds the average weekly deduction for Income Tax for the employees in the Records Unit
    (B) is less than the average weekly deduction for the Pension System for the employees in the Mail Unit
    (C) exceeds the average weekly deduction for Income Tax for the employees in the Accounting Unit
    (D) is less than the average weekly deduction for the Pension System for the employees in the Records Unit.

END OF TEST

If you finish before the allotted time is up, work on this part only.
When time is up, proceed directly to the next part and do not
return to this part.

TEST III. INTERPRETATION OF READING MATERIALS
IN THE NATURAL SCIENCES

TIME: 1 Hour

DIRECTIONS: Below each of the following passages of natural science reading material you will find one or more incomplete statements about the passage. Select the words or expressions that most satisfactorily complete each statement in accordance with the meaning of the paragraph.

Reading Passage I

Thorns are a nuisance in anybody's garden to-day. But to the paleolithic man they meant more than an unexpected jab in the foot or a prick in a finger. For when safety pins, buttons, snaps, and zippers were still undreamed of, he used the simple thorn to fasten his tunic and clasp his animal-skin cape. Thus he discovered the first pin, and the principle hasn't changed at all in 150,000 years. Even the history of the word *pin* itself is a striking clue to its background. It comes from the Latin *spina,* which means a thorn.

It took a New England Yankee, however, to make a pin-making machine. The first pin factory was set up in Derby, Connecticut, in 1835. To this day the Nutmeg State has continued its lead in the field. Of the eight companies which make almost all the pins in the United States, five are located in Connecticut. The others are in Chicago, New York, and Philadelphia.

Unlike hundreds of other items, pin sales just don't respond to a fast-talking, glittering advertising campaign. The housewife, it seems, goes out to buy pins only when she needs them. But even this has its consolations. Come what may, the market sells a steady 2,500,000 to 3,000,000 pounds of pins every year.

1. The title below that best expresses the main theme or subject of this selection is:
   (A) Selling pins
   (B) The Nutmeg State
   (C) The earliest fasteners
   (D) How pins were named
   (E) The history of pins

2. From this selection, a reader may conclude that a paleolithic man is one who
   (A) lived thousands of years ago
   (B) invented the metal safety pin
   (C) developed pin-making machinery
   (D) was jabbed continuously by pins
   (E) first used the Latin words for pin

3. Which statement is *true* according to the selection?
   (A) Early users of pins considered them a nuisance.
   (B) Plants supplied the material first used as pins.
   (C) Sales of pins are seriously affected by yearly business trends.
   (D) High-pressure advertising influences women to buy more pins than they can use.
   (E) Connecticut has lost its position as the state leading in the manufacture of pins.

S1675

Reading Passage II

The part of the ear which we see is only a trumpet to catch sound waves. The delicate apparatus which makes it possible for us to hear is buried for safekeeping in the bone at the base of the skull. A passage leads from the outer ear to a membrane called the eardrum. Sound waves striking the eardrum make it vibrate. On the other side of the eardrum lies a space called the middle ear. Across this a chain of three tiny bones carries sound vibrations onward to another space called the inner ear. The nerve of hearing (auditory nerve) picks up sound messages from the inner ear and carries them to the brain. The middle ear is connected with the throat by a tube about 1½ inches long, called the Eustachian tube. This tube ends near the throat opening of the nose and close to the tonsils. The middle ear also communicates with the mastoid or air cells in the bone back of the ear.

4. The eardrum is
   (A) a trumpet　　　　(C) a bone
   (B) an air cell　　　　(D) a tube
   　　　　(E) a membrane

5. In the middle ear there are
   (A) long passages
   (B) several 1½ inch tubes
   (C) networks of nerves
   (D) three small connected bones
   (E) mastoids

6. The Eustachian tube connects
   (A) the nose and throat
   (B) the middle ear and the throat
   (C) the inner ear and the eardrum
   (D) the middle ear and the outer ear
   (E) the inner ear and the base of the skull

Reading Passage III

Powdered zirconium is more fiery and violent than the magnesium powder which went into wartime incendiary bombs. Under some conditions, it can be ignited with a kitchen match, and it cannot be extinguished with water. Munitions makers once tried to incorporate it into explosives, but turned it down as too dangerous for even them to handle.

But when this strange metal is transformed into a solid bar or sheet or tube, as lustrous as burnished silver, its temper changes. It is so docile that it can be used by surgeons as a safe covering plate for sensitive brain tissues. It is almost as strong as steel, and it can be exposed to hydrochloric acid or nitric acid without corroding.

Zirconium is also safe and stable when it is bound up with other elements to form mineral compounds, which occur in abundant deposits in North and South America, India, and Australia. Although it is classified as a rare metal, it is more abundant in the earth's crust than nickel, copper, tungsten, tin, or lead. Until a few years ago, scarcely a dozen men had ever seen zirconium in pure form, but today it is the wonder metal of a fantastic new industry, a vital component of television, radar, and radio sets, an exciting structural material for chemical equipment and for superrockets and jet engines, and a key metal for atomic piles.

7. The title below that best expresses the main theme or subject of this selection is:
   (A) A vital component
   (B) A safe and stable substance
   (C) Zirconium's uses in surgery
   (D) Forming mineral compounds
   (E) Characteristics of zirconium

8. Zirconium is *not* safe to handle when it is
   (A) docile　　　　　(C) powdered
   (B) lustrous　　　　(D) in tubes
   　　　　(E) in bar form

9. The selection tells us that zirconium
   (A) is a metal
   (B) is fireproof
   (C) dissolves in water
   (D) is stronger than steel
   (E) is familiar to fewer than a dozen scientists

10. The selection makes it clear that
    (A) zirconium rusts easily
    (B) chemists are finding uses for zirconium
    (C) keys are frequently made of zirconium nowadays
    (D) zirconium is less abundant in the earth's crust than lead
    (E) makers of explosives are searching for ways to use zirconium

11. Zirconium is likely to be useful in all of the following fields *except*
    (A) surgery
    (B) television
    (C) atomic research
    (D) the manufacture of fireworks
    (E) the manufacture of jet engines

Reading Passage IV

When the first white men came to America, they found vast amounts of natural resources of tremendous value. Forests covered a large part of the nation; later gas, oil and minerals were found in unbelievable amounts. There was a great abundance of very fertile soil. Forests, prairies, streams and rivers abounded with wildlife. So vast were these resources, that it seemed that they could never be used up. So forests were destroyed to make way for farmland. Glasslands and prairies were plowed and harrowed. Minerals and oil were used in great quantities to supply a young industrial nation. Almost every river became the scene of factories, mills and power companies. Mammals and birds were slaughtered for food and sport.

Within a short time, the results were obvious. Floods caused millions of dollars worth of damage yearly. The very fertile soil washed away or blew up in great clouds. The seemingly inexhaustible oil and minerals showed signs of depletion. Rivers were filled with silt from eroding farms and wastes from factories. Many of the rivers were made unfit for fish. Several species of birds disappeared, and some mammals seemed on the verge of going. Future timber shortages were predicted. In short, Americans soon came to realize that some sort of conservation program must be set up, if future, as well as present, Americans were to share in the resources that are the heritage of every American.

12. The title below that best expresses the main theme or subject of this selection is:
    (A) What the first white men found in America
    (B) The cause of timber shortages
    (C) The loss of topsoil
    (D) The story of America's natural resources
    (E) Our share of the American heritage

13. It seemed to the early American settlers that
    (A) game was scarce
    (B) forests should not be cut
    (C) the natural resources were inexhaustible
    (D) there was a shortage of minerals
    (E) resources should be carefully used

14. The use of America's natural resources by the early settlers was
    (A) careless
    (B) scientific
    (C) unbelievable
    (D) predicted
    (E) unselfish

15. Much of the fertile soil of America has
    (A) sunk deep into the earth
    (B) been eroded by wind and water
    (C) been covered by lakes
    (D) caused millions of dollars worth of damage
    (E) become the scene of factories

16. One reason many of our rivers are no longer suitable living places for fish is that
    (A) too many fish have been caught
    (B) floods have caused much damage
    (C) fishermen have not been sportsmanlike
    (D) a conservation program has been set up
    (E) factories have dumped waste into the rivers

17. Americans have finally become aware of the fact that
    (A) no more factories should be built
    (B) our minerals will last forever
    (C) our natural resources must be conserved
    (D) animals must not be killed for food
    (E) it is too late to stop the destruction of our natural resources

Reading Passage V

Although man has known about asbestos for many hundreds of years, it was not until some eight decades ago that it was mined for the first time on the North American continent. H. W. Johns, proprietor of a New York City supply shop for roofers, was responsible for the opening of that first mine.

Mr. Johns was given a piece of asbestos which had been found in Italy. He experimented with the material and then demonstrated its miraculous powers to his astounded customers. After donning a pair of asbestos gloves, which looked much like ordinary workgloves, he took red-hot coals from the fireplace and juggled them in the air. How amazed the spectators were to discover that he was not burned at all! You can well imagine that he soon had a thriving business in asbestos roofing materials. However, because the transporting of the asbestos from Italy to the United States was very expensive, Mr. Johns sent out a young scientist to seek a source nearer home. This geologist located great veins in the province of Quebec in Canada.

Ever since 1881 Quebec has led the world in the production of this unusual mineral, which is a compound of magnesium, silicon, iron, and oxygen. When it is mined, the asbestos is heavy, just as you would expect a mineral to be. When it is picked apart, a strange thing happens: the rock breaks down into fine, soft, soapy fibers.

Geologists have not yet solved the riddle of this rock that can be separated easily into threads, but they have found thousands of uses for this fireproof material, often called the "cloth of stone."

18. The title below that best expresses the main theme or subject of this selection is:
    (A) Fireproof substances
    (B) The contributions of H. W. Johns
    (C) A "wonder" mineral
    (D) A new roofing material
    (E) Asbestos mining in Canada

19. Johns proved his ability as a salesman by
    (A) going into the roofing business
    (B) hiring a trained geologist
    (C) importing asbestos from Italy
    (D) demonstrating the use of asbestos gloves
    (E) proving to be a clever juggler

20. Johns sought a nearby source of asbestos in order to
    (A) impress his customers
    (B) locate better raw material
    (C) attract new business in Canada
    (D) make use of scientific help
    (E) lessen transportation costs

21. Which property of asbestos does the author emphasize?
    (A) its unusually great weight
    (B) its thread-like consistency
    (C) its composition of elements
    (D) its soapy taste
    (E) its tendency to burn easily

22. The author's chief purpose in writing this passage was to
    (A) show the need for more geologists
    (B) improve business relations with Canada
    (C) present facts about asbestos
    (D) increase the sales of asbestos
    (E) compare asbestos with other minerals

Reading Passage VI

When we say a snake "glides," we have already persuaded ourselves to shiver a little. If we say that it "slithers," we are as good as undone. Suppose we try saying, for our reassurance, what is the simple fact: a snake walks.

A snake doesn't have any breastbone. The tips of its ribs are freemoving and amount, so to speak, to feet. A snake walks along on its rib tips, pushing forward its ventral scutes at each "step," and it speeds up this mode of progress by undulating from side to side and by taking advantage of every rough "toehold" it can find in the terrain. Let's look at it this way: A man or other animal going forward on all fours is using a sort of locomotion that's familiar enough to all of us and isn't at all dismaying. Now: Suppose this walker is enclosed inside some sort of pliable encasement like a sacking. The front "feet" will still step forward, the "hind legs" still hitch along afterward. It will still be a standard enough sort of animal walking, only all we'll see now is a sort of wiggling of the sacking without visible feet. That's the snake-way. A snake has its covering outside its feet, as an insect has its skeleton on its outside, with no bones on the interior. There's nothing "horrid" about the one arrangement any more than about the other.

23. The title below that best expresses the main theme or subject of this selection is:
    (A) Snake's "legs"
    (B) Don't be afraid
    (C) How a snake moves
    (D) Snakes are like people
    (E) People and snakes move alike

24. A snake's "feet" are its
    (A) toes   (C) side
    (B) ribs   (D) sacking
              (E) breastbone

25. According to the selection we may conclude that the author
    (A) raises reptiles
    (B) dislikes snakes
    (C) is well informed about snakes
    (D) likes snakes better than people
    (E) thinks a snake "walks" better than man

END OF TEST

If you finish before the allotted time is up, work on this part only.
When time is up, proceed directly to the next part and do not
return to this part.

TEST IV. INTERPRETATION OF LITERARY MATERIALS

TIME: 1 Hour

DIRECTIONS: Below each of the following passages of literature you will find one or more incomplete statements about the passage. Each statement is followed by five words or expressions. Select the word or expression that most satisfactorily completes each statement in accordance with the direct or implied meaning of each passage.

Reading Passage I

Macbeth: Blood hath been shed ere now, i' the
    olden time,
Ere humane statute purg'd the gentle weal;
Ay, and since too, murders have been perform'd
Too terrible for the ear. The time has been,
That, when the brains were out, the man would die,
And there an end; but now they rise again,
With twenty mortal murders on their crowns,
And push us from our stools. This is more strange
Than such a murder is.

1. The thought of the quotation may best be
    expressed by:
    (A) all's well that ends well
    (B) a man without brains will die
    (C) murder will out
    (D) murders are ordinary things compared
        with ghosts
    (E) twenty murdered men cannot rest in
        peace.

2. The mood of the quotation may best be ex-
    pressed as:
    (A) sinister   (B) hilarious
    (C) fearful   (D) baleful
        (E) obdurate.

3. The expression " . . . . now they rise again"
    refers to:
    (A) trees   (B) revolutionaries
    (C) ghosts   (D) balloons
        (E) clouds.

4. The paragraphs may be said to be written in:
    (A) good prose   (B) good dialogue
    (C) verse   (D) dramatic prose
        (E) stilted English.

Reading Passage II

"There are few books which go with midnight, solitude and a candle. It is much easier to say what does not please us than what is exactly right. The book must be, anyhow, something benedictory by a sinning fellow man. Cleverness would be repellent at such an hour. Cleverness, anyhow, is the level of mediocrity today; we are all to infernally clever. The first witty and perverse paradox blows out the candle. Only the sick mind craves cleverness, as a morbid body turns to drink. The late candle throws its beams a great distance; and its rays make transparent much that seemed massy and important. The mind at rest beside that light, when the house is asleep, and the consequential affairs of the urgent world have diminished to their right proportions because we see them distantly from another and more tranquil place in the heavens, where duty, honor, witty arguments, controversial logic on great questions appear such as will hardly leave a trace of fossil in the indurated mud which will cover them—the mind then smiles at cleverness. For though at that hour the body may be dog-tired, the mind is white and lucid, like that of a man from whom a fever has abated. It is bare of illusions. It has a sharp focus, small and starlike, as a clear and lonely flame left burning by the altar of a shrine from which all have gone but one. A book which approaches that light in the privacy of that place must come, as it were, with open and honest pages."

5. The title that best expresses the ideas of this
    paragraph is:
    (A) Reading by Candlelight
    (B) Books for Convalescents
    (C) Not A Time to Read
    (D) Books for Tired Minds
    (E) Books for Midnight Reading.

6. To make good reading at bedtime, a book must be:
   (A) light   (B) witty
   (C) controversial   (D) historical
         (E) straightforward.

7. Naming the qualities of a book suitable for reading when one retires is:
   (A) logical   (B) a clever job
   (C) difficult   (D) like lighting a candle
         (E) tiresome.

8. The author considers the average book of today:
   (A) inane   (B) sinful
   (C) benedictory   (D) restful
         (E) open and honest.

Reading Passage III

"International cultural relations are not like a plant whose growth can be forced under glass; love for another country's stories and poems cannot be created by clever publicity, as if philosophy and art were an old brand of cigarettes under a new name. In all our efforts toward mutual appreciation we have to recognize that certain elements rooted in tradition, race and indigenous practices are not transferable. There are limits to the international to which we must pay heed, and these limits cannot be expanded; certain aspects of national culture can be comprehended only painstakingly. If a mere interchange of books by means of translation, or the import and export of scholars, were the key to mastery of another nation's culture, it might easily be proved that cultures are alike except for languages. Happily this is not the truth; the fascination of alien cultures lies in their inaccessibility. Therefore, a scheme that is directed toward conquering the superficial while it ignores the essential is without merit."

9. The title that best expresses the ideas of this paragraph is:
   (A) The Importance of Cultural Exchange
   (B) Dissimilarities of Cultural Backgrounds
   (C) Obstacles to Understanding Other Cultures
   (D) Methods of Mastering International Culture
   (E) The Futility of Cultural Exchange.

10. The author feels that the key to knowledge of other cultures is:
    (A) breaking down the barriers of language
    (B) a publicity drive
    (C) careful study
    (D) transferring indigenous ways
    (E) exchange of scholars.

Reading Passage IV

Among the men and women who have contributed to human happiness, advancement and welfare, must be included philosophers as well as statesmen, inventors, scientists and captains of industry. A philosopher helps people to seek truth and to inquire what are the most worth-while things that life affords. This is the way in which Ralph Waldo Emerson contributed to the greatness of America. Though he lived in an intellectual aristocracy, he had respect for the common man and his rights. He believed in democracy, in the dignity of human life, in the right and duty of each man to be independent and self-reliant and to follow the dictates of his conscience. He condemned slavery and sang the praises of those who had the courage to oppose it. He raised his voice in protest against the coming industrialism, which threatened to stifle the individual and to keep men and women from developing their various powers and capacities. His appeals for freedom of thought and action have as ringing force today as they did a century ago.

11. Emerson is noted for his
    (A) ideas   (C) experiments
    (B) inventions   (D) laws
          (E) industrial leadership

12. Emerson believed in
    (A) the importance of aristocracy
    (B) dictatorship
    (C) slavery
    (D) accumulation of wealth
    (E) freedom of thought

Reading Passage V

Men and women never stop learning. They all matriculate at the "university of hard knocks." Those who make the effort to learn are engaged in "adult education." Most adult education comes through the daily press, magazines, books, libraries, museums, the theater, concerts, the radio, motion pictures, conversation, travel and attendance at meetings and lectures. Government has touched certain parts of education very definitely through encouraging and supporting public libraries, providing classes—mostly in English—for foreign groups, arranging occasional lectures and supervising correspondence courses. The Federal Extension Service with its farm, home and club county agents is the largest adult education service in rural areas. No one can tell in advance what the adult education opportunities of any community will be as time goes on but the possibilities of television as an instrument of instruction should certainly be explored.

13. Adult education presupposes
    (A) graduation   (C) an effort to learn
    (B) leisure   (D) entering a university
         (E) plenty of money

14. The greatest educational aid for rural districts is
    (A) correspondence courses
    (B) travel
    (C) museums
    (D) English classes for foreigners
    (E) Federal Extension Service

15. The most important possibility for future adult education is the
    (A) club   (C) newspaper
    (B) television   (D) automobile
         (E) motion picture

Reading Passage VI

Considering that most friendships are made by mere hazard, how is it that men find themselves equipped and fortified with just the friends they need? We have heard of men who asserted that they would like to have more money, or more books, or more pairs of pajamas; but we have never heard of a man saying that he did not have enough friends. For, while one can never have too many friends, yet those one has are always enough. They satisfy us completely. The curious thing is that at any time and in any settled way of life a man is generally provided with friends far in excess of his dessert and also in excess of his capacity to absorb their wisdom and affectionate attentions.

16. Most friends are gained by
    (A) wealth   (C) intelligence
    (B) position   (D) wit
         (E) chance

17. People have _______ friends
    (A) too many   (C) too poor
    (B) too few   (D) wise
         (E) enough

18. A man _______ his friends
    (A) appreciates   (C) deserts
    (B) deserves   (D) provides
         (E) annoys

Reading Passage VII

A phase of my life which has lost something through refinement is the game of croquet. We used to have an old croquet set whose wooden balls, having been chewed by dogs, were no rounder than eggs. Paint had faded; wickets were askew. The course had been laid out haphazardly and eagerly by a child, and we all used to go out there on summer nights and play good-naturedly, with the dogs romping on the lawn in the beautiful light, and the mosquitoes sniping at us, and everyone in good spirits, racing after balls and making split shots for the sheer love of battle. Last spring we decided the croquet set was beyond use, and invested in a rather fancy new one with hoops set in small wooden sockets, and mallets with rubber faces. The course is now exactly seventy-two feet long and we lined the wickets up with a string, but the little boy is less fond of it now, for we make him keep still while we are shooting. A dog isn't even allowed to cast his shadow across the line of play. There are frequent quarrels of a minor nature, and it seems to me we return from the field of honor tense and out of sorts.

19. Refinement here means
    (A) politeness   (C) distinction
    (B) improvement   (D) his own dignity

20. The author of the paragraph above is
    (A) very angry   (C) deeply grieved
    (B) indifferent   (D) mildly regretful

21. The mood of the paragraph is
    (A) dogmatic   (C) very earnest
    (B) wistful   (D) belligerent

22. In comparing the earlier and later ways in which they played croquet, he considers the new way
    (A) more exact and less attractive
    (B) more beneficial for children
    (C) more conducive to happy family life
    (D) more fun for the dogs

23. The "quarrels of a minor nature" occur because
    (A) the dog chases the croquet balls
    (B) the balls do not roll well
    (C) efficiency has become more important than sociability
    (D) the little boy interrupts the game with his shouts

24. The author
    (A) is opposed to all progress
    (B) is very exact in everything he does
    (C) dislikes games
    (D) feels that undue attention to detail can lessen enjoyment

25. He thinks that
    (A) children should be seen and not heard
    (B) dogs are pleasant companions
    (C) dogs are a nuisance
    (D) children should not be trusted to arrange croquet wickets

END OF TEST

TEST V. GENERAL MATHEMATICAL ABILITY

TIME: 1 Hour

DIRECTIONS: In the following multiple choice questions, choose the correct answer from the choices offered.

Do not make any marks on the test itself. It is best to work out the solution to each question on a sheet of blank paper before looking at the suggested answers. This will help prevent you from being misled by answers that at first glance may look correct.

1. Of the following Roman numbers, the highest is
   (A) MXXX   (C) MXCI
   (B) MXXVIII   (D) MLIX

2. The best approximate answer for 8.4738 divided by $1\frac{3}{16}$ is
   (A) 4   (C) 10
   (B) 6   (D) 16

3. Of the following the largest is
   (A) $\frac{1}{2}$ (C) $0.37\frac{1}{2}$
   (B) 7%   (D) 0.099

4. The cost of sending a telegram is 52 cents for the first ten words and $2\frac{1}{2}$ cents for each additional word. The cost of sending a 14-word telegram is
   (A) 62 cents   (C) 69 cents
   (B) 66 cents   (D) 87 cents

5. 10% written as a decimal is
   (A) 1.0   (C) 0.001
   (B) 0.01   (D) 0.1

6. The number of half-pound packages of tea that can be weighed out of a box which holds $10\frac{1}{4}$ lbs. of tea is
   (A) 5   (C) 20
   (B) $10\frac{1}{2}$ (D) $20\frac{1}{2}$

7. Aluminum bronze consists of copper and aluminum, usually in the ratio of 10:1 by weight. If an object made of this alloy weighs 77 lbs., how many pounds of aluminum does it contain?
   (A) 7.7   (C) 70.0
   (B) 7.0   (D) 62.3

8. 0.004, written as a common fraction reduced to lowest terms is
   (A) $\frac{1}{5}$ (C) $\frac{1}{250}$
   (B) $\frac{1}{25}$ (D) $\frac{1}{2500}$

9. Mr. Jones bought stock at $60 a share. The par value of the stock is $100. If the stock pays $6 a year in dividends, what rate of interest is Mr. Jones getting on his money?
   (A) 10%   (C) 15%
   (B) 6%   (D) $4\frac{1}{2}$%

10. The New York State recent income tax was 2% on the first $1,000 of income subject to tax and 3% on the next $1,000 or any part thereof. By special law, the State allowed a deduction of $\frac{1}{4}$ of the tax computed on the above schedule. In 1944, $1,800 of Mrs. Smith's income was subject to tax. What was the amount of the tax?
    (A) $110   (C) $55
    (B) $33   (D) $11

11. How many miles can be traveled in 3 hours by a plane traveling at 117.2 miles per hour?
    (A) $390\frac{2}{3}$ (C) 272.4
    (B) 351.6   (D) 285.9

12. If a team wins 3 games and loses 2, what percentage of games played did the team win?
    (A) 40%   (C) 80%
    (B) 60%   (D) $66\frac{2}{3}$%

13. $\frac{3}{1000}$ written as a decimal is equal to
    (A) .03   (C) .0003
    (B) .003   (D) .00003

14. 1% of 8 =
    (A) 8   (C) .08
    (B) .8   (D) .008

15. 36 yd. and 12 feet divided by 3 =
    (A) 40 ft.   (C) 12¼ yds.
    (B) 124 ft.   (D) 12 yds.

16. Which fraction is *not* in its proper order in the series?
    (A) ¾   (C) ⅚
    (B) ⅘   (D) ⅔

17. 42 divided by .06 =
    (A) 7   (C) 700
    (B) 70   (D) .7

18. $2\frac{4}{17} \times \frac{1}{2} \times 11\frac{1}{3}$ =
    (A) 2   (C) 17⅓
    (B) 8   (D) 2⅓

19. $\frac{3}{2} \div \frac{2}{3}$ =
    (A) 1   (C) ⅞
    (B) ⁹⁄₂   (D) 2¼

20. If a man borrows $500 at 3% interest per year, how much does he owe in 3 years?
    (A) $45   (C) $545
    (B) $515   (D) $15

21. After spending two-thirds of her money, Mary has $1.50 left. The amount she had at first was
    (A) $1.00   (C) $3.50
    (B) $3.00   (D) $4.50

22. Some boys hiked 9 miles in 2¼ hours. The average rate in miles per hour was
    (A) 3   (C) 4¼
    (B) 4   (D) 6¾

23. Walnuts are selling at $2.19 for a 5-pound bag. The cost for 10 pounds is
    (A) $2.19 × 10   (C) $2.19 × 50
    (B) $2.19 × 2   (D) $2.19 × 5 ÷ 10

24. If six girls can paint a fence in two days, how many girls, working at the same uniform rate, can finish it in one day?
    (A) 2   (C) 12
    (B) 3   (D) 4

25. Two cars start from the same point at the same time. One drives north at 20 miles an hour and the other drives south on the same straight road at 36 miles an hour. How many miles apart are they after 30 minutes?
    (A) less than 10
    (B) between 10 and 20
    (C) between 20 and 30
    (D) between 30 and 40

END OF EXAMINATION

If you finish before the allotted time is up, check your work on this test only. Do not go back to earlier tests. When time runs out, compare your answers for this test and all the other tests in the examination with the correct key answers that follow.

CORRECT ANSWERS FOR SAMPLE EXAMINATION IV.

(Please try to answer the questions on your own before looking at our answers. You'll do much better on your test if you follow this rule.)

TEST I. CORRECTNESS AND EFFECTIVENESS OF EXPRESSION

PART A. ENGLISH USAGE

1.C	6.B	11.B	16.D	21.C	26.D
2.A	7.C	12.D	17.C	22.D	27.B
3.C	8.C	13.B	18.C	23.C	28.C
4.B	9.D	14.B	19.C	24.B	29.B
5.C	10.A	15.B	20.A	25.A	30.A

PART B. SPELLING

1.B	5.A	9.C	13.A	17.B
2.B	6.D	10.D	14.B	18.B
3.D	7.C	11.D	15.C	19.A
4.A	8.B	12.D	16.A	20.B

TEST II. INTERPRETATION OF READING MATERIALS IN THE SOCIAL STUDIES

PART A. SOCIAL STUDIES READINGS

1.D	6.C	11.B	16.C	21.D
2.E	7.D	12.C	17.E	22.E
3.B	8.D	13.D	18.B	23.E
4.B	9.D	14.E	19.B	24.A
5.C	10.A	15.C	20.C	25.E

PART B. GRAPH AND TABLE INTERPRETATION

1.A	3.C	5.B	7.B	9.A
2.C	4.B	6.D	8.D	10.D

TEST III. INTERPRETATION OF READING MATERIALS IN THE NATURAL SCIENCES

1.E	6.B	11.D	16.E	21.B
2.A	7.E	12.D	17.C	22.C
3.B	8.C	13.C	18.C	23.C
4.E	9.A	14.A	19.D	24.B
5.D	10.B	15.B	20.E	25.C

TEST IV. INTERPRETATION OF LITERARY MATERIALS

1.D	6.E	11.A	16.E	21.B
2.C	7.C	12.E	17.E	22.A
3.C	8.A	13.C	18.A	23.C
4.C	9.C	14.E	19.B	24.D
5.E	10.C	15.B	20.D	25.B

TEST V. GENERAL MATHEMATICAL ABILITY

1.C	6.D	11.B	16.D	21.D
2.C	7.B	12.B	17.C	22.B
3.A	8.C	13.B	18.B	23.B
4.A	9.A	14.C	19.D	24.C
5.D	10.B	15.A	20.C	25.C

V. FINAL SAMPLE EXAM FOR PRACTICE

Based on all the information available before going to press we have constructed this examination to give you a comprehensive and authoritative view of what's in store for you. To avoid any misunderstanding, we must emphasize that this test has never been given before. We devised it specially to provide a final opportunity of employing all you've learned in a situation that closely simulates the real thing.

The time allowed for the entire examination is 5 hours.

TEST I. CORRECTNESS AND EFFECTIVENESS OF EXPRESSION

TIME: 1 Hour

PART A. ENGLISH USAGE

DIRECTIONS: Read each Theme through carefully to get the general meaning. Then go back and look at the underlined and numbered portions of the story. Some of the underlined words and phrases contain errors in grammar, punctuation or choice of words. Others are correct as written. Study the suggested corrections in the right-hand column and choose the one you think is best. All of the suggestions may be grammatically correct, but one is always more effective than the others.

THEME I.

It is not right that we should force people to retire because of <u>oldness</u>, if they are willing and <u>able</u> to continue working. Age in years <u>is not no longer</u> a dependable <u>measuring</u> to decide <u>if</u> a person is ca-

1. (A) NO CHANGE   (C) aging
   (B) age   (D) oldness of age

2. (A) NO CHANGE   (C) with ability
   (B) have ability   (D) can seem

3. (A) NO CHANGE   (C) is no longer
   (B) is not longer   (D) are no longer

4. (A) NO CHANGE   (C) measurer
   (B) measurement   (D) measure

5. (A) NO CHANGE   (C) about
   (B) why   (D) whether

pable <u>of working</u>. The <u>Second World War</u> proved
this point when it became necessary to hire older

<u>experienced workers</u> to take the places of the
younger workers called away to serve <u>there</u> country.

The records <u>showed</u> that the older workers helped
us maintain a high level <u>on</u> production.

It is also interesting <u>in noting</u> that our <u>life ex-</u>
<u>pectancy</u> is increasing. The over-65 group will jump
to twenty million in 1975. A good many of these
people are able to produce and have a desire to
work, but they are not allowed to <u>work. Because</u>
many employers think that only young people can
give good service. It is true that a young person has
more action and <u>speed</u>. On the other hand, there is
much to be gained from the experience, loyalty, and
judgment of the older worker.

THEME II.

<u>For you to know</u> the meaning of words <u>are im-</u>
<u>portant</u> for your future <u>success</u>—socially, scholas-
tically, and in <u>business</u>'. You must have a good
choice of words <u>in</u> your command in order to get

6. (A) NO CHANGE   (C) in working
   (B) for working   (D) for to work

7. (A) NO CHANGE
   (B) Second world war
   (C) second World War
   (D) second world War

8. (A) NO CHANGE
   (B) workers of experience
   (C) experience workers
   (D) workers from experience

9. (A) NO CHANGE   (C) they're
   (B) thier   (D) their

10. (A) NO CHANGE   (C) are shown
   (B) has showed   (D) is showing

11. (A) NO CHANGE   (C) of
   (B) from   (D) by

12. (A) NO CHANGE   (C) to note
   (B) for noting   (D) to be noting

13. (A) NO CHANGE
   (B) expectancy in live
   (C) expectancy in living
   (D) living expectancy

14. (A) NO CHANGE   (C) work, because
   (B) work; because   (D) work; Because

15. (A) NO CHANGE   (C) is speedier
   (B) speediness   (D) can speed more

16. (A) NO CHANGE   (C) For to know
   (B) For your knowing   (D) Knowing

17. (A) NO CHANGE   (C) is important
   (B) am important   (D) have importance

18. (A) NO CHANGE   (C) successes
   (B) success'   (D) successment

19. (A) NO CHANGE   (C) business
   (B) busines's   (D) businesses

20. (A) NO CHANGE   (C) by
   (B) on   (D) at

ANSWER SHEET FOR SAMPLE EXAMINATION V.

Make only ONE mark for each answer. Additional and stray marks may be counted as mistakes.

TEST I. CORRECTNESS AND EFFECTIVENESS OF EXPRESSION

PART A. ENGLISH USAGE

PART B. SPELLING

TEST II. INTERPRETATION OF READING MATERIALS IN THE SOCIAL STUDIES

PART A. SOCIAL STUDIES READINGS

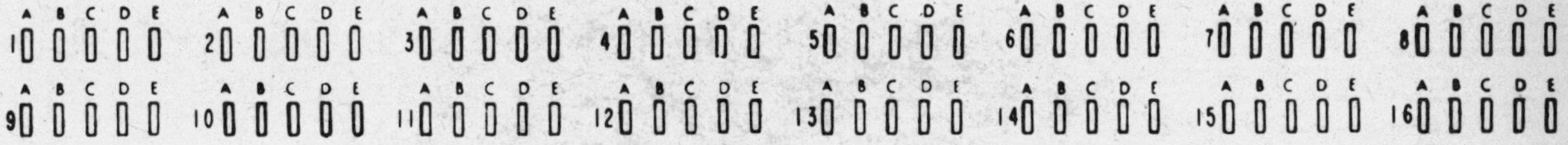

PART B. GRAPH AND TABLE INTERPRETATION

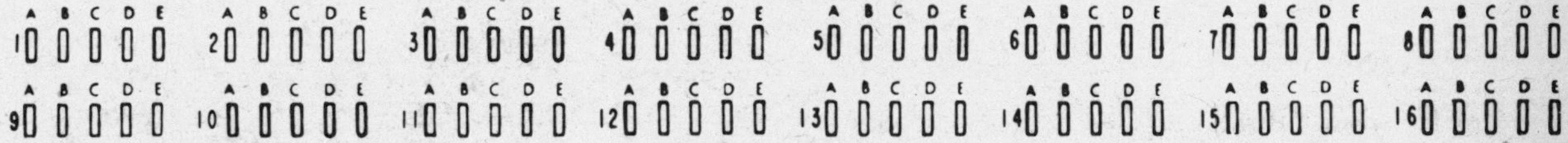

TEST III. INTERPRETATION OF READING MATERIALS IN THE NATURAL SCIENCES

TEST IV. INTERPRETATION OF LITERARY MATERIALS

TEST V. GENERAL MATHEMATICAL ABILITY

along <u>good</u> with your friends. Statistics <u>shows</u> that
₂₁   ₂₂

a strong vocabulary ties up <u>close with</u> school and
₂₃

business results in our <u>country</u>. That was what an
₂₄

organization <u>finded</u> out when it tested the vocab-
₂₅

ulary of different <u>kinds of a groups</u>. High school
₂₆

students averaged seventy-six errors; <u>college gradu-</u>
₂₇

<u>ates</u>, forty errors; college <u>professors'</u> scores showed
₂₈

eight errors; and business executives, seven errors.

The business executives were <u>them</u> that <u>held</u> the
₂₉   ₃₀

post of president or vice-president of a big com-

pany. Mind you, they scored even higher than the

professors.

21. (A) NO CHANGE   (C) well
    (B) o.k.   (D) swell

22. (A) NO CHANGE   (C) is showing
    (B) show   (D) does show

23. (A) NO CHANGE   (C) close in
    (B) closely with   (D) close to

24. (A) NO CHANGE   (C) Country
    (B) countryland   (D) country land

25. (A) NO CHANGE   (C) find
    (B) founded   (D) found

26. (A) NO CHANGE   (C) group kinds
    (B) kinds of groups (D) kind of a groups

27. (A) NO CHANGE
    (B) College graduates
    (C) college Graduates
    (D) College Graduates

28. (A) NO CHANGE   (C) professors
    (B) professor's   (D) professor'es

29. (A) NO CHANGE   (C) they
    (B) them ones   (D) those ones

30. (A) NO CHANGE   (C) was holding
    (B) holded   (D) helded

END OF PART

Go on to the next Test in the Examination, just as you would do on the actual exam. Check your answers when you have completed the entire Examination. The correct answers for this Test, and all the other Tests, are assembled at the conclusion of this Examination.

TEST I. CORRECTNESS AND EFFECTIVENESS
OF EXPRESSION

PART B. SPELLING

DIRECTIONS: In this test all words but one of each group are spelled correctly. Indicate the misspelled word in each group.

1. (A) executive   (B) rainbow   (C) irigation   (D) multiply

2. (A) acquarium   (B) aerial   (C) liver   (D) delivered

3. (A) final   (B) deoderant   (C) foundation   (D) hardships

4. (A) salary   (B) weekley   (C) swallow   (D) wilderness

5. (A) seashore   (B) chopping   (C) recieving   (D) lipstick

6. (A) inkwell   (B) boxing   (C) hickery   (D) major

7. (A) quantities   (B) toilet   (C) spinach   (D) servent

8. (A) ragged   (B) subtract   (C) pajammas   (D) paragraph

9. (A) unhappy   (B) zebra   (C) sheperd   (D) per cent

10. (A) sucessful   (B) tuberculosis   (C) splash   (D) playground

11. (A) thrown   (B) ugly   (C) temprature   (D) wondering

12. (A) poisen   (B) pressure   (C) whenever   (D) wrapped

13. (A) therefore   (B) windmills   (C) weapons   (D) slipery

14. (A) choir   (B) method   (C) entirely   (D) arguement

15. (A) independant   (B) booklet   (C) expensive   (D) extremely

16. (A) fisherman   (B) grease   (C) meanwile   (D) crime

17. (A) judicial   (B) haystack   (C) mayor   (D) atentive

18. (A) grapefruit   (B) earlier   (C) effect   (D) jewlery

19. (A) declaration   (B) companion   (C) expidition   (D) overcoat

20. (A) complection   (B) conversation   (C) dragon   (D) platform

TEST II. INTERPRETATION OF READING MATERIALS IN THE SOCIAL STUDIES

TIME: 1 Hour

PART A. SOCIAL STUDIES READINGS

DIRECTIONS: Below each of the following passages of social science reading material you will find one or more incomplete statements about the passage. Select the words or expressions that most satisfactorily complete each statement in accordance with the meaning of the paragraph.

Reading Passage I

All this activity and taking of responsibility runs right down into the smallest villages. There are at least 200,000 organizations, associations, clubs, societies, and lodges in the United States, along with innumerable social groups and *ad hoc* committees formed for specific causes. Except for the few intellectuals who don't believe in "joining," and the very, very poor who can't afford to, practically all adult Americans belong to some club or other, and most of them take part in some joint effort to do good. This prodigious army of volunteer citizens, who take time from their jobs and pleasure to work more or less unselfishly for the betterment of the community, is unique in the world. It is, in a way, the mainspring as well as the safeguard of democracy. For the volunteers are always ready to work and fight for what they think is right.

1. The title below that best expresses the ideas of this passage is
   (A) The busy citizen and his activities
   (B) The joiner
   (C) Group action in a democracy
   (D) Soldiers as civilians
   (E) America's smallest communities.

2. An *ad hoc* committee is one appointed
   (A) under parliamentary rules
   (B) to enlist volunteers
   (C) for a particular service
   (D) on a permanent basis
   (E) to supervise other organizations.

3. The author states that Americans who join clubs are interested in
   (A) the welfare of society
   (B) making friends
   (C) a unique organization
   (D) using their leisure profitably
   (E) maintaining American leadership.

Reading Passage II

The American Revolution is the only one in modern history which, rather than devouring the intellectuals who prepared it, carried them to power. Most of the signatories of the Declaration of Independence were intellectuals. This tradition is ingrained in America, whose greatest statesmen have been intellectuals—Jefferson and Lincoln, for example. These statesmen performed their political function, but at the same time they felt a more universal responsibility, and they actively defined this responsibility. Thanks to them there is in America a living school of political science. In fact, it is at the moment the only one perfectly adapted to the emergencies of the contemporary world, and one which can be victoriously opposed to communism. A European who follows American politics will be struck by the constant reference in the press and from the platform to this political philosophy, to the historical events through which it was best expressed, to the great statesmen who were its best representatives.

4. The title below that best expresses the ideas of this passage is
   (A) Fathers of the American Revolution
   (B) Jefferson and Lincoln—ideal statesmen
   (C) Democracy versus communism
   (D) The basis of American political philosophy
   (E) The responsibilities of statesmen.

5. According to this passage, intellectuals who pave the way for revolutions are usually
   (A) destroyed
   (B) misunderstood
   (C) honored
   (D) forgotten
   (E) elected to office.

6. Which statement is true according to the passage?
   (A) Adaptability is a characteristic of American and political science
   (B) The signers of the Declaration of Independence were all well educated
   (C) Jefferson and Lincoln were revolutionaries
   (D) America is a land of intellectuals
   (E) Europeans are confused by American politics.

Reading Passage III

Since 1750, about the beginning of the Age of Steam, the earth's population has more than tripled. This increase has not been an evolutionary phenomenon with biological causes. Yet there was an evolution—it took place in the world's economic organization. Thus 1,500,000,000 more human beings can now remain alive on the earth's surface, can support themselves by working for others who in turn work for them. This extraordinary tripling of human population in six short generations is explained by the speeded-up economic unification which took place during the same period. Thus most of us are now kept alive by this vast cooperative unified world society. Goods are the great travelers over the earth's surface, far more than human beings. Endlessly streams of goods crisscross, as on Martian canals, with hardly an inhabited spot on the globe unvisited.

7. The title below that best expresses the ideas of this passage is
   (A) Modern phenomena
   (B) The Age of Steam
   (C) Increasing population
   (D) Our greatest travelers
   (E) Our economic interdependence.

8. A generation is considered to be
   (A) 20 years
   (B) 25 years
   (C) 33 years
   (D) 40 years
   (E) dependent on the average age at marriage.

9. The writer considers trade necessary for
   (A) travel
   (B) democracy
   (C) political unity
   (D) self-preservation
   (E) the theory of evolution.

10. The basic change which led to the greatly increased population concerns
    (A) a revolution
    (B) economic factors
    (C) biological factors
    (D) an increase in travel
    (E) the growth of world government.

Reading Passage IV

The propaganda of a nation at war is designed to stimulate the energy of its citizens and their will to win, and to imbue them with an overwhelming sense of the justice of their cause. Directed abroad, its purpose is to create precisely contrary effects among citizens of enemy nations and to assure to nationals of allied or subjugated countries full and unwavering assistance.

11. The title below that best expresses the ideas of this passage is
    (A) Propaganda's failure
    (B) Designs for waging war
    (C) Influencing opinion in wartime
    (D) The propaganda of other nations
    (E) Citizens of enemy nations and their allies.

12. This passage implies that a nation's wartime propaganda is
    (A) dangerous to its nationals
    (B) useful to some of its enemies
    (C) unjustified
    (D) doubtful procedure
    (E) varied.

END OF PART

Go on to the next Test in the Examination, just as you would do on the actual exam. Check your answers when you have completed the entire Examination. The correct answers for this Test, and all the other Tests, are assembled at the conclusion of this Examination.

TEST II. INTERPRETATION OF READING MATERIALS IN THE SOCIAL STUDIES

PART B. GRAPH AND TABLE INTERPRETATION

DIRECTIONS: Read each question in this test carefully. Answer each one on the basis of the following table. Select the best answer among the given choices.

VALUE OF PROPERTY STOLEN— 1963 and 1964
LARCENY

CATEGORY	1963		1964	
	Number of Offenses	Value of Stolen Property	Number of Offenses	Value of Stolen Property
Pocket - picking	20	$ 1,950	10	$ 950
Purse - snatching	175	5,750	120	12,050
Shoplifting	155	7,950	225	17,350
Automobile thefts	1040	127,050	860	108,000
Thefts of automobile accessories	1135	34,950	970	24,400
Bicycle thefts	355	8,250	240	6,350
All other thefts	1375	187,150	1300	153,150

1. Of the total number of larcenies reported for 1963, automobile thefts accounted for, most nearly,
   (A) 5% (B) 15% (C) 25%
   (D) 50% (E) 75%

2. The largest percentage decrease in the value of the stolen property from 1963 to 1964 was in the category of
   (A) bicycle thefts
   (B) automobile thefts
   (C) thefts of automobile accessories
   (D) pocket-picking
   (E) all other thefts

3. In 1964 the average amount of each theft was lowest for the category of
   (A) pocket-picking
   (B) purse-snatching
   (C) thefts of automobile accessories
   (D) shoplifting
   (E) bicycle thefts

4. The category which had the largest numerical reduction in the number of offenses from 1963 to 1964 was
   (A) pocket-picking
   (B) automobile thefts
   (C) thefts of automobile accessories
   (D) bicycle thefts
   (E) all other thefts

5. When the categories are ranked, for each year, according to the number of offenses committed in each category (largest number to rank first), the number of categories which will have the same rank in 1963 as in 1964 is
   (A) 3 (B) 4 (C) 5
   (D) 6 (E) 7

6. For the two years combined (1963 and 1964), the average value of property stolen by pocket-picking was approximately
   (A) $25 (B) $30 (C) $150
   (D) $97 (E) $74

Answer the following questions solely on the basis of
this chart.

Number of Persons Receiving Public Assistance and Cost of Public Assistance in 1961 and 1962

Category of Assistance	Monthly average number receiving assistance during		Total Cost for Year in Millions of Dollars		Cost Paid by New York City for Year in Millions of Dollars	
	1961	1962	1961	1962	1961	1962
H R	36,097	38,263	$19.2	$17.4	$9.7	$8.7
V A	6,632	5,972	2.5	1.6	1.3	.8
O A A	32,545	31,804	33.7	29.7	6.5	5.0
M A A	13,992	11,782	13.2	21.3	3.3	5.3
A D C	212,795	228,795	108.3	121.4	27.5	31.3

7. Assume that the *total* cost of the Home Relief program decreases by 10% each year for the next three years after 1962. Then the total cost of the Home Relief program for 1965 will be, most nearly,
   (A) $11.5 million   (C) $12.7 million
   (B) $14.1 million   (D) $14.5 million
         (E) $36.0 million

8. The category for which New York City paid the smallest percentage of the total cost was
   (A) O A A in 1961   (C) V A in 1961
   (B) A D C in 1961   (D) O A A in 1962
         (E) A D C in 1962

9. The *monthly* cost to the city for each person receiving MAA during 1962 was, most nearly,
   (A) $18 more than in 1961
   (B) $26 less than in 1961
   (C) $20 more than in 1961
   (D) $67 more than in 1961
   (E) $18 less than in 1961

10. Assume that 40% of the number of persons receiving ADC in 1961 were adults caring for minor children, but the city's contribution towards maintaining these adults was only 36% of its total contribution to the ADC program in 1961, then the amount paid by the city for each adult per month in 1961 is, most nearly,
    (A) $10   (B) $14   (C) $31   (D) $36
          (E) $107

11. Assume that 10% of the persons receiving OAA in 1962 will be transferred to MAA in 1963, and 6% of the persons receiving MAA in 1962 will no longer need any public assistance in 1963, then the percentage change from 1962 to 1963 in the monthly average number receiving MAA would be, most nearly,

    (A) an increase of 4%
    (B) an increase of 27%
    (C) a decrease of 6%
    (D) an increase of 21%

END OF TEST

If you finish before the allotted time is up, work on this part only.
When time is up, proceed directly to the next part and do not
return to this part.

TEST III. INTERPRETATION OF READING MATERIALS
IN THE NATURAL SCIENCES

TIME: 1 Hour

DIRECTIONS: Below each of the following passages of natural science reading material you will find one or more incomplete statements about the passage. Select the words or expressions that most satisfactorily complete each statement in accordance with the meaning of the paragraph.

Reading Passage I

A need for beauty, lightness, corrosion resistance, or other specific properties must be present before plastics can even be considered as competitors of brick, window glass, cement, cast iron, or steel, since volumetric prices are so low for the last substance and for wood. It is not particularly unfortunate that plastics do not appear economical for every use. There is no reason why industry should want to replace wood, brick, concrete, and metals when the latter are adequate and inexpensive. Too much has been written about the coming "Plastics and Light Metal Age," which is prophesized as the successor to the Stone Age, the Bronze Age, and the Iron Age. In the historical sequence of these earlier periods, there is logic in the quantitive sense; one age gave way to another when the use of a new material exceeded in quantity that of its predecessor. For the plastics and light metals, however, a different picture presents itself; less than 3,000,000 tons of all these materials are being produced annually, while steel production exceeded 90,000,000 tons last year and will probably not recede to less than 60,000,000 tons for many years. This is still the Iron Age—or rather the Steel Age.

1. The title below that best expresses the ideas of this passage is
   (A) New uses for plastics
   (B) How one age succeeds another
   (C) Advantages of plastics
   (D) Limitations on the use of plastics
   (E) New demands in a postwar world.

2. The writer considers that the Bronze Age succeeded the Stone Age because
   (A) there was a scarcity of wood and other building materials
   (B) bronze was less expensive than stone
   (C) stone was no longer available
   (D) more bronze than stone came into use
   (E) the use of bronze was a step toward the Steel Age.

3. The writer regards the change to a "Plastics and Light Metal Age" in the near future as
   (A) necessary
   (B) desirable
   (C) improbable
   (D) economical
   (E) logical.

Reading Passage II

Many observers have commented on what seems to be the fact that fear plays a much smaller part than we should think it must in the life of an animal which lives dangerously. Terror he can know, and perhaps he knows it frequently. But it seems to last only a little longer than the immediate danger it helps him to avoid, instead of lingering, as in the human being it does, until it becomes a burden and a threat. The frightened bird resumes his song as soon as danger has passed and so does the frightened rabbit his games. It is almost as if they knew that "cowards die many times before their deaths; the valiant never taste of death but once."

4. The title below that best expresses the ideas of this passage is
   (A) A comparison of fear and terror
   (B) A comparison of man and the lower animals
   (C) Animal traits
   (D) Fear in animals
   (E) The nature of courage.

5. The writer believes that
   (A) terror is a permanent form of fear
   (B) fear is almost unknown in animals
   (C) fear has a permanent effect on animals
   (D) animals live less dangerously than men
   (E) animals remember fear only a short time.

6. "Cowards die many times before their deaths"
   means
   (A) many times the coward is almost caught
       in his misdeeds
   (B) the coward is frequently seriously ill
   (C) the coward's frequent fears are often as
       bad as death
   (D) cowards many times wish they were dead
   (E) the coward has several lives.

Reading Passage III

It takes no calendar to tell root and stem that the calm days of midsummer are here. Last spring's sprouted seed comes to fruit. None of these things depends on a calendar of the days and months. They are their own calendar, marks on a span of time that reaches far back into the shadows of time. The mark is there for all to see, in every field and meadow and treetop, as it was last year and ten years ago and when the centuries were young.

The time is here. This is that point in the great continuity when these things happen, and will continue to happen year after year. Any summer arrives at this point, only to lead on to the next and the next, and so to summer again. These things we can count on; these things will happen again and again, so long as the earth turns.

7. The title below that best expresses the ideas
   of this passage is
   (A) The appeal of spring
   (B) The march of time
   (C) Earth cycles
   (D) The beauty of wild flowers
   (E) The continuity of nature.

8. The passage indicates that the author experiences a feeling of
   (A) frustration
   (B) fear of the forces of nature
   (C) pessimism
   (D) regret at the rapid passage of time
   (E) serene confidence.

Reading Passage IV

The horse is far superior to the camel for every kind of work except traveling over a desert. The peculiar shape of the camel's feet enables him to walk over the sand of the desert without sinking as deeply as a horse would. Also, a camel can go without water for a period of time in which a horse would die of thirst. The horse is affectionate and loyal to his owner, but the camel is treacherous and often dangerous. He also has the reputation of being exceedingly stupid. On ground which is not soft sand, the horse is swifter than the camel. The camel has one valuable characteristic: he sheds his hair once a year, and thereby provides materials which can be made into tents and clothing. Camel's hair is far more serviceable than horsehair, and comes off in such a way that it can be easily gathered.

9. The camel is
   (A) treacherous   (C) affectionate
   (B) loyal   (D) swift
            (E) graceful

10. The camel is the best animal for desert travel
    because of
    (A) his size   (C) the shape of his feet
    (B) his speed   (D) his long neck
             (E) his appetite

11. The hair of the camel is
    (A) used for fertilizer
    (B) buried in desert sands
    (C) scattered widely
    (D) used in making clothing
    (E) burned for fuel

Reading Passage V

You all know of the Natural Bridge in Virginia and perhaps have heard how the first President of the United States, in the athletic vigor of his youth, climbed and carved his name high on its cliff. If a score of such bridges, however, were thrown together side by side, they would not be so large as the Natural Bridge of Pine Creek, Arizona, which is to the world's natural bridges what the Grand Canyon of the Colorado is to the world's chasms—the greatest, grandest and most bewildering. The actual span of the Arizona bridge is over 500 feet, five times the span of the Virginia bridge, and the breadth is over 600 feet or more than 12 times as wide as the one in Virginia. There are also countless minor bridges in the southwest, including a curious natural bridge near Fort Defiance, New Mexico. This is small but unusual, for it was carved not by rock particles carried in water but by sand-laden winds.

12. The largest natural bridge in the world is located in the state of
    (A) Virginia   (C) Arizona
    (B) Colorado   (D) New Mexico
             (E) California

13. Natural bridges are usually made by the action of
    (A) sand-laden winds
    (B) substances carried by streams
    (C) water
    (D) fragments of wood
    (E) frost

14. The largest natural bridge is notable for the fact that it
    (A) is made of pine
    (B) was climbed by George Washington
    (C) is five times as high as any other natural bridge
    (D) is 500 feet wide
    (E) is more than 12 times as broad as the first bridge mentioned

Reading Passage VI

Parachutes have been used in saving our forests from their worst enemy—fire. About fifteen million acres of forest can not be easily reached by roads or trails. Fires in these areas have the opportunity to get a good start before firefighters can penetrate the wilderness. Time is an important factor in fire fighting. Two or three smoke jumpers quickly brought to the scene by plane and parachute can control a small fire and prevent serious damage, whereas in the old days by the time a ground crew arrived many more men were needed to control a much enlarged fire.

Smoke jumping is a unique profession. The men, first of all, are trained foresters who know exactly what to do and are ready to start fighting a fire within a few minutes after they land. They have also been trained in jumping practices. Smoke jumpers in working clothes look as if they might be men from Mars. They wear special clothing to protect them when they land by parachute. Jumping suits are made of heavy canvas, zippered for immediate disrobing. The suits are well padded. Smoke jumpers also wear exaggerated football helmets with heavy wire masks. Ankle braces are worn over ordinary boots to prevent spraining ankles. Thus protected, landing on a treetop is as safe for the jumper as landing on the ground. In the pocket of his uniform he carries a strong rope to lower himself from trees. In a pocket on the pack carrying the 30-foot parachute is a miniature high-frequency radio for communication. Supplies and other equipment are also dropped by parachute, sufficient for at least two days. By that time a ground crew will have come to the assistance of the smoke jumpers.

Though smoke jumping is still in its infancy, plans for at least five squads of eight jumpers each have been developed. The records of the U. S. Forest Service show that this is a safe, cheap and effective way of controlling certain forest fires, especially those caused by lightning in out-of-the-way places. There is every chance that the parachute corps will remain a permanent and important part of the Forest Service.

15. The best of the following titles for this selection is:
    (A) Improved technique in fighting forest fires
    (B) How to be a smoke jumper
    (C) Fire-fighting equipment
    (D) A new kind of parachute
    (E) Dangerous fire fighting

16. The chief factor in preventing the spread of forest fires is:
    (A) area
    (B) roads
    (C) time
    (D) cost
    (E) number of men

17. The name "smoke jumpers" is applied to some of the forest rangers because they
    (A) stamp out fires
    (B) look like men from another planet
    (C) know how to live in the forest
    (D) use parachutes to reach fires
    (E) burn waste timber

18. Smoke jumpers are protected from injury when landing by
    (A) zippers
    (B) padded clothes
    (C) ropes
    (D) ordinary boots
    (E) pocket radios

19. The number of smoke jumpers that the government plans to employ is at least
    (A) 15
    (B) 8
    (C) 30
    (D) 40
    (E) 5

Reading Passage VII

Milk is a suspension of nourishing materials in water, which constitutes about 86 per cent of the total weight. The 14 per cent of nutrient solids consist of milk sugar five per cent, fat about four per cent, protein just a fraction less than that, and finally minerals and vitamins. It can readily be seen that milk is a kind of natural combination containing most of the body's requirements for growth and health. What is unique about milk is its richness in minerals and vitamins. Fat, sugar and protein can come from other sources, but the vitamin A and the minerals of milk can not be easily obtained elsewhere. It is also rich in the vitamin B group so urgently needed for health. Calcium and phosphorus are two minerals contained in milk that are of primary importance. These minerals are essential for normal development and maintenance of bones and teeth. Not only is milk rich in bone-forming calcium and phosphorus but it carries them in a form that is much more readily assimilated than the same minerals found in vegetables. Yet it is fortunate for us that we do not have to subsist on milk alone. Milk does not supply the body with the iron needed to prevent anemia. Milk also lacks vitamin D, although sunshine easily compensates for that shortage. Under our conditions of preparing milk, it also lacks vitamin C, which is the anti-scurvy vitamin of many fruits and vegetables. Cream and butter contain the fat of the milk, while cheese contains its solidified protein plus some fat, its vitamin A and some minerals. We also have, of course, the concentrated forms of milk, such as evaporated, condensed and powdered. These are whole milk equivalents minus some or all of the water.

20. The title that best expresses the main theme or subject of this selection is:
    (A) A history of milk
    (B) The sources of milk
    (C) Milk, a perfect food
    (D) Food values in milk
    (E) Popular milk products.

21. The largest part of milk is composed of
    (A) fat   (C) water
    (B) sugar   (D) minerals
         (E) vitamins

22. Milk is an especially important food because
    (A) it is cheap
    (B) it is easily available
    (C) it contains so much protein
    (D) its fat content is so large
    (E) its minerals can not be readily obtained otherwise

23. Milk is deficient in
    (A) phosphorus   (C) fat
    (B) iron   (D) protein
         (E) vitamin A

24. In order to have good teeth, a person should have plenty of
    (A) calcium
    (B) iron
    (C) protein
    (D) sugar
    (E) cheese

25. Sunshine is a good source of
    (A) vitamin A
    (B) vitamin C
    (C) vitamin D
    (D) phosphorus
    (E) calcium

END OF TEST

If you finish before the allotted time is up, work on this part only.
When time is up, proceed directly to the next part and do not
return to this part.

TEST IV. INTERPRETATION OF LITERARY MATERIALS

TIME: 1 Hour

DIRECTIONS: Below each of the following passages of literature you will find one or more incomplete statements about the passage. Each statement is followed by five words or expressions. Select the word or expression that most satisfactorily completes each statement in accordance with the direct or implied meaning of each passage.

Reading Passage I

Education was free. That subject my father had written about repeatedly, as comprising his chief hope for us children, the essence of American opportunity, the treasure that no thief could touch, not even misfortune or poverty. It was the one thing he was able to promise us when he sent for us, surer, safer than bread or shelter. On our second day I was thrilled with the realization of what this freedom of education meant. A little girl from across the alley came and offered to conduct us to school. My father was out, but we five between us had a few words of English by this time. We knew the word school. We understood. This child, who had never seen us till yesterday, who could not pronounce our names, who was not much better dressed than we, was able to offer us the freedom of the schools of Boston! The doors stood open for every one of us. The smallest child could show us the way. This incident impressed me more than anything I had heard in advance about the freedom of education in America. It was a concrete proof—almost the thing itself. One had to experience it to understand it.

1. The title below that best expresses the main theme or subject of this selection is:
   (A) My first day in America
   (B) The schools of Boston
   (C) My father's education
   (D) Our greatest opportunity in America
   (E) The little girl next door

2. When the father sent for his children, the only thing he could surely promise them was
   (A) bread   (D) schooling
   (B) friends   (E) wealth
   (C) shelter

3. The father believed that
   (A) he should have stayed in Europe
   (B) education was not worth while
   (C) the children could not learn English
   (D) he would always live in poverty
   (E) education was one possession that could not be stolen

4. The word *school*
   (A) was unknown to the children
   (B) frightened the children
   (C) was one of the first English words the children had learned
   (D) reminded the children of unhappy days in Europe
   (E) was difficult for the children to understand

5. The children fully realized the meaning of their father's words when they discovered that
   (A) the little girl across the way had better clothes than they did
   (B) they could not understand the little girl
   (C) the Boston schools didn't want them
   (D) in America even a little girl could take them to school
   (E) the little girl could not pronounce their names

Reading Passage II

Some of you still enjoy reading fairy tales, but you are not so deeply absorbed in them as you were a few years ago. It is an interesting part of growing up to keep adding to our enthusiasms, never wholly discarding what we outgrow, but tying on new pieces of muslin to the tail of our kite. The age of fairy tales belongs to a period when we are interested chiefly in a world of unreality. Goblins, wizards, dwarfs—all those creatures of the imagination—seem to children so much more engaging than water lilies or tadpoles or bread and butter.

Grown people find pleasure in remembering their childish imaginings. But other interests have displaced those early flights of fancy. In fairy tales, you know, all one needs for success or happiness is a fairy godmother. Then everything always turns out all right for the hero or heroine. But as we grow older, these imaginary victories which once satisfied us lose their power of enchantment. We want real success and real happiness. It is this growing interest in a real world, in contrast to the fanciful world of fairy lore, that marks the first great advance made in reading taste. An interest in *The Adventures of Alice in Wonderland* gives way to an interest in deep-sea diving. The fascination of "Jack the Giant Killer" is lost to a keen interest in Commander Byrd on his Antarctic exploration. The world of real people, real problems, real victories, real facts—these are the reading interests of a mind growing up.

6. The title that best expresses the main idea of this selection is:
    (A) Fairy tales
    (B) Growing up in reading taste
    (C) Real happiness
    (D) Our interest in goblins
    (E) Winning imaginary victories

7. "Tying new pieces of muslin to the tail of our kite" means
    (A) adding new interests to our lives
    (B) finding new excuses
    (C) forgetting the past
    (D) making up stories
    (E) flying a kite rather than reading

8. According to the selection, grown people remember their childish imaginings with
    (A) difficulty   (C) enthusiasm
    (B) enchantment   (D) pleasure
            (E) regret

9. In a fairy tale all one needs for success or happiness is a
    (A) wizard   (C) fairy godmother
    (B) hero   (D) heroine
            (E) goblin

10. According to the author, realistic stories appeal chiefly to a person who is
    (A) childish   (C) successful and happy
    (B) undeveloped   (D) becoming mature
            (E) reading fairy tales

Reading Passage III

The Greek teacher and philosopher Pythagoras was born about 580 B.C. on the island of Samos, whence his title of the "Samian Sage." Most of his later life was passed at Croton in southern Italy, where he became the founder of a celebrated brotherhood or association. It is to Pythagoras that we are indebted for the word *philosopher*. Being asked of what he was master, he replied that he was simply a "philosopher," that is, "a lover of wisdom." In astronomy the Pythagoreans held views which anticipated by two thousand years those of Copernicus and his school. The Pythagoreans taught that the earth is a sphere and that it, together with the other planets, revolves about a central globe of fire, "the hearth or altar of the universe."

11. The best of the following titles for this paragraph is:
    (A) Life and teachings of Pythagoras
    (B) How the word "philosopher" came about
    (C) The astronomy of Pythagoras
    (D) Famous Greek philosophers
    (E) Astronomy of the early Greeks

12. Pythagoras spent most of his later life in
    (A) Samos   (C) Greece
    (B) Rome   (D) Copernicus
            (E) Italy

13. Pythagoras taught that the
    (A) sun revolves around the earth
    (B) planets are balls of fire
    (C) earth is the center of the universe
    (D) earth revolves around the sun
    (E) planets revolve around the earth

14. Pythagoras was born in what century B.C.?
    (A) 2nd   (C) 4th
    (B) 3rd   (D) 5th
            (E) 6th

Reading Passage IV

My acquaintance among ferrymen is not extensive, but I can not remember any that were cheerful. Perhaps there were none. The one over there at this moment, on the other side, for whom we are waiting and who is being so deliberate—he certainly has no air of gaiety. There is a wealth of reasons for this lack of mirth. To begin with, a boat on a river is normally a vehicle of pleasure; but the ferryman's boat is a drudge. Then, the ordinary course of a boat on a river is up or down, between banks that can provide excitement, and around bends, each one of which may reveal adventure; but the ferryman's boat must constantly cross from side to side, always from the same spot to the same spot and back again. All that the ferryman knows of the true purposes of a river he gains from observation of others, who gaily pass him, pulling with the stream or against it and singing, perhaps, as they row.

15. The purpose of a ferryboat is
    (A) work   (C) observation
    (B) dredging (D) exploring
       (E) pleasure

16. The course of the ferryboat is
    (A) around the island
    (B) up the river
    (C) down the river
    (D) around the bends
    (E) across the river

17. The ferryman seems to be
    (A) pleasant (C) talkative
    (B) adventurous (D) gay
       (E) unhurried

Reading Passage V

The *Readers' Guide to Periodical Literature* tells you the names of authors who write for magazines, the titles of many of the articles and especially the subjects of all the articles. It lists all these in alphabetical order just as the card catalog does. Of course, it does not include all the magazines but you will find those most commonly used in libraries, schools and homes. The *Readers' Guide* appears first as a semimonthly magazine and has a paper cover much like any other magazine. You can readily see that an index to magazines which come out at regular periods such as weekly, monthly or quarterly would also have to appear at regular intervals. Some months the guide is much thicker than other months because it consolidates the information of several months in one number. At the end of the year all the information in all the issues for the whole year is published in book form. After three or four years the material is consolidated still further into a very large volume which contains all the information in the yearly volumes. This large volume is about as big as an unabridged dictionary.

18. The *Readers' Guide* contains
    (A) helps to housewives
    (B) condensed articles
    (C) lists of magazine articles
    (D) serial stories
    (E) recommendations of good books

19. The *Readers' Guide*
    (A) is always the same size
    (B) varies slightly in size
    (C) varies greatly in size
    (D) is issued twice a week
    (E) is issued weekly

20. The *Readers' Guide* is found in
    (A) hotels   (C) drugstores
    (B) homes   (D) libraries
       (E) churches

Reading Passage VI

In Thessaly there is a mountain named Olympus, the snowy peaks of which tower high into the sky. On the summits of this mountain, so the Greeks thought, were the shining palaces of the gods. To be sure, they never saw either the gods or the palaces but they explained this by saying that the encircling clouds shut off the wonderful vision from the eyes of mortals. In general the gods resembled mortals in appearance, although they were much larger and stronger. The Greeks imagined the gods as living much the same kind of life as did their own nobles. The gods required food and drink, although this did not consist of bread and wine but of a delicious substance called "ambrosia" and a liquid known as "nectar." While the fragrance of the sacrifices was pleasing to the gods, they never cooked or prepared any food for themselves.

21. Olympus was
    (A) a volcano
    (B) the home of the gods
    (C) a beautiful valley
    (D) a battle ground
    (E) a place for athletic games

22. The gods drank
    (A) wine   (C) ambrosia
    (B) nectar (D) milk
       (E) brandy

23. The gods were like the nobles in
    (A) size   (C) place of abode
    (B) length of life (D) power
       (E) way of living

TEST V. GENERAL MATHEMATICAL ABILITY

TIME: 1 Hour

DIRECTIONS: In the following multiple choice questions, choose the correct answer from the choices offered.

1. Multiply $1.08 by $6\frac{1}{4}$
   (A) $2.64
   (B) $3.98
   (C) $4.26
   (D) $6.75

2. Divide 73.44 by 2.4
   (A) 30.6
   (B) 3.06
   (C) .306
   (D) .0306

3. Change $\frac{5}{8}$ to a per cent
   (A) 50%
   (B) 60%
   (C) $62\frac{1}{2}$%
   (D) 75%

4. Subtract $941.20 from $1,000
   (A) $58.80
   (B) $48.60
   (C) $39.70
   (D) $25.40

5. Add $8\frac{9}{16}$, $4\frac{1}{2}$, $6\frac{3}{4}$
   (A) $18\frac{3}{8}$
   (B) $19\frac{13}{16}$
   (C) $20\frac{1}{4}$
   (D) $21\frac{1}{2}$

6. If 1 pound 4 ounces of meat costs $1.05, what is the cost of the meat per pound?
   (A) 62¢
   (B) 74¢
   (C) 84¢
   (D) 92¢

7. What is the interest for 3 months on a loan of $1,200 at a yearly rate of 5%?
   (A) $10
   (B) $12
   (C) $15
   (D) $18

8. How many square yards of linoleum are needed to cover a floor having an area of 270 square feet?
   (A) 20
   (B) 24
   (C) 28
   (D) 30

9. A boy took an examination on which there were 20 examples. If he had 18 of them correct, what percentage of the examples did he do correctly?
   (A) 70%
   (B) 80%
   (C) 90%
   (D) 95%

10. Six girls sold the following number of boxes of cookies: 42, 35, 28, 30, 24, 27. What was the average number of boxes sold by each girl?
    (A) 26
    (B) 29
    (C) 30
    (D) 31

11. $25.726 \times .04 =$
    (A) 10.2904
    (B) 1.02904
    (C) .0102904
    (D) 2.12904

12. $111111111 \div 9 =$
    (A) 12345678
    (B) 12345679
    (C) 11191119
    (D) 11235679

13. $2\frac{1}{2} \div 3 =$
    (A) $6\frac{1}{2}$
    (B) $7\frac{1}{2}$
    (C) $\frac{5}{6}$
    (D) 3

14. $.04 + .004 + 12.3 + 17 + .009 + 2.0 =$
    (A) 3.1353
    (B) 31.353
    (C) 313.53
    (D) 32.353

15. $+ 1 - 1 + 1 - 1 + 1 \ldots$, and so on where the last number is $+ 1$, has a sum of
    (A) 0
    (B) $- 1$
    (C) $+ 1$
    (D) 2

16. If $1,000 is invested at 5% interest, how much money will be accumulated in 5 years?
    (A) $2,500
    (B) $250
    (C) $1,050
    (D) $1,250

17. $\frac{1}{4} - \frac{1}{7} =$
    (A) $\frac{3}{28}$
    (B) $\frac{1}{3}$
    (C) $\frac{3}{7}$
    (D) $\frac{11}{28}$

18. If a pie is divided into 40 parts, what per cent is one part of the whole pie?
    (A) 40
    (B) 25
    (C) 4.0
    (D) 2.5

19. A man can dig 3 ditches in 2 hours. How many ditches can he dig in 8 hours?
    (A) 12
    (B) 8
    (C) 4
    (D) 2

20. 5% of 5% of 100 is
    (A) 25
    (B) .25
    (C) 2.5
    (D) 100

21. How many yards of ribbon will it take to make 45 badges if each badge uses 4 inches of ribbon?
    (A) 5
    (B) 9
    (C) 11
    (D) 15

22. Three pounds of popcorn are to be put into paper bags each holding $\frac{1}{8}$ of a pound. The number of bags required is
    (A) 8
    (B) 10
    (C) 16
    (D) 24

23. (A) Sam sells newspapers at 5 cents each and pays $3\frac{3}{4}$ cents for each paper that he sells. His profit on 100 papers is
    (A) $8.75
    (B) $1.25
    (C) $3.75
    (D) $12.50

24. If you pay $2 for a piece of cloth $1\frac{1}{4}$ yards long, the price per yard is
    (A) less than 50 cents
    (B) between 50 cents and $1.00
    (C) $1.25
    (D) $1.60

25. In making a bracelet Sally uses three 10-inch strips of cord. How many bracelets can she make from a 5-yard roll of cord?
    (A) 2
    (B) 5
    (C) 6
    (D) 15

END OF EXAMINATION

If you finish before the allotted time is up, check your work on this part only. When time runs out, compare your answers for this test and all the other tests in the examination with the correct key answers that follow.

CORRECT ANSWERS FOR SAMPLE EXAMINATION V.

(Please try to answer the questions on your own before looking at our answers. You'll do much better on your test if you follow this rule.)

TEST I. CORRECTNESS AND EFFECTIVENESS OF EXPRESSION

PART A. ENGLISH USAGE

1.B	6.A	11.C	16.D	21.C	26.B
2.A	7.C	12.C	17.C	22.B	27.A
3.C	8.A	13.A	18.A	23.B	28.A
4.D	9.D	14.C	19.C	24.A	29.C
5.D	10.A	15.A	20.D	25.D	30.A

PART B. SPELLING

1.C	5.C	9.C	13.D	17.D
2.A	6.C	10.A	14.D	18.D
3.B	7.D	11.C	15.A	19.C
4.B	8.C	12.A	16.C	20.A

TEST II. INTERPRETATION OF READING MATERIALS IN THE SOCIAL STUDIES

PART A. SOCIAL STUDIES READINGS

1.C	3.A	5.A	7.E	9.D	11.C
2.C	4.D	6.A	8.C	10.B	12.E

PART B. GRAPH AND TABLE INTERPRETATION

1.C	3.C	5.C	7.C	9.A	11.D
2.D	4.B	6.D	8.D	10.A	

TEST III. INTERPRETATION OF READING MATERIALS IN THE NATURAL SCIENCES

1.D	6.C	11.D	16.C	21.C
2.D	7.E	12.C	17.D	22.E
3.C	8.E	13.B	18.B	23.B
4.D	9.A	14.E	19.D	24.A
5.E	10.C	15.A	20.D	25.C

TEST IV. INTERPRETATION OF LITERARY MATERIALS

1.D	5.D	9.C	13.D	17.E	21.B
2.D	6.B	10.D	14.E	18.C	22.B
3.E	7.A	11.A	15.A	19.C	23.E
4.C	8.D	12.E	16.E	20.D	

TEST V. GENERAL MATHEMATICAL ABILITY

1.D	6.C	11.B	16.D	21.A
2.A	7.C	12.B	17.A	22.D
3.C	8.D	13.C	18.D	23.B
4.A	9.C	14.B	19.A	24.D
5.B	10.D	15.C	20.B	25.C

PART THREE

Verbal Ability and Reading

3

AFTER TAKING THE FINAL EXAM

Recording your score on the exams in this book is important to your success. Use the Table below to record these scores and track your progress.

EXAM NUMBER	NUMBER OF QUESTIONS	YOUR CORRECT ANSWERS	YOUR SCORE
I.	Total: 151	Total:	$\dfrac{\text{NO. CORRECT}}{\text{NO. OF QUESTIONS}}$ ...... %
II.	Total: 150	Total:	$\dfrac{\text{NO. CORRECT}}{\text{NO. OF QUESTIONS}}$ ...... %
III.	Total: 158	Total:	$\dfrac{\text{NO. CORRECT}}{\text{NO. OF QUESTIONS}}$ ...... %
IV.	Total: 160	Total:	$\dfrac{\text{NO. CORRECT}}{\text{NO. OF QUESTIONS}}$ ...... %
V.	Total: 146	Total:	$\dfrac{\text{NO. CORRECT}}{\text{NO. OF QUESTIONS}}$ ...... %

The Pinpoint Practice chapters which follow provide all the drill material you need for every phase of the Examination. Plan your attack systematically. Concentrate on your weaknesses. Answer the practice questions in these areas. As you will discover, the material is presented so that the areas tested in the actual exam are individually treated in this book.

TEST____ PART_________________________

DATE_________________

RATING

(Slightly reduced from standard size used with many tests)

USE THE SPECIAL PENCIL.   MAKE GLOSSY BLACK MARKS.

Make only ONE mark for each answer.   Additional and stray marks may be
counted as mistakes.   In making corrections, erase errors COMPLETELY.

TEAR OUT ALONG THIS LINE AND MARK YOUR ANSWERS AS INSTRUCTED IN THE TEXT

BETTER LANGUAGE AND UNDERSTANDING

The questions contained in this section are designed to test your knowledge of grammar, sentence structure, correct usage and punctuation, and to point out some of the main sources of errors that have confounded candidates on past examinations.

STOP THE "CRIME WAVE"!

A person may make a few mistakes in English and yet be considered a fairly good speaker or writer. The errors he commits, however—few as they are—must not be of a serious nature.

Let us draw a court room analogy. A judge may have several offenders appearing before him. Each one has been charged with a different violation— one offense may be more serious than another. That is the reason His Honor must pass sentence according to the wrong done—"twenty years," "three months," "thirty days," "suspended sentence," and so on. Likewise, offenses in the use of English are punishable by Public Opinion, according to the seriousness of the "crime." "I will (for shall) do it shortly," though incorrect, may get a "suspended sentence" because it is not a serious mistake. But "the balloon has busted" and "he don't understand" deserve "twenty years."

If you were a Good English Judge, how well would you know the "criminal code"? We cite here additional offenses with the suggested terms of punishment.

Suspended Sentence

1. Can I borrow your pen for a moment?
2. Neither of the salesmen are married.
3. Will you loan me a quarter?
4. We will attend to it soon.

30 Days

5. This is just between the three of us.
6. I wonder if it's going to rain.

7. My brother and I don't get along with one another.
8. It's me.

3 Months

9. Due to the storm, I'll have to postpone the trip.
10. He went in the next room.
11. Who did you give it to?
12. Leave me do it.

20 Years

13. Joe and me are going.
14. They prefer these kind of paper bags.
15. Do it like you were told.
16. He's the man which called.

Life

17. She done it.
18. We was robbed.
19. He ain't going.
20. I seen him.

CORRECTIONS

1. May (not can); 2. is (not are); 3. lend (not loan); 4. shall (not will); 5. among (not between); 6. whether (not if); 7. each other (not one another); 8. I (not me); 9. Because of (not Due to); 10. into (not in); 11. Whom (not Who); 12. Let (not Leave); 13. I (not me); 14. this (not these); 15. as (not like); 16. who (not which); 17. did (not done); 18. were (not was); 19. isn't (not ain't); 20. saw (not seen).

25 English Traps*

You will, in this section, find many principles of good English which will help you to avoid many errors, including the above. Some of the rules and facts you will read about are more important to know that others. But if you wish to be singled out and respected as a person who really knows his English, you should learn every rule and principle herein. It will give you that wonderful feeling of being "guiltless."

Don't get caught. Use the right word or expression.

1. ACCEPT - EXCEPT . . . accept means to receive; except means to leave out.
   "I accepted the job."
   "We cannot except any employee from the regulation."

2. BESIDE - BESIDES . . . beside means at the side of; besides means in addition.
   "Put the coffee table beside the sofa."
   "Besides Jim, Harry also went."

3. BETWEEN - AMONG . . . between applies to two objects; among to more than two.
   "The profits will be shared only between the two of us."
   "The business of the Texas area will be divided among three salesmen."

4. BRING - TAKE . . . bring means to carry toward the person who is speaking; take means to carry away from the speaker.
   "Bring the contracts to me when you return."
   "Please take this letter to the second floor desk."

5. CAN - MAY . . . can means physically able; may gives the idea of permission.
   "I can lift this chair over my head."
   "You may leave after you finish your work."

6. CONTINUOUSLY - CONTINUALLY . . . continuously means without a stop; continually means stopping and starting.
   "It rained continuously for seven days without a moment of dry weather."
   "It is hard to accomplish a job with continual interruptions."

7. DIFFERENT FROM - DIFFERENT THAN . . . never say different than; always say different from.
   "This typewriter ribbon is much different from the old one."

8. DUE TO - BECAUSE OF . . . due to is always wrong at the beginning of a sentence; say because of.
   "Because of unwise speculation, he lost every cent he had."
   "The loss of his money was due to unwise speculation."

9. EACH OTHER - ONE ANOTHER . . . each other refers to two; one another to more than two.
   "You and I ought to cooperate with each other."
   "The three players tossed the ball to one another."

10. EFFECT - AFFECT . . . they both mean influence; effect is a noun; affect is a verb.
    "The climate has an effect on people's lives."
    "How does the new tax law affect you?"
    Note: effect as a verb means bring about.
    "His plan effected a rise in sales."

11. FEWER - LESS . . . fewer is used when things are countable; less for a quantity that is considered as bulk.
    "We have fewer customers this week than last week."
    "I have less money in my pocket than you have."

12. IF - WHETHER . . . if is used to express a condition; whether to express a choice.
    "If I see Jack, I shall tell him."
    "I wonder whether this adding machine has been repaired."

13. IMPLY - INFER . . . the speaker implies something by his remarks; the listener infers something from what the speaker says.
    "Your words imply that I am dishonest."
    "I infer from what he says that he distrusts me."

14. IN - INTO . . . in usually refers to a state of being (no motion); into is used for motion from one place to another.
    "The records are in that drawer."
    "I put the records into that drawer."

15. INVITE - INVITATION . . . invite is a verb; invitation is a noun.
    "I shall invite ten people to dinner."
    "Let's send an invitation to Joe and his wife."

16. LAY - LIE . . . lay means place or put; lie means rest or relax.
    "The chicken (1) lays (2) laid (3) has laid an egg."
    "The child (1) lies (2) lay (3) has lain down to rest."

17. LEAVE - LET . . . leave means depart, abandon; let means permit, allow.
    "Don't leave him all alone."
    "The nurse won't let me see the patient."
    Note: "leave" takes no verb.
    "let" must take a verb ("see" in above sentence).

18. LEND - LOAN . . . lend is a verb; loan is a noun.
    "Please lend me a dollar."
    "May I have a loan of a dollar?"
    Note: lend-borrow . . . the one who has the money, lends; the one who needs the money, borrows.
    "I have no carfare. May I borrow a dime from you?"

19. PERSECUTE - PROSECUTE . . . to persecute is to make life miserable for someone; to prosecute is to attempt to right a wrong by legal means.
    "The persecution of minorities is characteristic of dictatorships."
    "Anyone disobeying the law will be prosecuted."

20. PRINCIPAL - PRINCIPLE . . . principal means main or chief; principle means rule or policy.
    "Cotton is one of the South's principal products."
    "Newton discovered the principle of gravity."

21. REASON IS THAT - REASON IS BECAUSE . . . never say the reason is because; always the reason is that.
    "The reason for my being late is that I had a flat tire."

22. ROB - STEAL . . . one robs a person but steals a thing.
    "I have been robbed!" he shouted.
    "The thief stole my wallet."
    Note: "The gunman robbed the National Bank" is correct because the Bank constitutes persons—president, cashier, etc. But —"The thieves stole the child's bank."

23. THESE KIND - THIS KIND . . . never say these kind; always this kind.
    "I am very fond of this kind of apples."

24. TRY TO - TRY AND . . . never say try and; always try to.
    "Try to come."

25. UNINTERESTED - DISINTERESTED . . . uninterested means bored; disinterested means fair, impartial.
    "I am uninterested in this slow-moving game."
    "Let us ask a disinterested person to settle this argument."

Test on 25 English Traps

Avoid the traps. Choose the correct form in the parentheses.

1. I (EXCEPT, ACCEPT) your offer; it sounds good.
2. Veterans are (EXCEPTED, ACCEPTED) from certain requirements.
3. We can't ship your order today; (BESIDE, BESIDES) we must check your credit before a shipment is made.
4. Don't put the sweet cream (BESIDE, BESIDES) the radiator.
5. Our buying is split up (BETWEEN, AMONG) four different manufacturers.
6. I'm going to "let you in" on something, but this is just (BETWEEN, AMONG) you and me.
7. Which samples are you going to (BRING, TAKE) to Chicago?
8. On your return from lunch, please (BRING, TAKE) back a bar of chocolate.
9. You (MAY, CAN) apply to our Personnel Division if you're interested in a position.
10. Salesmen are (CONTINUALLY, CONTINUOUSLY) coming to our showroom with that same idea.
11. Our neighbor's radio has been playing (CONTINUALLY, CONTINUOUSLY) with no let-up since this morning.
12. Your appearance is much different (THAN, FROM) what it was before your hair was cut.
13. (DUE TO, BECAUSE OF) the strike situation, deliveries have been slowed up considerably.
14. The members of the Board of Directors often consult (EACH OTHER, ONE ANOTHER).
15. An executive and his secretary must get along with (EACH OTHER, ONE ANOTHER).
16. The Stock Market trend seems to (EFFECT, AFFECT) business in general.
17. Consumers are now feeling the (EFFECT, AFFECT) of increased production.
18. Lowering of prices will naturally (EFFECT, AFFECT) an increase in the number of customers.
19. There have been (FEWER, LESS) requests for gabardine suits this year than last.
20. I am not sure (IF, WHETHER) to buy now or later.
21. I (INFER, IMPLY) from your attitude that you no longer care to work here.
22. By his remarks, he (IMPLIED, INFERRED) that he was looking for another position.
23. We always put the outgoing mail (IN, INTO) that tray.
24. Let's send (INVITES, INVITATIONS) to all the employees.
25. I felt so tired this afternoon that I (LAY, LAID) down for awhile.
26. The disgruntled workers (LAID, LAY) the whole matter before the Arbitration Committee yesterday.
27. The dog was (LAYING, LYING) helpless in the street.
28. Jim has (LIED, LAIN) down for a few minutes.
29. The truckmen have (LAIN, LAID) the cartons on the sidewalk.
30. (LEAVE, LET) us face the fact that competition is getting keener.
31. Don't (LEAVE, LET) the customer alone at the counter.
32. The Bank will (LEND, LOAN) me up to $5,000.
33. Will you be good enough to (BORROW, LEND) me a quarter?
34. If you're "up against it" and you want to (BORROW, LEND) some money, speak up.
35. The District Attorney will (PERSECUTE, PROSECUTE) the defendants in this case.
36. The Nazis (PERSECUTED, PROSECUTED) millions of helpless people.
37. Its (PRINCIPAL, PRINCIPLE) selling point is its low cost.
38. Our firm subscribes to the (PRINCIPAL, PRINCIPLE) of promoting those who show tangible results.
39. The reason for my not wishing to take on another typist is (THAT, BECAUSE) business doesn't warrant it.
40. Someone has (ROBBED, STOLEN) the sales records.
41. The crooks that (ROBBED, STOLE) the Exchange Bank, escaped with $100,000.
42. He prefers (THIS, THESE) kind of materials.
43. Try (TO, AND) visit me on your next trip East.
44. The organization is (DISINTERESTED, UNINTERESTED) in these articles at the present time.

45. The wage dispute is to be settled by a committee of three (DISINTERESTED, UNINTERESTED) persons.

Correct Answers

1. accept; 2. excepted; 3. besides; 4. beside; 5. among; 6. between; 7. take; 8. bring; 9. may; 10. continually; 11. continuously; 12. from; 13. Because of; 14. one another; 15. each other; 16. affect; 17. effect; 18. effect; 19. fewer; 20. whether; 21. infer; 22. implied; 23. into; 24. invitations; 25. lay; 26. laid; 27. lying; 28. lain; 29. laid; 30. let; 31. leave; 32. lend; 33. lend; 34. borrow; 35. prosecute; 36. persecuted; 37. principal; 38. principle; 39. that; 40. stolen; 41. robbed; 42. this; 43. to; 44. uninterested; 45. disinterested.

A Letter-Writer Who Was Trapped

The writer of this letter fell into a dozen different traps. Are you able to find them?

Dear Mr. Jamieson:

Please except my apology for my not having written to you sooner. If I can explain, the oversight was attributable to the rush of local business. But this is besides the point.

Due to the trucking strike, I cannot affect immediate shipment of your order. Please leave me know if you can wait another month. You realize these kind of delays can happen now and then. If you are disinterested in a future shipment under these circumstances, please try and notify me at once.

Incidentally, I imply from your last letter that you may come to town soon. I wish to extend a standing invite for nine holes of golf and dinner at my home.

Cordially,

Correct Answers

1. accept (not except); 2. may explain (not can explain); 3. beside (not besides); 4. Because of (not Due to); 5. effect (not affect); 6. let me know (not leave me know); 7. know whether (not know if); 8. this kind (not these kind); 9. uninterested (not disinterested); 10. try to (not try and); 11. infer from (not imply from); 12. invitation (not invite).

<table>
<tr><td>SCORE</td><td>........................... %</td></tr>
<tr><td colspan="2">NO. CORRECT ÷ NO. OF QUESTIONS</td></tr>
</table>

Grammar Is Not Hard to Learn

Research has indicated that a great many errors in grammar may be traced to a lack of understanding of only ten simple grammatical principles—and these ten principles may be learned thoroughly by any person of average intelligence in a surprisingly short period of time. But before we give you these rules, let us see how well you know your grammar. Maybe you are so smart that you do not have to study the rules.

Here, then, are 25 questions that will test your grammar "health." Twenty to 25 correct means that you are quite healthy; 14 to 19 correct means that you are in good condition, but you can stand some improvement. If you score under 14—oh, my! —you are "grammar sick." In that event, be sure that you learn the rules that follow the test. It won't take you long to do so.

Grammar Test

Directions: Underline the correct word. Answers appear at the end of the test.

Example: (<u>This</u>, These) kind of oranges will give plenty of juice.

1. To date, only one in five persons (has, have) paid his tax.
2. It is I who (is, am) the youngest employee here.
3. Use the machine (as, like) you've been told to.
4. The four salesmen, each of whom (has, have) just returned from a tour, will report to the President of the firm.
5. This is a matter to be settled between the boss and (I, me).
6. Neither the owner nor the foreman (considers, consider) this man qualified for the vacancy.
7. The typist (which, who) was ill is feeling better.
8. I've (risen, rose) at 6 A.M. every morning this week.
9. I absolutely (shall, will) refuse to sign this agreement.
10. (Who, Whom) do you think should make the Western trip?
11. Are these the shopkeepers (whom, who) you believe should be reported to the Board of Health?
12. The secret was known only to Jack and (I, me).
13. Without (us, we) Yanks, the war would never have been won.
14. (Who, Whom) are you betting on to win the Series?
15. I feel as if I (was, were) floating on clouds.
16. You and I (shall, will) find out soon what Smith intends to do.
17. You ought to phone Ellen; everybody's here but (her, she).
18. You squander money as if you (was, were) a rich man.
19. Don't rush; they can t start without you and (I, me).
20. What would the men do without (we, us) women?
21. After selecting the garment, the customer discovered that he (lost, had lost) his wallet.
22. Every worker promised that (he, they) would contribute.
23. It was (he, him) who filled the order, not (I, me).
24. Yesterday my brother (laid, lay) down right after supper.
25. Why don't you (set, sit) down for awhile?

Correct Answers

(You'll learn more by writing your own answers before comparing them with these.)

If you want to know the reasons, the rule number is given after each answer—refer to the Rules following.

1. has (#8) 2. am (#3) 3. as (#7) 4. has (#8) 5. me (#2) 6. considers (#8) 7. who (#5) 8. risen (#10) 9. will (#1) 10. Who (#4) 11. who (#4) 12. me (#2) 13. us (#2) 14. whom (#4) 15. were (#6) 16. shall (#1) 17. her (#2) 18. were (#6) 19. me (#2) 20. us (#2) 21. had lost (#9) 22. he (#8) 23. he, I (#2) 24. lay (#10) 25. sit (#10).

SCORE	.... **%**
NO. CORRECT ÷ NO. OF QUESTIONS	

TEN BASIC GRAMMAR RULES

1. SHALL or WILL
Rule: Say I shall, we shall. Otherwise, say will (you will, he will, she will, they will).
   "I think that I shall stop work now."
   "The officers will announce their policy shortly."
Note: In cases of <u>determination</u>, reverse the above rule.
   "I certainly will insist upon full payment."
   "They shall not pass."
SHOULD and WOULD follow the same rules as SHALL and WILL. In addition:
(1) <u>would</u> is always used for habitual action.
   "Last summer at Lake George, I <u>would</u> take a mile walk every morning before breakfast."
(2) <u>should</u> is always used for <u>obligation</u> (ought to).
   "You <u>should</u> check your bills before mailing them."

2. I or ME
Rule: With a preposition (little words like in, on, upon, from, between, with) always use the so-called object form of the pronoun—<u>me</u> (not I), <u>him</u> (not me), <u>her</u> (not she), <u>us</u> (not we), <u>them</u> (not they).
   "They divided the receipts between Joe and (I, me)."
   Correct: <u>me</u>—because it is the object of the preposition <u>between</u>.

3. WHO IS or WHO AM
"It is I who (is, am) the most experienced."
Suggestion:
   Find the word that comes before <u>who</u> which <u>who</u> refers to.
   They call this "coming before" word the antecedent of <u>who.</u>
   I is the antecedent in this sentence. You say <u>I am</u> (not I is)—therefore, say <u>who am</u> in the sentence above.

   "It is he who (is, am) filling the order."
   You say <u>he is</u> (not he am)—therefore, say <u>Who is</u> in this case.
Note these sentences:
   "It is he or I who am to go."
   "It is I or he who is to go."
   (<u>is</u> or <u>am</u> is used depending on which antecedent is closer to the <u>who</u> part of the sentence)
   "It is he and I who are to go."
   (the antecedent—<u>he plus I</u>—is <u>plural</u>; therefore, the plural verb <u>are</u> must be used)

4. WHO or WHOM
"Tell me (who, whom) you think should represent our Company at the Convention."
Suggestion: 2 steps for "who-whom" trouble:
   Step #1) turn the sentence around to its natural order
   ". . . you think (who, whom) should represent . . ."
   Step #2) substitute <u>he</u> (or they) for <u>who</u>; <u>him</u> (or them) for <u>whom</u>
   ". . . you think (he, him) should represent . . ."
   You would, of course, say ". . . he should represent . . .";
   Therefore, "Tell me <u>who</u> you think should represent our Company . . ." is correct.
"Please let me know (who, whom) that letter is for."
   Step #1) Natural Order: ". . . that letter is for (whom, who)."
   Step #2) ". . . that letter is for (he, him)."
   ". . . for him" is correct; therefore, the correct sentence reads . . .
   "Please let me know <u>whom</u> that letter is for."

5. WHO or WHICH
"The woman (<u>who</u>, which) dresses well, is usually well received."
Rule: who refers to persons
   Correct: "The woman <u>who</u> dresses well . . ."
   "The mink (who, which) is used for expensive garments, is raised in different parts of the world."
Rule: which refers to animals and things.
   Correct: "The mink, <u>which</u> is used for . . ."

6. WAS or WERE
Rule: If something is <u>contrary to fact</u> (not a fact), use <u>were</u>—not was.
   "I wish I (was, were) in Bermuda."
   Correct: <u>were</u>—because the sentence is not a fact.

7. LIKE or AS

Like is a preposition

"My brother looks like me."

Note: like is followed by the object form me not I).

As is a conjunction—a verb must follow. "I made out the invoice as you told me to."

Note this sentence:

"He is as tall as I (am tall)."

The verb am is understood.

8. VERB NUMBER

"Each of the managers (requires, require) a secretary."

Rule: When the subject is singular, the verb is singular.

When the subject is plural, the verb is plural.

Since the subject each (managers is not the subject) is singular, the verb form must be singular—requires.

Correct: "Each . . . requires a secretary."

"Everyone of these men (is, are) applying for the job."

Correct: "Everyone . . . is applying . . ."

"Not a single one of the five applicants (has, have) met the requirements."

Correct: "Not a single one . . . has met . . ."

9. VERB TIME

a) "The foreman asked what (happened, had happened) to my eye."

Correct: had happened

Rule: When an action in the past (had happened above) is even "more past" than another past action (asked above), use the past perfect tense (had come, had gone, had seen, etc.)—not the past tense (came, went, saw).

b) "I'm glad you're here at last. I (waited, have waited) an hour for you to come."

Correct: have waited

Rule: When an action was begun in the past, but extends to the present, use the present perfect tense (have waited, have run, have left, etc.)—not the past tense (waited, ran left).

10. VERB PART

Each verb has 3 principal parts. Learn them and you can't go wrong on which part to use. Here are the principal parts of 25 trouble-making verbs:

PRESENT*	PAST	PRESENT PERFECT**
1. begin	began	has (have) begun
2. blow	blew	has blown
3. break	broke	has broken
4. bring	brought	has brought
5. burst	burst	has burst
6. choose	chose	has chosen
7. do	did	has done
8. draw	drew	has drawn
9. drink	drank	has drunk
10. drive	drove	has driven
11. fly	flew	has flown
12. freeze	froze	has frozen
13. ride	rode	has ridden
14. ring	rang	has rung
15. raise (elevate)	raised	has raised
16. rise (get up)	rose	has risen
17. shrink	shrank	has shrunk
18. strive	strove	has striven
19. spring	sprang	has sprung
20. swim	swam	has swum
21. write	wrote	has written
22. lay (put down)	laid	has laid
23. lie (rest)	lay	has lain
24. sit (have a seat)	sat	has sat
25. set (place)	set	has set

* gives us future form also . . . will begin

** gives us past perfect form also . . . had begun

VERB PART TEST

(Answers appear below the test)

1. Our firm has already (began, begun) to show a profit.
2. The wind howled and (blew, blowed).
3. This week's sales have (broke, broken) previous records.
4. He has (brought, brung) the accounts up to date.
5. Inflation will cause the financial bubble to (bust, burst).
6. Mr. Davis has (chose, chosen) not to remain with the company.
7. The employees (did, done) a fine job.
8. We have (overdrawed, overdrawn) our bank account.
9. I've (drank, drunk) six cupfuls of water already.
10. They (drived, drove) the trucks recklessly.
11. Miss James has (flied, flown) to Kansas City.
12. Their assets have been (froze, frozen).
13. I have (rode, ridden) 25,000 miles on these tires.
14. The office boy has (rung, rang) for Western Union.
15. They (rose, raised) our salaries last week.
16. Our expenses have (rose, risen) 50% over last year.
17. The material (shrank, shrunk).
18. The salesman (strived, strove) to increase his sales.
19. The boiler (sprang, sprung) a leak.
20. How many persons have (swum, swam) the English Channel?
21. The secretary has (wrote, written) a letter of collection.
22. The child has (laid, lain) down to rest.
23. When you finish reading the report, (lie, lay) it on the table.
24. I'm so tired, I have to (sit, set) down for awhile.
25. Please (sit, set) my cup of tea right there.

Correct Answers

(You'll learn more by writing your own answers before comparing them with these.)

1. begun; 2. blew; 3. broken; 4. brought; 5. burst; 6. chosen; 7. did; 8. overdrawn; 9. drunk; 10. drove; 11. flown; 12. frozen; 13. ridden; 14. rung; 15. raised; 16. risen; 17. shrank; 18. strove; 19. sprang; 20. swum; 21. written; 22. lain; 23. lay; 24. sit; 25. set.

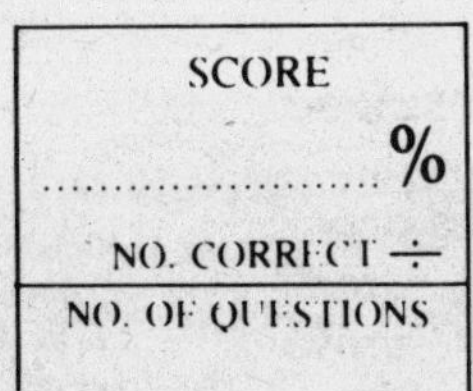

ENGLISH USAGE

DIRECTIONS: A passage is given in which words or phrases are underlined. Following the passage are four choices for each word or phrase underlined.   If the underlined part is correct as it stands, write the answer A. If you believe that the underlined part is incorrect, select from the other choices (B or C or D) whichever you think is correct. Grammar, sentence structure, word usage, and punctuation are to be considered in your decision. Regardless which choice you make, the original meaning of the sentence must be retained.

The following tests will determine how much you have improved in English Usage after studying the preceding pages. The form of the questions that follow is the same as the form of the questions in the actual test.   These questions, however, are easier.

ENGLISH USAGE TEST 1

Readers took there first trip to the moon 1,800 years' ago. They read about moon journeys in stories from Lucian of Samosta. He may, therefore, be called the father of science fiction. In one of his tales, titled "True History," a ship sailing in mysterious waters West of the Pillars of Hercules was blowed to the moon due to a sudden storm. In the other story, Icaromenippus practiced continually with the wings of large birds. He finally become airborne and flapped to his destination. Like we said, Lucian was the first storyteller to write of a trip into space.

1. (A) NO CHANGE   (C) they're
   (B) their   (D) thier

2. (A) NO CHANGE   (C) yea'rs
   (B) year's   (D) years

3. (A) NO CHANGE   (C) by
   (B) in   (D) on

4. (A) NO CHANGE   (C) science and fiction
   (B) scientific fiction   (D) fiction science

5. (A) NO CHANGE   (C) westerly
   (B) west   (D) in the West

6. (A) NO CHANGE   (C) was blown
   (B) was blewed   (D) were blowed

7. (A) NO CHANGE   (C) because of
   (B) due from   (D) on account

8. (A) NO CHANGE   (C) with continuation
   (B) continuously   (D) with continualness

9. (A) NO CHANGE   (C) was become
   (B) became   (D) was became

10. (A) NO CHANGE   (C) Like what
    (B) Like as   (D) As

Correct Answers

1. B	4. A	6. C	8. A
2. D	5. B	7. C	9. B
3. C			10. D

ENGLISH USAGE TEST 2

Next morning I <u>seen</u> for the first time an animal
¹
which I <u>hadn't never</u> met face to face. It was a
²
wolverine. He is <u>different than</u> most other dan-
³
gerous animals. <u>First off</u>, he is very small and weighs
⁴
less than 40 <u>pounds, he</u> is a fine tree climber and
⁵
a vicious destroyer. He <u>lays</u> quiet and then springs
⁶
on his prey. The wolverine has <u>kind of a</u> hunch-
⁷
back way of walking and <u>don't</u> easily tire. Before
⁸
he attacks, he <u>raises himself</u> on his hind legs and
⁹
then sways from side to side <u>like</u> a bear would
¹⁰
before charging.

1. (A) NO CHANGE   (C) saw
   (B) sawed   (D) seed

2. (A) NO CHANGE   (C) had not never
   (B) hadn't ever   (D) never

3. (A) NO CHANGE   (C) differing from
   (B) differing than   (D) different from

4. (A) NO CHANGE   (C) Number one
   (B) First   (D) One

5. (A) NO CHANGE   (C) pounds: he
   (B) pounds he   (D) pounds. He

6. (A) NO CHANGE   (C) lies
   (B) is laying   (D) has laid

7. (A) NO CHANGE   (C) kinda
   (B) kind of   (D) a

8. (A) NO CHANGE   (C) doesn't
   (B) dont   (D) do not

9. (A) NO CHANGE   (C) raises hisself
   (B) rises himself   (D) rises hisself

10. (A) NO CHANGE   (C) like about
    (B) like as   (D) as

Correct Answers

1. C	4. B	6. C	8. C
2. B	5. D	7. D	9. A
3. D			10. D

SCORE

.... %

NO. CORRECT ÷

NO. OF QUESTIONS
ON THIS TEST

ENGLISH USAGE TEST 3

There are some <u>people which</u> don't know how
1
to be happy. The <u>reason is because</u> they <u>haven't</u>
2
<u>never</u> sat down to think what really makes a person
3
happy. The average person <u>makes a big fuss</u> about
4
the <u>importance</u> of money. But money can give you
5
<u>plenty problems</u>. When you have money, others
6
<u>lend</u> from you. They can <u>rob</u> everything you own,
7   8
too. <u>Like</u> the old saying goes, "Money <u>isnt</u> every-
9   10
thing."

1. (A) NO CHANGE   (C) people who
   (B) folks what   (D) guys what

2. (A) NO CHANGE
   (B) reason is account of
   (C) reason is that
   (D) reason is why

3. (A) NO CHANGE   (C) haven't not
   (B) have never   (D) ain't never

4. (A) NO CHANGE
   (B) makes a big spiel
   (C) kicks up a big to-do
   (D) raises heck

5. (A) NO CHANGE
   (B) important thing
   (C) import
   (D) important

6. (A) NO CHANGE
   (B) plenty of problems
   (C) plenty headaches
   (D) plentiful problems

7. (A) NO CHANGE   (C) are lending
   (B) loan   (D) borrow

8. (A) NO CHANGE   (C) steal
   (B) hook   (D) swipe

9. (A) NO CHANGE   (C) Just like
   (B) As   (D) Like as

10. (A) NO CHANGE   (C) isn't
    (B) is'nt   (D) ain't

Correct Answers

(You'll learn more by writing your own answers before comparing them with these.)

1. C	4. A	6. B	8. C
2. C	5. A	7. D	9. B
3. B			10. C

SCORE

.... %

NO. CORRECT ÷

NO. OF QUESTIONS
ON THIS TEST

SPELLING IMPROVEMENT

The material in this chapter has appeared repeatedly on past examinations. It's all quite relevant, and well worth every minute of your valuable study time.

GETTING THE "SPELL" OUT OF SPELLING

A poor speller can, in almost every case, become an excellent speller. But he must go about it *diagnostically*. That means he must first locate the words that cause him trouble. The most wretched speller will discover that his spelling trouble is due to a limited number of words that he repeatedly spells incorrectly. Once he isolates these trouble-makers and gets to work on them, his spelling troubles are over.

LEARN TO SPELL A WORD

STEP ONE: Pronounce each syllable clearly, as you look at the word.

STEP TWO: Without looking at the word, try to see a picture of the word. Write the word in the air—then write it on a piece of paper.

STEP THREE: Compare the written word with the printed word in the book.

STEP FOUR: If you wrote the word incorrectly, write the word again correctly at least three times. Practice makes perfect. Writing the word will do you more good than spelling it out loud. Your purpose in learning how to spell the word is not to recite the correct spelling—it is to write the word correctly on an exam, in a letter, on a report, etc.

GET TO WORK

Have someone dictate to you the following one hundred words. They are considered among the most frequently misspelled words in the English language and they often appear on tests. After you have written the words, compare what you have written with this printed list. Place an X before each word that you got wrong (also before each word that you got right but which you were not sure of). Then write the incorrect words three times each *correctly*.

Keep a list of the words which you spelled incorrectly. Call them your Spelling Devils. Every once in a while have someone test you on this list till you get these Devils out of your system. Note that each word in these lists has at least one catch (underlined).

50 Big Devils

1. absence
2. accessible
3. achieve
4. allotted
5. all right (2 words)
6. analyze
7. annual
8. apology
9. appreciation
10. argument
11. assistant
12. commercial
13. committee
14. definitely
15. description
16. desirable
17. development
18. disappear
19. disappoint
20. exceed (like succeed, proceed)
21. existence
22. extension
23. forfeit
24. forty
25. indispensable
26. insistent
27. insurance
28. interfere
29. irrelevant
30. license
31. mortgage
32. necessary (unnecessary, necessity)
33. noticeable
34. occasion
35. occurrence (but occur)
36. possesses
37. precede (like concede, recede, secede)
38. preferred (like referred; but prefer, refer)
39. privilege
40. receive
41. recommend
42. repetition
43. ridiculous
44. schedule
45. separate
46. sincerely
47. stationery (means paper; stationary means in one position)
48. successful
49. supersede (only word that ends in sede)
50. truly

50 Little Devils

1. acceptable
2. accidentally
3. accommodate
4. accordance
5. accounts
6. acknowledge
7. across
8. actually
9. addressed
10. affairs
11. almost
12. alter (change)
13. analysis
14. apparel
15. apparently
16. appearance
17. arrangement
18. assistance
19. balance
20. beginning
21. bookkeeper
22. bulletin
23. bureau
24. customer
25. destroy
26. embarrassing
27. exaggerate
28. exhausted
29. familiar
30. foreign
31. happiness
32. hoping
33. humorous
34. interest
35. interrupt
36. irresistible
37. maintenance
38. naturally
39. omission
40. opportunities
41. originally
42. parallel
43. personnel (not personal)
44. prejudice
45. reference
46. seize
47. spoonful (cupful, mouthful, etc.)
48. too (means also; two is the number; to is a preposition —to the store, to the park
49. until
50. Wednesday

Devil Test

Twenty-five words, taken from the preceding "Devil Lists," have been misspelled in the following paragraph. Find the misspelled words, then spell them correctly in the spaces provided below the paragraph (answers appear below).

On this ocasion, it is highly desireable for our comittee to make refference to the indispensible assistence rendered by certain of our employees. Their sucessful efforts in the developement of our business should recieve our sincerly expressed appreshiation. It is truely a privelige to reccommend them, to, for their custemer intrest, and their servicing of acounts. We must not forfit this oportunity to give a discription of their personel accomplishments, and to acknowlidge their seperate achievements of the various tasks alotted them.

1. _______________
2. _______________
3. _______________
4. _______________
5. _______________
6. _______________
7. _______________
8. _______________
9. _______________
10. _______________

11. _______________
12. _______________
13. _______________
14. _______________
15. _______________
16. _______________
17. _______________
18. _______________
19. _______________
20. _______________
21. _______________
22. _______________
23. _______________
24. _______________
25. _______________

Correct Answers

1. occasion; 2. desirable; 3. committee; 4. reference; 5. indispensable; 6. assistance; 7. successful; 8. development; 9. receive; 10. sincerely; 11. appreciation; 12. truly; 13. privilege; 14. recommend; 15. too; 16. customer; 17. interest; 18. accounts; 19. forfeit; 20. opportunity; 21. description; 22. personal; 23. acknowledge; 24. separate; 25. allotted

100 More Spelling Troublemakers

Try this test. One word in each group is misspelled. Find the word and spell it correctly in the space provided at the right (answers appear below).

1. partial, business, through, comission
2. accounts, financial, reciept, answer
3. except, conection, altogether, credentials
4. whose, written, strenth, therefore
5. catalogue, familiar, formerly, secretery
6. debtor, shipment, fileing, correspond
7. courtesy, dictionery, extremely, exactly
8. probaly, directory, acquired, hurriedly
9. hauled, freight, hankerchief, millionaire
10. goverment, mileage, scene, ninety
11. written, permenent, similar, convenent
12. cooperation, duplicate, negotiable, Febuary
13. experience, interupt, cylinder, campaign
14. cordialy, completely, sandwich, respectfully
15. generaly, purpose, oppose, intelligence
16. judgment, miscelaneous, enforceable, opinion
17. restaurant, pleasent, organization, individual
18. picnicking, quantity, mispell, usual
19. typewriter, whenever, weapon, grammer
20. o'clock, practical, misstake, preparation
21. several, gauranteed, height, merely
22. question, remittence, dyeing, consequently
23. criticism, undoutedly, precious, reference
24. proffessional, period, immediately, gratefully
25. complexion, recollect, permissable, skillful

Correct Answers For The Foregoing Questions

(Please make every effort to answer the questions on your own before looking at these answers. You'll make faster progress by following this rule.)

1. commission; 2. receipt; 3. connection; 4. strength; 5. secretary; 6. filing; 7. dictionary; 8. probably; 9. handkerchief; 10. government; 11. permanent; 12. February; 13. interrupt; 14. cordially; 15. generally; 16. miscellaneous; 17. pleasant; 18. misspell; 19. grammar; 20. mistake; 21. guaranteed; 22. remittance; 23. undoubtedly; 24. professional; 25. permissible

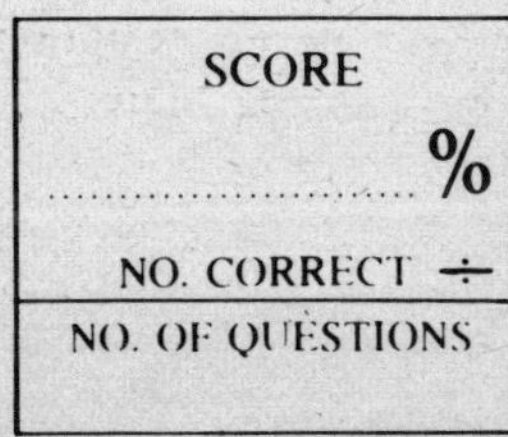

WORDS THAT LOOK EASY---OFTEN MISSPELLED

Following are four lists of what look like very simple words. They are on the elementary school Sixth Grade Level, Seventh Grade Level, Eighth Grade, and Ninth Grade Level. Yet adults very often misspell these words. Use the four steps to learn every one of these words.

SIXTH GRADE LEVEL

account	beef	cherry	dining
adopted	beg	chocolate	direction
adventure	bench	chores	disappointed
afterwards	blind	chosen	district
agreed	bodies	cleaning	ditch
agreement	bomb	clerk	donkey
aid	boss	cliff	double
aisle	bother	closet	Dr.
alive	bouquet	cocoa	drank
ancient	branch	coconut	drawn
ant	breast	collar	dressing
anxious	breath	colony	drill
anywhere	bringing	comfortable	drinking
appeared	brook	commerce	driver
apron	bubbles	committee	
area	bug	community	easier
artist	burst	considered	eastern
ashes	bush	continued	eighty
atom	butterfly	control	enemies
attack	button	copper	enemy
attic	buying	copy	energy
August		correct	engineer
author		costume	enjoying
auto	cabinet	cottage	excitement
avenue	calendar	crack	exercise
average	calves	crew	expected
awake	canal	criminal	expecting
awfully	canyon	crop	explain
ax	capture	crowded	extra
	caravan	curly	
	carefully	current	
bags	carriage		fact
bait	carries		failed
bake	cement		fairies
baked	cent	daily	fan
banana	century	dam	fasten
bang	chalk	date	favor
bare	character	dearest	fear
barrel	chart	decide	fever
bathing	chasing	deck	fierce
bay	check	decorate	figure
becoming	cherries	department	firecrackers
		dime	

flashlight
float
follows
fond
fool
forced
fork
forward
frost
froze
fuel
further
future

gang
gasoline
gathering
geese
generally
goldfish
goose
governor
greatly
groceries
grounds
growth
guard
guide
gum
gymnasium

handed
handle
happily
happiness
harbor
harvest
haunted
hearing
height
herd
here's
hiding
hoe
hog
hollow
holy
honest
human
hunter

immediately
information
inn
invitation
itself

jacks
jelly

jet
join
joke
judge

keen
keeper
kid
kindergarten
kiss
knee
knives

lad
ladies
lamb
lap
lard
lately
lawn
lawyer
length
letting
level
liberty
lightning
limb
liquid
list
lit
lock
lonely
lose

machinery
magazine
maid
manager
Mar.
march
mat
meant
measles
medicine
member
men's
message
midnight
mineral
mining
mischief
missile
model
motive
motor
musical

nap
native
natural
nature
naughty
navy
nearer
neighborhood
nephew
net
nicely
niece
nineteen
notice
noticed
noun

oasis
oatmeal
obey
object
October
offered
officers
oldest
opening
orchard
ordered
ourselves
oven
overalls
owl

pages
pain
pal
palace
pardon
parties
passing
paste
pat
patch
peaches
peak
peas
penmanship
pennies
per
perfect
phrase
pillow
pilot
pirate
pitcher
plantation

player
playhouse
playmates
plow
pocketbook
poison
polite
ponies
pop
popular
pot
pour
practicing
prepare
press
prevent
price
prince
princess
print
prison
process
produce
project
promise
proper
property
protection
pup
puppies
pure
purpose
purse

rag
raising
rake
rapidly
raw
reader
reasons
record
refused
regular
rent
ribbon
ringing
roast
roller
rolling
rooster
rule
ruler
rum
rush
rushed

saddle	signed	tame	ugly
safely	silly	tan	umbrella
sailing	simple	tank	unknown
sailor	single	tar	uses
salmon	sink	tardy	usual
sandwiches	sister's	tariff	various
sandy	sixty	taste	vase
Sat.	ski	tax	vegetable
scarf	slave	tear	vine
scenery	slip	temperature	visitor
scissors	slippery	tennis	visitors
scooter	smile	term	walrus
score	smooth	territory	waste
scratch	snowman	therefore	wave
search	social	they're	weak
section	solid	throat	weapons
seek	soup	thrown	wedding
Sept.	space	thus	weigh
September	spirit	ticket	weighed
serve	spoon	timber	we've
service	St.	toast	whale
sets	stable	toe	what's
settle	stationery	tomatoes	whenever
settlement	steal	tore	whip
settlers	steep	torn	windmills
seventeen	stiff	towards	wine
shadow	stole	towel	wishes
shape	streetcar	tractor	witch
sheets	stuff	training	within
shelter	success	tramp	wolves
shine	sulphur	transportation	wondering
shook	supplies	treat	worry
shoulder	supply	treated	worse
shovel	surrounded	treaty	worshiped
showing	swam	trimmed	wrap
sickness	sweep	tub	wrapped
signal	sword	twenty-five	wrist

SEVENTH GRADE LEVEL

aboard
ache
acquainted
action
adjective
advantage
adverb
advice
agree
agriculture
aim
alfalfa
alike
alley
alligator
allow
altogether
amendment
amusement
angel
ankle
answering
apartment
apiece
appearance
appreciated
appreciation
argument
arrive
article
ashamed
aside
assignment
attacked
attend
attended
attractive
aviator

backwards
bacon
bacteria
bakery
baking
barley
bean
beaver
begged
begun
bend

beneath
bent
blown
bluebird
boil
booklet
border
borrow
bound
boundary
bracelet
brake
breaking
breathe
bridle
buck
bud
bulb
bulldog
bump
bundle
burnt

cafeteria
camera
cannon
Capitol
cardboard
careless
carols
cast
cedar
ceiling
celery
chapter
cheap
checkers
cheerful
chew
choir
chorus
civil
cloudy
clover
coach
cocoon
collect
collection
collie
colonial

colt
comical
command
commercial
complete
completed
composition
concert
condition
confederation
consider
contain
continent
convention
council
counter
courage
covering
cranberries
crash
crawl
crazy
crept
crime
crow
cruel
curtain

damp
dandy
darkness
darling
dates
dawn
degree
delicious
delighted
deliver
design
destination
destroyed
development
diamond
dictionary
difference
difficult
digest
dip
dipped
discovery

dive
divide
division
dock
dolly
dot
downtown
dozen
dreaming
dresser
driven
drowned
due
dull
duties
duty
dwarf
dye
dying

eagle
earn
earned
election
elevator
embroidery
entertainment
entirely
envelope
equal
equip
equipment
eraser
event
exactly
example
excellent
exchange
executive
exhibit
expensive
explore
express
extremely

fairly
fairyland
falling
feather
fertile

figures
filling
fireman
fireworks
fisherman
flax
flight
flow
fold
folk
foolish
force
ford
forever
forgive
fortune
fountain
frame
freight
fried
furnace
furnish
furnished

gain
garters
gentle
gobble
golf
goodness
grab
graceful
gradually
grammar
grave
grazing
grease
greater
grey

habit
ham
happiest
harm
harness
harp
hatch
hatched
hatchet
hated
haul
hawk
heaven
hero
heroes
highway

holly
holster
hoped
hose
household
hygiene

iceberg
icy
idle
igloo
importance
impossible
improve
improvement
including
increased
indeed
independence
independent
index
industries
insects
instance
instrument
intelligent
invention
ironing
irrigation

jacket
jam
jealous
jewels
justice

kettle
keys
knight
knob
knot
knowing
knowledge

labor
lack
lame
lantern
lariat
league
lies
lift
likely
lime
linen
lungs

magic
mailbox
majority
manners
manual
manufacture
maple
marked
mass
mate
meadow
meanwhile
measure
melt
memory
metal
method
mighty
military
miner
minister
mirror
mistake
mistress
mittens
mix
moisture
moonlight
moth
mountainous
mule
multiply
mumps
mystery

nearest
necklace
Negroes
nervous
ninety
ninth
northwest
notebook
notes

obtained
occupation
occupied
odor
onions
opera
operation
opposite
orbit
organ
organized

outline
ox
oxen
oxygen

paddle
pajamas
palm
pantry
paragraph
parlor
particular
partner
pavement
paw
peep
per cent
permission
petroleum
phone
pier
pigeon
pioneer
pistol
pitch
playful
playground
P.M.
poet
political
port
potato
pray
prepared
preparing
principle
printed
printing
prisoner
private
problem
production
progress
pronoun
proved
provide
provided
pudding
puzzle

quack
quantities
quilt

raft
ragged

rail
rainbow
rainfall
realize
recreation
regards
religion
religious
remain
respect
result
revolution
reward
rid
ripe
rise
rising
robber
rocky
rod
roofs
root
rub
runner

salad
salute
satisfied
scarce
schoolroom
scream
screen
seldom
semester
sense
serious
servant
seventy
share
shelf
shepherd
shipped
shone
shout

shower
shown
silence
silent
skirt
skunk
smallpox
smoking
snowy
soda
somewhere
sour
spade
spare
speaking
spear
spending
spices
spin
spinach
splash
splendid
split
sprained
statement
statue
steer
stem
stir
stolen
stool
stoop
stranger
stratosphere
strawberries
streamline
strength
strike
student
subtract
succeeded
successful
suggested

sum
sunset
support
swept
swift
Swiss

tadpoles
tap
teaspoon
teepee
telegraph
tender
tenth
thanking
thirsty
thoughts
thrifty
throne
throughout
thunder
tip
title
toad
toilet
tomato
tongue
tonsils
tool
tough
tower
trading
traffic
trim
trousers
trout
truth
tube
tuberculosis
tulips
tune
twin
type

unhappy
unit
united
untie
upset
uptown

vacant
value
varnish
verses
view
vitamins
voyage

waist
wander
wanting
watermelon
wax
wealth
wealthy
weave
weaving
whatever
whipping
willing
windmill
windy
wipe
worn
worried
worst
wound
wreath
wreck

yell
younger

zebra
zero
zone

EIGHTH GRADE LEVEL

absence	bandage	checked	delight
accept	banner	chin	delightful
accepted	barber	choice	delivered
accessories	barefooted	chop	dense
accommodate	barely	chopping	dentist
accurate	basin	chum	deodorant
achieve	bass	churn	depend
activity	bathe	cider	depot
adding	batter	civilization	describe
adolescent	beard	civilized	description
advertisement	beast	clever	desire
aerial	beaten	closely	destroy
afford	beyond	closing	determined
agricultural	birch	code	dew
air conditioned	biscuits	colonist	diameter
alarm	bison	comfort	diary
alcohol	bitter	companies	diet
allegiance	blade	companion	directly
alphabet	blond	completely	distant
A.M.	blossom	complexion	distributed
ambition	blueberries	compound	dizzy
ambulance	bold	conductor	document
announce	boom	cone	doubt
antenna	boxing	connected	dough
anyhow	brand	consent	drag
ape	breaks	considerable	dragon
appear	breeze	constant	drain
appointed	broad	content	drawer
appointment	brownie	continue	dreadful
apprentice	bugle	conversation	drug
Apr.	bullet	cooky	drunk
apt	bunk	coop	dumb
aquarium	butcher	cord	dump
armies		cough	dungarees
armistice	cafe	cradle	dusty
arose	campus	crown	
arranged	canned	curb	eager
artificial	carbon	cure	earlier
ashore	carpenter	curious	effect
astonished	carpet	curl	elect
attached	carrot		elements
attempt	carve	daintiness	elf
attentive	cash	dainty	empire
Aug.	catalogue	damage	enclose
aviation	catcher	dare	enforce
	caterpillar	daylight	entire
background	cereal	debt	entrance
baggage	certificate	declaration	erase
baker	changing	deed	errand
balance	cheaper	defense	evergreen

expedition
experiment
explained
export
expression

faint
faith
faithful
false
fancy
farmer's
fault
favorable
female
fiddle
file
final
finest
firm
fitted
flakes
flash
flesh
flint
fluffy
forehead
former
fortunate
foundation
fraction
friendship
fright
frighten
fry
fudge
funeral

gallon
garbage
gentleman
gentlemen
giraffe
glaciers
globe
glove
glue
goal
good night
gown
graders
graduate
granite
grapefruit
grasshopper

gravel
gravy
grind
groomed
grove
guest
guitar
gulf

hail
handsome
handy
happier
hardships
haystack
headache
heap
helpful
hem
hickory
highly
historical
hitch
hobbies
hopping
horrible
howl
how's
humbug

icebox
ideal
ignorance
image
imagination
impatient
import
improved
incident
income
incorrect
indent
industrial
influence
inkwell
innocent
insect
intend
intended
interior
intestines
inventor
investigate
iodine
issued
itch

jaw
jerk
jewelry
judicial
junk

kindly
kindness
kingdom
knit
knitting

laboratory
lane
latter
lbs.
leak
lean
legislature
lemon
lemonade
license
lick
lid
lilies
liner
lip
lipstick
literature
liver
local
location
lodge
lowest

mailman
major
male
manner
mansion
marriage
marshmallows
mask
mayor
meantime
medium
mend
mentioned
meow
merchant
merely
mess
messenger
mild
mission

moist
monument
mop
mosquito
motion
motorboat
motto
movement
multiplication
murder
muscles

napkin
naturally
necktie
noble
noisy
nowadays
numerous

oars
odd
olden
onto
opinion
opossum
opportunity
ordinary
organic
organization
original
orphan
otherwise
ouch
overcoat
overflow
owe
oyster

pageant
pale
pansies
papoose
parachute
parrot
partly
passage
passenger
patient
pattern
paying
peaceful
peach
pear
pearl
peasants

pecans	rack	select	stump
peck	racket	selected	stunts
peculiar	raincoat	selfish	style
pepper	range	series	subscription
permanent	rank	serving	substance
petals	rate	shack	succeed
phosphorus	rattle	shady	suck
physical	rattlesnake	shark	suggest
planet	reaching	shelves	suitable
plank	rear	shiny	suitcase
plaster	receiving	shipping	superintendent
platform	recently	shock	surrender
plaything	redwood	showman	swallow
pledge	refreshments	shrubs	swamp
plum	refugees	silkworms	switch
plural	register	similar	swung
poisonous	regret	singer	syrup
policy	relief	singular	
polish	reply	skillful	
pork	reported	skip	tablecloth
porous	republic	slick	tack
porter	request	slim	tackle
possession	requested	smelting	tale
postmaster	required	snap	tallow
pottery	rescue	snowflakes	target
poultry	resources	snowshoes	task
practically	restaurant	somewhat	tavern
prairie	riddle	source	teacups
prayer	rider	southeastern	tease
preacher	rim	southwest	telegram
preamble	rink	sparrow	telescope
precious	roar	speaker	temple
preposition	rosy	spider	tend
Pres.	rotten	spied	terms
presence	rubbish	spill	thrift
presents	rude	spit	thumb
pressure	rusty	spite	Thurs.
prettier	rye	spoil	tickled
primary		spool	tide
primitive		sprang	ties
product	sake	spun	tinsel
professor	salary	stack	toboggan
promote	salty	stake	toothache
propelled	sample	stalk	toothbrush
proteins	sandwich	startled	total
prove	sank	stationary	tournament
published	satellite	steady	trailer
puddle	sauce	sting	transport
puff	scale	stopping	trash
pulp	schoolmate	stormy	travelers
purchase	scrub	strain	tray
purchased	scrubbing	strap	treatment
	seaports	streak	trial
quail	seashore	stretch	troop
quarrel	secure	strip	tropical
quart	seesaw	stroke	tusks

twelfth	vapor	weary	woodpecker
twigs	vast	Wed.	woolen
typhoid	verse	weed	worker
	vessel	weekly	woven
unable	victory	welfare	writer
underground	victrola	wharf	
underneath	vinegar	wherever	yarn
understood		wicked	you'd
unexpected		wigwam	youth
uniform	wade	wilderness	you've
university	walnut	willow	
unloaded	warn	winner	
unusual	waterfalls	winning	zinc

NINTH GRADE LEVEL

ability
abundance
abundant
abuse
accidentally
accompanied
according
accused
acorn
acre
active
activities
actually
additional
addressed
adjustment
administration
admire
admission
admitted
adoption
adult
advance
advanced
advertise
advertising
advise
advised
affair
affected
afterward
agent
agreeable
alas
ale
alien
aloud
amazement
ammunition
amusing
anchor
angle
anniversary
annual
apologize
appears
appendicitis
appetite
applied
apply

appoint
appropriate
approximately
apricots
armor
arrange
arrangement
arrest
arrival
arts
assistance
assistant
assortment
athletic
atmosphere
attendance
attending
attorney
audience
available
avoid
aye

bachelor
bamboo
banjo
banquet
bantam
bathtub
battery
bead
beautifully
beet
beggar
behave
belief
beloved
benefit
benefited
berry
bid
bind
blame
blank
blaze
bleed
bless
blessing
blizzard
bloody

bond
bonfire
bore
bounce
brain
brass
bride
brilliant
bronze
buckle
bulletin
burglar
bury
bushy
buyer
buzz

cable
cactus
caddie
calm
canvas
capable
cape
caring
carol
carrier
celebration
cemetery
chairman
chapel
charged
check
chemical
chemistry
chestnut
cigarette
civic
claim
clamp
clan
claws
cleanliness
clearly
click
cloak
coarse
coastal
coin
coke

colonel
commander
commence
commission
communication
compass
concerning
concrete
conduct
conference
connect
connection
conquer
constantly
construction
containing
continental
contract
convenience
cooperate
copies
copyright
cork
corpuscles
cot
courteous
coward
coyote
crab
cracker
cranberry
crank
crayons
create
credit
creep
crepe
cripple
crochet
crocodile
crust
crystal
cultivate
cunning
curve
cushion
custom

daisies
daisy

dandelion
dash
deaf
debate
deceived
decent
decision
declare
decoration
defects
defend
delicate
delivery
demand
depth
derrick
described
desired
dessert
detective
develop
devil
dike
dine
dipper
direct
disappear
disappointment
discover
discuss
discussed
discussion
disgusted
disposition
dissolve
distinct
disturb
dodge
dole
dome
domestic
dominoes
dose
dove
drama
dread
dreary
drift
drown

earliest
ease
easiest
edition
editor
effort

electrical
eleventh
elk
elm
embarrassed
enormous
entertain
entitled
equator
equipped
essay
essential
establish
evil
exact
exceedingly
exhausted
expense
expenses
extend
extended
extent
extreme

fade
fail
fairground
fame
familiar
fare
farewell
fashion
fatten
feature
federal
feeble
fern
ferry
festival
film
fingernail
fist
flame
fled
fleet
flock
flop
fluid
flute
foe
foggy
footsteps
foreigners
forenoon
formerly
fowl

frequently
Fri.
frontier
fully
fuzzy

gaily
galoshes
generation
geysers
gin
gladly
glance
glands
glassware
glee
gloomy
glorious
gnat
goblins
goddess
gorgeous
graduation
grant
grateful
gravity
graze
greedy
greet
grip
grocer
growl
guessed
guilty
gusher

hammock
handful
happening
hardware
harpoon
harsh
headquarters
healthful
heel
hesitate
hippopotamus
hire
historic
homesick
honorable
hood
horizon
hound
huckleberries
hug
hum

humorous
hump
hurrah
hurriedly
hydrogen

ignorant
illness
immigrants
imp
impolite
impression
include
increase
individual
indoor
industrious
informed
injure
inquire
inspection
instantly
instruction
insurance
interfere
international
interview
introduce
invalid
invent
irrigate
ivory

jay
joint
joyful
joyous
juicy
jury

kidnaped
kimonos
kit
kneel
knelt
kodak

lain
latch
latest
laundry
layer
lb.
leap
leapfrog
legal
lend
lever

liable
lieutenant
lighthouse
lily
limestone
limp
lining
liquor
lively
livestock
loaf
locate
locker
locomotive
lone
loop
lord
loses
loss
lover
lowlands
loyal
lump

macaroni
magnificent
malaria
manage
mane
manhole
manicure
manly
marvelous
mash
mathematics
mattress
mechanical
medal
medical
membership
mention
mercy
merrily
microscope
midway
mink
minstrel
minus
mischievous
miserable
missionary
mist
mixture
moccasins
mockingbird
mold

mole
Mon.
monitor
monks
monster
morn
mount
mummy
musician
mustard
mysterious

narcissus
navigation
nerve
newsboys
New Year's
nickname
nightgown
normal
northeast
notify
nuisance
nursery

obedient
objection
obtain
occur
occurred
offer
official
olive
operate
opportunities
oral
originally
oriole
ostrich
outfit
overboard

pad
painter
pane
panther
patent
patience
patrol
patter
paving
peddler
peddles
peel
peninsula
perch
perfectly

performance
permit
personal
pest
petrified
pheasants
phonograph
pill
pinch
pineapple
pint
pity
plateau
pleasing
plentiful
pneumonia
pod
poetry
politics
polo
poorly
porcupine
portion
positive
possibly
postage
posters
posture
practical
prairies
praise
predicate
prefer
pretend
previous
pride
priest
printer
privilege
profit
prominent
promptly
propeller
properly
proposed
prosperous
publish
punch
punish
punishment
pussy

quality
quantity
quintuplets

rabbi
radiator
railway
ram
rapid
rare
rascal
recent
recognize
reddish
reflection
refrigerator
refuse
reins
relation
release
remove
repair
reporter
represent
representative
reservation
reserve
reservoirs
reside
resort
respiration
review
revolver
rhinoceros
rhyme
ridge
rinse
risen
rob
robe
rodeo
rowboat
royal
ruin
rung
rust

sacred
salesman
salve
sandals
sandpaper
sash
satin
satisfactory
saucer
sausage
scarcely
scarlet
scary

scatter
scheme
scholar
scientist
scold
scrap
scrapbook
scrape
screw
scribbling
seaweed
secured
seize
senior
seriously
sermon
session
severe
sewage
shallow
shame
sheriff
shield
shingle
shoemaker
shortly
shotgun
shove
shrimp
sigh
signature
silkworm
sill
silverware
simply
sin
sincere
sincerity
skeleton
skill
skinny
skull
slap
slay
sleet
sleeve
slender
slice
slight
sling
slope
sly
snail
sneak
sneeze
soak

society
sock
sofa
sole
somehow
somersaults
sorrow
soul
southwestern
sow
spank
spark
species
specimen
speller
spray
springtime
sprinkle
spruce
spy
squash
squaw
squeak
squeeze
stagecoach
stairway
stall
standard
stare
starter
starve
stately
steak
steamboat
steamer
steamship
stenographer
sticky
stitch
storage
storekeeper
stout
straighten
strait
strawberry
stray
strict
struggle
supermarket

taffy
tailor
tangled
taxi
taxicab

teapot
tearing
temper
terrific
testimony
textile
theory
thermometer
thief
thorn
thorough
thoughtful
thrill
thump
tickle
timid
tiresome
tomb
ton
tone
tonsillitis
topic
torch
touchdown
tourist
tow
trace
transfer
transferred
trapeze
traveler
treasurer
triangle
trigger
tripped
trot
trough
trust
tucked
Tues.
tumble
turnip
twine
twinkle
twisted

umpire
uncomfortable
unconscious
unconstitutional
underline
underwear
unfortunate
unite

unload
unlocked
unnecessary
unpleasant
upward
urn

vaccinated
vaccination
vanilla
vanished
vanity
variety
vats
vegetation
velvet
venison
vest
vicinity
viking
violet
visible
volcanoes
volley

wages
ward
warrant
warrior
westward
wharves
wheelbarrow
whiskers
whisper
whoever
wholesome
wick
widow
width
wiener
wig
wildcat
wink
wireless
witness
wives
woody
workshop
worthy
wren

yeast
yield
yolk

INTERPRETATION OF VARIED READING PASSAGES

Skill with reading interpretation questions is an important knack for master test-takers. This chapter provides plenty of practice with the kind of reading questions you are likely to face. Although the questions cover a variety of topics, you won't have to memorize any information to select the correct answer. Clear thinking is the key to success in interpreting each passage correctly. Practice now and profit later.

Concentration, speed, retentiveness, ability to associate the ideas you read ... these are the hallmarks of the master test-taker. It doesn't matter what they give you to read, these capabilities will help you score high. That's why this chapter tests your reading in a variety of fields. It asks that you flex your mental muscles and acquire competence through flexibility.

These varied reading passages question you in several ways. Can you quickly grasp the main idea? Can you remember and associate specific details? Can you judge the truth or falsity of what you read? Can you make reasonable inferences from your reading?

If you bear in mind that a good piece of writing usually has a central thought, and that each paragraph in that piece has its own important idea, the following suggestions should help you.

1. Read the paragraph through quickly to get the general sense.

2. Reread the paragraph, concentrating on the central idea, and try to picture it as a unit.

3. Examine the various choices carefully but rapidly, *eliminating immediately* those which are far-fetched or irrelevant.

4. Be sure to consider only the facts given in the paragraph to which the choice refers!

5. Be especially careful of trick expressions or "catch-words" which sometimes destroy the validity of a seemingly true statement. These include the expressions: "under all circumstances," "at all times," "never," "always," "under no conditions," "absolutely," "completely," and "entirely."

6. In this sort of question you may correctly infer an answer from the information given, even if it's not actually stated.

In questions that test your ability to single out details and facts, answer *solely* on the basis of the information given.

In questions that test your ability to judge truth or falsity, your answer should also be based *solely* on the information given. If you must make inferences, infer cautiously, because these questions test your ability to spot precisely what *is* and what *is not* stated.

In most reading questions, a paragraph is followed by one or more statements based upon the paragraph. Each statement is in turn followed by several choices that will complete the statement. You may never have seen the paragraph before, but you must now read it carefully so that you understand it.

Then read the statements and choices. Choose the one that is most correct. Try to pick the one that is most complete, most accurate . . . the one that is best supported by and necessarily flows from the paragraph. *Be sure* that it contains nothing false so far as the paragraph itself is concerned. When you've answered all the questions, score yourself faithfully by checking with our answers that follow the last question. But please don't look at those answers until you've written your own. You just won't be helping yourself if you do that. Besides you'll have ample opportunity to do the questions again, and to check with our answers, in the event that your first try results in a low score.

TEST I. READINGS IN SOCIAL CHANGE

TIME: 20 minutes

This reading comprehension test consists of a number of different passages. One or more questions are based on each passage. The questions are composed of incomplete statements about the passage. Each incomplete statement is followed by five choices lettered (A) (B) (C) (D) (E). Mark your answer sheet with the letter of that choice which best completes the statement, and which best conveys the meaning of the passage.

Correct key answers to these sample questions are given at the conclusion of the test. Please don't peek at our key answers until you've answered all the questions on your own.

Reading Passage

Poverty in itself is seldom the cause of revolution. It is the sense of inequality in the distribution of wealth that breeds discontent. When the rich are indifferent to this inequality, and no effort is made to ease the economic burden of the poor, the sense of inequality grows into enmity.

The chief task of good administration is to secure internal peace through orderly growth. Many factors contribute to the economic growth or decay of a country: climate, natural resources, agriculture and industry to mention a few. To insure that economic growth benefits all citizens, not just a few, government must deal with and regulate those factors.

1. The title that best epitomizes this passage is

    (A) Changes in the early society of our country
    (B) The monopoly of wealth by a special class
    (C) Insuring internal peace
    (D) Enmity resulting from social burdens
    (E) Governmental regulations

2. Good administration should

    (A) distribute wealth equally
    (B) regulate those factors which affect the economy
    (C) control economic life
    (D) help the poor by promoting government economy
    (E) make the poorer citizens happy

3. Discontent is chiefly the result of

   (A) poverty
   (B) inevitable social and economic changes
   (C) increase in wealth of the country
   (D) class competition
   (E) uneven distribution of wealth

Reading Passage

I suppose that I might connect this with another myth: that since most Chinese are illiterate they are, therefore, ignorant. Actually there is surprisingly little connection between illiteracy and ignorance. I learned this in my forty years in China from many friends who, though illiterate, were wise and sophisticated. I learned it again in my own country, where I found literacy and ignorance in frequent combination. Knowing how to read does not mean that one reads or thinks. Wisdom is the essential element of civilization, and of wisdom the Chinese have much.

4. The title below that best expresses the idea of this passage is

   (A) Illiteracy, a myth   (B) Illiteracy and wisdom
   (C) Forty years in China   (D) Characteristics of the illiterate
   (E) Wisdom through reading

5. The writer considers the Chinese on the whole

   (A) ignorant but friendly   (B) literate
   (C) wise   (D) satisfied with their illiteracy
   (E) less mythical than Americans

Reading Passage

Television has just about reached in 20 years the goal toward which print has been working for 500: to extend its audience to include the entire population. In 1973 in the United States, nine out of ten families watched 45 million sets going an average of five hours a day.

6. According to the above paragraph

   (A) the entire nation has TV sets
   (B) nine out of ten individuals watch an average of five hours a day
   (C) the TV viewing public grew much more rapidly than did the reading public
   (D) there are more TV sets in the United States than in other countries
   (E) the total possible TV audience is larger than the reading public

Reading Passage

The problem in adult education seems to be not the piling up of facts but practice in thinking.

7. According to the above paragraph

   (A) educational methods for adults and young people should differ
   (B) adults do not seem to retain new facts
   (C) adults seem to think more than young people
   (D) a well-educated adult is one who thinks but does not have a store of information
   (E) adult education should stress ability to think

Reading Passage

Approximately 19,000 fatal accidents in 1972 were sustained in industry. There were approximately 130 non-fatal injuries to each fatal injury.

8. According to the above paragraph, the number of non-fatal accidents during 1972 was approximately

   (A) 146,000   (B) 190,000   (C) 1,150,000
   (D) 2,500,000   (E) 3,200,000

Reading Passage

The capacity of banks to grant loans depends, in the long run, on the amount of money deposited with them by the public. In the short run, however, it is a well known fact that banks not only can, but do lend more than is deposited with them. If such lending is carried to excess, it leads to inflation.

9. On the basis of the preceding paragraph it is most reasonable to conclude that

    (A) banks often indulge in the vicious practice of lending more than is deposited with them
    (B) in the long run, a sound banking policy operates for the mutual advantage of the bankers and the public
    (C inflation is usually the result of excess lending by the banks
    (D) the public must guard against inflation
    (E) bank lending is always in direct ratio with bank deposits

Reading Passage

Neither the revolution in manufacturing nor that in agriculture could have proceeded without those brilliant inventions in transportation and communication which have bound country to city, nation to nation, and continent to continent.

10. Judging from the contents of the preceding paragraph it can most precisely be indicated that

    (A) nations have been brought together more closely by transportation than by manufacturing and agriculture
    (B) progress in communication and transportation has been essential to progress in manufacturing and agriculture
    (C) changes in manufacturing and agriculture are characterized by a revolutionary process
    (D) industrial changes must be preceded by brilliant inventions in communication
    (E) both industry and transportation serve to bind country to city, nation to nation, and continent to continent

Reading Passage

Of the 300 cars owned in 1895, only four were manufactured in this country. Of the 100 million registered in 1973, most were manufactured in American plants.

11. The paragraph notes that cars registered in this country in 1973

   (A) were far in excess of those manufactured abroad in 1895
   (B) were manufactured in the United States
   (C) increased considerably over the preceding decade
   (D) improved greatly in construction over the 1895 model
   (E) were largely of domestic construction

Reading Passage

The labor required to produce a bushel of wheat in 1830 was three hours. Today it takes less than ten minutes. Further, it has been estimated that fifty men, employing modern farm machinery and agricultural methods, can do the work of five hundred peasants toiling under the conditions of the eighteenth century.

12. On the basis of the facts presented above, one could best conclude that

   (A) the increase of efficiency in agriculture is almost as great as that in manufacturing
   (B) peasants in the eighteenth century worked much harder than today's farmers
   (C) modern farm machinery has resulted in serious unemployment among farmers
   (D) more than 18 times as much wheat is produced today than in 1830
   (E) modern farm machinery is labor-saving

Reading Passage

The railroads, building trades, mineral industries, and automotive works normally take two-thirds of our annual production of steel. The remaining third has been around 16 million tons. For this last third of our output the farmers have been the best customers with farm machinery, tools, and wire constituting their chief demands.

13. Judging from the above facts it would be most reasonable to assume that

   (A) there is an increasing demand for the newer and more efficient farm machinery and tools
   (B) the growth of the steel industry has made possible the growth of all of our basic industries that depend upon steel
   (C) the farmers are our best steel customers
   (D) our normal annual steel output is about 48 million tons
   (E) only one-third of our steel output is exported with the remaining two-thirds consumed by our own industries

Reading Passage

Although rural crime reporting is spottier and less efficient than city and town reporting, sufficient data is collected to support the statement that rural crime rates are lower than those of urban communities.

14. According to the above paragraph

   (A) better reporting of crime occurs in rural areas than in cities
   (B) there appears to be a lower proportion of crime in rural areas than in cities
   (C) cities have more crime than towns
   (D) crime depends on the amount of reporting
   (E) no conclusions can be drawn regarding crime in rural areas because of inadequate reporting

Reading Passage

Prior to the Civil War, the steamboat was the center of life in the thriving Mississippi towns. With the war came the railroads. River traffic dwindled and the white-painted vessels rotted at the wharves. During World War I, the government decided to relieve rail congestion by reviving the long-forgotten waterways. Today, steamers, diesels, and barges ply the Mississippi.

15.   According to the above paragraph

(A)   the railroads were once the center of thriving river towns on the Mississippi River

(B)   the volume of river transportation was greater than the volume of rail transportation during World War I

(C)   growth of river transportation greatly increased the congestion on the railroads

(D)   business found river transportation more profitable than railroad transportation during World War I

(E)   since the Civil War, the volume of transportation on the Mississippi has varied

CONSOLIDATE YOUR KEY ANSWERS HERE

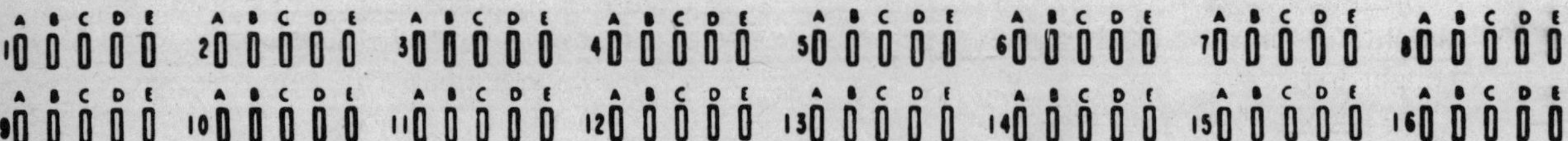

CORRECT KEY ANSWERS: READINGS IN SOCIAL CHANGE

To assist you in scoring yourself we have provided Correct Answers alongside your Answer Sheet. May we therefore suggest that while you are doing the test you cover the Correct Answers with a sheet of white paper.....to avoid temptation and to arrive at an accurate estimate of your ability and progress.

1.C	4.B	7.E	10.B	13.D
2.B	5.C	8.D	11.E	14.B
3.E	6.C	9.C	12.E	15.E

TEST II. SCIENCE READINGS

TIME: 25 minutes

This reading comprehension test consists of a number of different passages. One or more questions are based on each passage. The questions are composed of incomplete statements about the passage. Each incomplete statement is followed by five choices lettered (A) (B) (C) (D) (E). Mark your answer sheet with the letter of that choice which best completes the statement, and which best conveys the meaning of the passage.

Correct key answers to these sample questions are given at the conclusion of the test. Please don't peek at our key answers until you've answered all the questions on your own.

Reading Passage

Influenza travels exactly as fast as man. In oxcart days its progress was slow. In 1918 man could girdle the globe in eight weeks, and that is exactly the time it took influenza to complete its encirclement of the earth. Today, by jets and air transport, man moves at higher speed. This modern speed makes influenza's advent unpredictable from day to day. It all means that our control over this disease must be commensurately swift.

1. The title below that best expresses the idea of this paragraph is

   (A) Influenza around the world
   (B) The world epidemic of influenza in 1918
   (C) How jets spread influenza
   (D) Unpredictability of influenza
   (E) The effect of speed upon the spread of influenza

2. The author states that more adequate control of influenza is necessary nowadays because

   (A) it may occur during any season
   (B) it may occur anywhere on earth
   (C) the germs can travel as fast as an airplane
   (D) man can not travel fast enough to escape it
   (E) man carries it about more quickly

Reading Passage

The coastal area of North Africa is a land of great contrast. The climate is almost as pleasant as Southern California's. In the lowlands, summers are hot and dry, the winters, temperate but rainy. Temperatures in the coastland's higher altitudes fall below freezing on winter nights. The forested mountains of Morocco and Algeria have a heavy winter snowfall, and excellent skiing grounds. South of the mountains and plateaus is the true desert. However, it is not a continuous sea of flat, barren land. Vast stretches of picturesque dunes are followed by miles of gravel studded with outcroppings of rim rock. One can travel for days and see scarcely any sand. On the desert, rains fall rarely but so heavily that bivouac commanders should be especially careful not to make camp in a ravine. Winter nights on the desert are bitterly cold.

3. The title that best epitomizes this passage is

    (A) The coastal area of North Africa
    (B) The deserts of North Africa
    (C) Contrasts in the climate and topography of North Africa
    (D) The weather in Algeria
    (E) Difficulties of travel in North Africa

4. Travelers in the North African desert should not camp in ravines because of the danger of

    (A) rock slides   (B) sand storms   (C) floods
    (D) extreme cold   (E) attacks from Arabs

5. The climate of North Africa

    (A) is fine for tourists
    (B) is similar to that of California
    (C) varies in different sections
    (D) causes many difficulties for soldiers
    (E) is unpleasant

Reading Passage

If you watch a lamp which is turned on and off very rapidly, and keep your eyes open, "persistence of vision" will bridge the gaps of darkness between the flashes of light. The lamp will seem to be continuously lit. This "optical afterglow" explains the magic of the stroboscope, an instrument which seems to freeze the swiftest motions while they are still going on, and to stop time dead in its tracks. The "magic" is all in the eye of the beholder.

6. The "magic" of the stroboscope is due to

   (A) continuous lighting   (B) intense cold
   (C) slow motion   (D) behavior of the human eye
   (E) a lapse of time

7. "Persistence of vision" is explained by

   (A) darkness   (B) winking   (C) rapid flashes
   (D) gaps   (E) afterimpression

Reading Passage

The toplofty United States elm is yet another victim of World War II. Today, thousands of these trees are marked for death by the activities of the tiny European elm bark beetle. The beetles, however, do not do the fatal damage. Death is caused by another importation, Dutch elm disease, a fungus infection which the beetles carry from tree to tree. Prior to the War, quarantine and tree sanitation measures confined the disease within a 150-mile radius of New York City. War curtailed these measures, and allowed the spread of Dutch elm disease. Now, every household and village that prizes an elm-shaded lawn or commons must watch for it. Since there is as yet no cure, infected trees must be pruned or felled, and the wood burned to protect the healthy trees.

8. The title below that best summarizes this paragraph is

   (A) A menace to our elms   (B) Pests and diseases of the elm
   (C) Our vanishing elms   (D) The need to protect Dutch elms
   (D) How elms are protected

9. The danger of spreading the Dutch elm disease was increased by

   (A) destroying infected trees   (B) World War II
   (C) the lack of a cure   (D) a fungus infection
   (E) quarantine measures

10. The European elm bark beetle is a serious threat to our elms because it

    (A) chews the bark
    (B) kills the trees
    (C) is particularly active near New York City
    (D) carries infection
    (E) cannot be controlled

Reading Passage

As the market for hay declined, farmers looked west and saw the farmers of the flat lands growing rich raising corn and hogs. Without knowlege of scientific farming they decided, "If they can do it, we can." So they plowed the grass, meadowlands, and even the pastures of that rolling hilly country and planted corn. They planted the corn in rows, running more often than not up and down slopes and hills. Every time it rained, each furrow between the standing corn became a miniature gully carrying off not only the precious rainfall, but the topsoil and fertilizer as well.

11. The title that best epitomizes this passage is

    (A) Waste of the soil
    (B) Rotating crops
    (C) Rainfall and the corn crop
    (D) Why farmers become discouraged
    (E) The reward of courage

12. The author implies that corn was a less satisfactory crop in the more easterly section because the land in this section was less

    (A) fertile   (B) moist   (C) flat
    (D) thoroughly fertilized   (E) arid

13. The farmers were unwise in

    (A) not using flat land
    (B) not raising hogs
    (C) not plowing furrows across the slope
    (D) not using more fertilizer
    (E) filling the gullies

Reading Passage

Even when sheep are raised as a principal business rather than a farm by-product, it is extremely difficult to produce wool of uniform quality. On a single sheep there are at least four grades. In one season, no two sheep in a flock yield exactly the same grade of wool. In addition, since quality is affected by the food the sheep eat, by the soil over which they graze, and by the weather, no two flocks in one year produce the same grade of wool. And the same flock will change from year to year.

14. On the basis of the preceding paragraph one could most reasonably conclude that

    (A) soil is a factor in the quality of wool
    (B) sheep raising is usually a by-product of the meat-producing industries
    (C) sheep in one season usually yield exactly the same grade of wool
    (D) there is a consistent change in the seasonal quality of wool
    (E) flocks of sheep will change from year to year

CONSOLIDATE YOUR KEY ANSWERS HERE

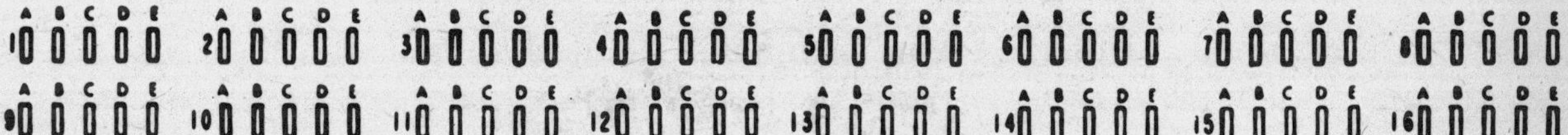

CORRECT KEY ANSWERS: SCIENCE READINGS

To assist you in scoring yourself we have provided Correct Answers alongside your Answer Sheet. May we therefore suggest that while you are doing the test you cover the Correct Answers with a sheet of white paper.....to avoid temptation and to arrive at an accurate estimate of your ability and progress.

1.E	3.C	5.C	7.E	9.B	11.A	13.C
2.E	4.C	6.D	8.A	10.D	12.C	14.A

TEST III. PHILOSOPHICAL AND HUMOROUS READINGS

TIME: 25 Minutes

This reading comprehension test consists of a number of different passages. One or more questions are based on each passage. The questions are composed of incomplete statements about the passage. Each incomplete statement is followed by five choices lettered (A) (B) (C) (D) (E). Mark your answer sheet with the letter of that choice which best completes the statement, and which best conveys the meaning of the passage.

Correct key answers to these sample questions are given at the conclusion of the test. Please don't peek at our key answers until you've answered all the questions on your own.

Reading Passage

For centuries we have enjoyed certain blessings: a stable law, before which the poor man and the rich man were equal; freedom within that law to believe what we pleased; a system of government which gave the ultimate power to the ordinary man. We have lived by toleration, rational compromise and freely expressed opinion, and we have lived very well. But we have come to take these blessings for granted, like the air we breathe. They have lost all glamour for us since they have become too familiar. Indeed, it is a mark of the intellectual to be rather critical and contemptuous of them. Young men have acquired a reputation by sneering at the liberal spirit in politics, and questioning the value of free discussion, toleration, and compromise.

1. The title below that best expresses the idea of this paragraph is
   (A) The value of free discussion
   (B) Respect for law
   (C) The weakness of the democratic way of life
   (D) Characteristics of democracy
   (E) Unappreciated advantages of democratic life

2. The writer resents the growing criticism of freedom—an attitude which results from

   (A) questioning the rightness of democracy
   (B) being too accustomed to freedom
   (C) too much freedom of speech
   (D) living in poverty too long
   (E) the conservatism of young intellectuals

3. The writer's attitude toward young intellectuals is

(A) indifferent (B) critical
(C) very contemptuous (D) generous
(E) angry

Reading Passage

The pessimist was good enough to·explain. He had been reading about sulfa drugs and penicillin and plasma and other miracle cures and techniques. He had been reading about the marvels of the plastic surgeon who rebuilds broken men. Then he could not help thinking that it was not all gain. Men have gone on building better machines for the protection and enhancement of life, better mousetraps to conquer typhus, better mosquito netting to conquer malaria and yellow fever, better houses and better diets to conquer the wasting diseases. But all this time nature counterattacks with bigger wars and bigger human feuds and hates. The pessimist said it was hardly necessary to mention the airplane. Whether it was a machine to build One World still remained to be seen. That the airplane did its share to make bigger and better World Wars has been demonstrated.

4. The title below that best expresses the idea of this paragraph is

(A) Improvements in civilization (B) The world of the future
(C) Technological advance (D) World Wars of tomorrow
(E) The problem of progress

5. In this article the attitude of the pessimist toward the future use of the airplane is one of

(A) questioning (B) condemnation (C) defense
(D) deploring (E) praise

6. The person mentioned in the paragraph is referred to as a pessimist because he

(A) doubts the value of medicine
(B) denies that the world can be united
(C) believes that technical progress is too slow
(D) fears that human nature will misuse new discoveries
(E) questions our ability to continue to advance technically

Reading Passage

Spring is one of those things that man has no hand in, any more than he has a part in sunrise or the phases of the moon. Spring came before man was here to enjoy it, and it will go right on coming even if man isn't here some time in the future. It is a matter of solar mechanics and celestial order. And for all our knowledge of astronomy and terrestrial mechanics, we haven't yet been able to do more than bounce a radar beam off the moon. We couldn't alter the arrival of the spring equinox by as much as one second, if we tried.

Spring is a matter of growth, of chlorophyll, of bud and blossom. We can alter growth and change the time of blossoming in individual plants; but the forests still grow in nature's way, and the grass of the plains hasn't altered its nature in a thousand years. Spring is a magnificent phase of the cycle of nature; but man really hasn't any guiding or controlling hand in it. He is here to enjoy it and benefit by it. And April is a good time to realize it; by May perhaps we will want to take full credit.

7. The title below that best expresses the idea of this passage is

   (A) The marvels of the spring equinox
   (B) Nature's dependence on mankind
   (C) The weakness of man opposed to nature
   (D) The glories of the world
   (E) Eternal growth

8. The author of the passage states that

   (A) man has a part in phases of the moon
   (B) April is a time for taking full credit
   (C) April is a good time to enjoy nature
   (D) man has a guiding hand in spring
   (E) spring will cease to be if civilization ends

Reading Passage

Character is a respect for human beings and their right to interpret experience differently. Character admits self-interest as a natural trait, but pins its faith on man's hesitant but heartening instinct to cooperate. Character is allergic to tyranny, irritable with ignorance and always open to improvement. Character implies the ability to laugh wholeheartedly and weep unashamedly. Character is, above all, a tremendous humility before the facts—an automatic alliance with truth even when that truth is a bitter medicine.

9. The title below that best conveys the idea of this paragraph is

  (A) The bitter medicine of truth
  (B) Respect for character
  (C) Character and experience
  (D) A definition of character
  (E) Character as a type of self-interest

10. A quality of character *not* mentioned by the author is

  (A) sympathy (B) humbleness (C) humor
  (D) patience (E) truthfulness

11. The author indicates that the man of character

  (A) expects people to be entirely unselfish
  (B) recognizes selfishness as the dominating trait of all mankind
  (C) realizes that people are naturally interested in themselves
  (D) admits that tyranny and ignorance are worse than selfishness
  (E) needs to recognize honesty when he sees it

Reading Passage

Why people choose varying ways to solve their problems is not known. Yet what an individual does when he is thwarted remains a reasonably good key to understanding his personality. If his responses to thwartings are emotional explosions and irrational excuses, he is tending to live in an unreal world. He may need help to regain the world of reality, the cause-and-effect world recognized by generations of thinkers and scientists. Perhaps he needs encouragement to redouble his efforts. Perhaps, on the other hand, he is striving for the impossible and needs to substitute a worth-while activity within the range of his abilities. It is wise to learn the nature of the world and of oneself in relation to it, and to meet each situation as intelligently and as adequately as one can.

12. The title below that best expresses the idea of this paragraph is

  (A) Adjusting to life (B) Escape from reality
  (C) Understanding personality (D) Emotional control
  (E) The nature of the world

13.　The writer argues that all should

    (A)　substitute new activities for old
    (B)　analyze their relation to the world
    (C)　seek encouragement from others
    (D)　redouble their efforts
    (E)　avoid thwartings

Reading Passage

It is elemental that the greater the development of man, the greater the problems he has to concern him. When he lived in a cave with stone implements, his mind no less than his actions was grooved into simple channels. Every new invention, every new way of doing things, posed fresh problems for him. And, as he moved along the road, he questioned each step, as indeed he should, for he trod upon the beliefs of his ancestors. It is equally elemental to say that each step upon this later road posed more questions than the earlier ones. It is only the educated man who realizes the results of his actions; it is only the thoughtful one who questions his own decisions.

14.　The title below that best conveys the idea of this paragraph is

    (A)　Channels of civilization
    (B)　The mark of a thoughtful man
    (C)　The cave man in contrast with man today
    (D)　The price of early progress
    (E)　Man's never-ending challenge

Reading Passage

Humanity is by no means so materialistic as foolish talk asserts it to be. Judging by what I have learned about men and women, I am convinced that there is far more idealism in them than ever comes to the surface of the world. Just as the water of streams is scant compared with that which flows underground, so the idealism which becomes visible is scant compared to that which men and women bear in their hearts, unreleased or scarcely released. To unbind what is bound, to bring the underground waters to the surface—mankind is waiting for men who can do that.

15. The title that best epitomizes this passage is

    (A) Releasing underground waters
    (B) The good and bad in man
    (C) Materialism in humanity
    (D) The surface and the depths of idealism
    (E) Unreleased energy

16. Human beings are more idealistic than

    (A) the water in underground streams
    (B) their waiting and longing proves
    (C) outward evidence shows
    (D) the world
    (E) other living creatures

Reading Passage

It is said that I am chasing after my youth. This is true. And not only after my own. Even more than beauty, youth attracts me with an irresistible appeal. I believe the truth lies in youth; I believe it is always right against us. I believe that, far from trying to teach it, it is in youth that we, the elders, must seek out lessons. I am well aware that youth is capable of errors; I know that our role is to forewarn youth as best we can; but I believe that often, in trying to protect youth, we impede it. I believe that each new generation arrives bearing a message that it must deliver; our role is to help that delivery. I believe that what is called experience is often but an avowed fatigue, resignation, blighted hope.

17. The title below that best expresses the idea of this passage is

    (A) The lessons youth offers   (B) The needs of youth
    (C) The nature of experience   (D) Advice to youth
    (E) A new generation

18. The writer's attitude toward the progress of each new generation is

    (A) skeptical   (B) questioning   (C) bitter
    (D) optimistic   (E) indifferent

Reading Passage

I consider that a man's brain originally is like a little empty attic, and you have to stock it with such furniture as you choose. A fool takes in all the lumber of every sort that he comes across. Then the knowledge which might be useful to him gets crowded out, or is jumbled up with a lot of other things, so that he has difficulty laying his hands upon it. It is a mistake to think that that little room has elastic walls and can distend to any size. Depend upon it, there comes a time when for every addition of knowledge, you forget something that you knew before.

19. According to the preceding paragraph, knowledge

   (A) should be sought for its own sake
   (B) is always valuable
   (C) should be avoided
   (D) should be acquired only if it is necessary
   (E) may be acquired without limitation

CONSOLIDATE YOUR KEY ANSWERS HERE

CORRECT KEY ANSWERS: PHILOSOPHICAL & HUMOROUS READINGS

To assist you in scoring yourself we have provided Correct Answers alongside your Answer Sheet. May we therefore suggest that while you are doing the test you cover the Correct Answers with a sheet of white paper.....to avoid temptation and to arrive at an accurate estimate of your ability and progress.

1.E	4.E	7.C	10.D	13.B	16.C	19.D
2.B	5.A	8.C	11.C	14.E	17.A	
3.B	6.D	9.D	12.A	15.D	18.D	

PART FOUR

Mathematics Review
and
Final Advice

4

APPROXIMATE CONVERSION FACTORS FOR CHANGING FROM CUSTOMARY UNITS TO METRIC UNITS.

Symbol	When You Know	Multiply by	To Find	Symbol
LENGTH				
in	inches	2.54	centimeters	cm
ft	feet	30	centimeters	cm
yd	yards	0.9	meters	m
mi	miles	1.6	kilometers	km
AREA				
in^2	square inches	6.5	square centimeters	cm^2
ft^2	square feet	0.09	square meters	m^2
yd^2	square yards	0.8	square meters	m^2
mi^2	square miles	2.6	square kilometers	km^2
	acres	0.4	hectares	ha
MASS (weight)				
oz	ounces	28	grams	g
lb	pounds	0.45	kilograms	kg
	short tons (2000 lb)	0.9	tonnes	t
VOLUME				
tsp	teaspoons	5	milliliters	ml
Tbsp	tablespoons	15	milliliters	ml
fl oz	fluid ounces	30	milliliters	ml
c	cups	0.24	liters	l
pt	pints	0.47	liters	l
qt	quarts	0.95	liters	l
gal	gallons	3.8	liters	l
ft^3	cubic feet	0.03	cubic meters	m^3
yd^3	cubic yards	0.76	cubic meters	m^3
TEMPERATURE (exact)				
°F	Fahrenheit temperature	5/9 (after subtracting 32)	Celsius temperature	°C

°F 32   98.6   °F 212
-40   0   40   80   120   160   200
-40   -20   0   20   40   60   80   100
°C   37   °C

SPEEDING UP YOUR BASIC MATH

BY FREDERICK L. MACOMBER

Designed as a short self-teaching course in basic mathematics, this chapter will improve your proficiency in multiplication, addition, subtraction, and division. Short cuts and improved work habits which bypass long and tedious traditional problem-solving methods are taught through explanations, examples, and drills.

Short cuts to bypass traditional problem-solving methods in Addition • Subtraction   Multiplication • Division

Speed can be gained in doing basic addition, subtraction, multiplication, and division by using various means.

Any method chosen may increase your speed in doing problems. But you can gain greater speed by doing the following things:

1. Increase your speed in recall of the multiplication table through 9.
2. Improve upon your ability to remember a number that has been read.
3. Improve your work habits.
4. Gain a better understanding of problem solving.

5. Learn when it might be advantageous to work from left to right in solving problems.
6. Improve upon the method used in working with zeros.

Requirements

1. A working knowledge of basic math.
2. Some experience in problem solving.
3. Passing a test on the multiplication table.

Answers

All answers to Problems and Tests are given.

MULTIPLICATION TABLE

Knowing the multiplication table is very important for an understanding of basic mathematics. It is always used in solving multiplication and division problems, and it can also be used in some addition and subtraction problems.

Study the multiplication table until you can get 100 percent accuracy in a maximum of three minutes. Then take the Introductory Multiplication Test that follows the table.

$0 \times$ any number $= 0$

$1 \quad \times 1 = 1 \quad \times 2 = 2 \quad \times 3 = 3 \quad \times 4 = 4$
$\quad \times 5 = 5 \quad \times 6 = 6 \quad \times 7 = 7 \quad \times 8 = 8 \quad \times 9 = 9$

$2 \quad \times 2 = 4 \quad \times 3 = 6 \quad \times 4 = 8 \quad \times 5 = 10$
$\quad \times 6 = 12 \quad \times 7 = 14 \quad \times 8 = 16 \quad \times 9 = 18$

$3 \quad \times 3 = 9 \quad \times 4 = 12 \quad \times 5 = 15 \quad \times 6 = 18$
$\quad \times 7 = 21 \quad \times 8 = 24 \quad \times 9 = 27$

$4 \quad \times 4 = 16 \quad \times 5 = 20 \quad \times 6 = 24 \quad \times 7 = 28$
$\quad \times 8 = 32 \quad \times 9 = 36$

$5 \quad \times 5 = 25 \quad \times 6 = 30 \quad \times 7 = 35 \quad \times 8 = 40$
$\quad \times 9 = 45$

$6 \quad \times 6 = 36 \quad \times 7 = 42 \quad \times 8 = 48 \quad \times 9 = 54$

$7 \quad \times 7 = 49 \quad \times 8 = 56 \quad \times 9 = 63$

$8 \quad \times 8 = 64 \quad \times 9 = 72$

$9 \quad \times 9 = 81$

Notice that the table becomes smaller as the base number increases. It does not matter which way a problem is stated, it is still the same problem. That is, $\underline{2 \times 9}$ is the same as $\underline{9 \times 2}$.

Multiplication Exercise One

Introductory Multiplication Table

Write down only the problem number and the answer. Do not copy the problem. The test should be completed in three minutes or less.

1) $1 \times 1 =$	26) $9 \times 2 =$
2) $2 \times 4 =$	27) $6 \times 1 =$
3) $6 \times 0 =$	28) $8 \times 9 =$
4) $7 \times 8 =$	29) $7 \times 7 =$
5) $8 \times 5 =$	30) $3 \times 4 =$
6) $9 \times 4 =$	31) $1 \times 9 =$
7) $0 \times 3 =$	32) $2 \times 6 =$
8) $7 \times 1 =$	33) $4 \times 5 =$
9) $6 \times 3 =$	34) $5 \times 6 =$
10) $4 \times 8 =$	35) $3 \times 5 =$
11) $4 \times 7 =$	36) $4 \times 0 =$
12) $6 \times 4 =$	37) $2 \times 2 =$
13) $8 \times 6 =$	38) $6 \times 6 =$
14) $7 \times 5 =$	39) $4 \times 4 =$
15) $8 \times 2 =$	40) $3 \times 3 =$
16) $9 \times 3 =$	41) $4 \times 1 =$
17) $6 \times 7 =$	42) $7 \times 2 =$
18) $9 \times 9 =$	43) $9 \times 5 =$
19) $8 \times 8 =$	44) $2 \times 1 =$
20) $6 \times 9 =$	45) $3 \times 2 =$
21) $5 \times 1 =$	46) $8 \times 1 =$
22) $3 \times 8 =$	47) $5 \times 2 =$
23) $7 \times 9 =$	48) $7 \times 0 =$
24) $5 \times 5 =$	49) $3 \times 1 =$
25) $7 \times 3 =$	50) $6 \times 8 =$

Correct Answers For The Foregoing Questions

1) 1	7) 0	13) 48	18) 81	23) 63	29) 49	34) 30	39) 16	45) 6
2) 8	8) 7	14) 35	19) 64	24) 25	30) 12	35) 15	40) 9	46) 8
3) 0	9) 18	15) 16	20) 54	25) 21	31) 9	36) 0	41) 4	47) 10
4) 56	10) 32	16) 27	21) 5	26) 18	32) 12	37) 4	42) 14	48) 0
5) 40	11) 28	17) 42	22) 24	27) 6	33) 20	38) 36	43) 45	49) 3
6) 36	12) 24			28) 72			44) 2	50) 48

Multiplication Exercises

Work with the following problems to build
up your accuracy and speed.

A. This set of problems should be completed in
one and one half minutes. Write down only the
problem number and the answer. Do not copy the
problem.

1) $1\times1=$		14) $7\times5=$
2) $2\times4=$		15) $8\times2=$
3) $6\times0=$		16) $9\times3=$
4) $7\times8=$		17) $6\times7=$
5) $8\times5=$		18) $9\times9=$
6) $9\times4=$		19) $8\times8=$
7) $0\times3=$		20) $6\times9=$
8) $7\times1=$		21) $5\times1=$
9) $6\times3=$		22) $3\times8=$
10) $4\times8=$		23) $7\times9=$
11) $4\times7=$		24) $5\times5=$
12) $6\times4=$		25) $7\times3=$
13) $8\times6=$		

B. This set of problems should be completed in
one and one half minutes. Write down the problem
number and answer; do not copy the problem.

1) $9\times2=$		14) $4\times4=$
2) $6\times1=$		15) $3\times3=$
3) $8\times9=$		16) $4\times1=$
4) $7\times7=$		17) $7\times2=$
5) $3\times4=$		18) $9\times5=$
6) $1\times9=$		19) $2\times1=$
7) $2\times6=$		20) $3\times2=$
8) $4\times5=$		21) $8\times1=$
9) $5\times6=$		22) $5\times2=$
10) $3\times5=$		23) $7\times0=$
11) $4\times0=$		24) $3\times1=$
12) $2\times2=$		25) $6\times8=$
13) $6\times6=$		

C. This set of problems will not be timed. It is to
be used for practice only. You need write down
only the number of the problem and the answer,
but you may copy down the problem if necessary.

1) $9873\div9=$		5) $6275\div5=$
2) $6376\div8=$		6) $8396\div4=$
3) $5691\div7=$		7) $2367\div3=$
4) $4524\div6=$		8) $1374\div2=$

D. This set of problems is for practice. Write
down only the problem number and the answer.

1) $1\times8=$		14) $3248\div4=$
2) $7\times6=$		15) $3642\div6=$
3) $8\times9=$		16) $3545\div5=$
4) $7\times8=$		17) $2846\div2=$
5) $6\times9=$		18) $6390\div3=$
6) $8\times6=$		19) $4\times8=$
7) $9\times7=$		20) $7\times5=$
8) $7\times7=$		21) $6\times4=$
9) $8\times8=$		22) $4\times9=$
10) $9\times9=$		23) $5\times8=$
11) $8172\div9=$		24) $7\times4=$
12) $4984\div7=$		25) $6\times6=$
13) $6416\div8=$		

Correct Answers For The Foregoing Questions

*(Please make every effort to answer the questions on your own before look-
ing at these answers. You'll make faster progress by following this rule.)*

Problems A

1)	1	14)	35
2)	8	15)	16
3)	0	16)	27
4)	56	17)	42
5)	40	18)	81
6)	36	19)	64
7)	0	20)	54
8)	7	21)	5
9)	18	22)	24
10)	32	23)	63
11)	28	24)	25
12)	24	25)	21
13)	48		

Problems B

1)	18	14)	16
2)	6	15)	9
3)	72	16)	4
4)	49	17)	14
5)	12	18)	45
6)	9	19)	2
7)	12	20)	6
8)	20	21)	8
9)	30	22)	10
10)	15	23)	0
11)	0	24)	3
12)	4	25)	48
13)	36		

Problems C

1)	1097	5)	1255
2)	797	6)	2099
3)	813	7)	789
4)	754	8)	687

Problems D

1)	8	14)	812
2)	42	15)	607
3)	72	16)	709
4)	56	17)	1423
5)	54	18)	2130
6)	48	19)	32
7)	63	20)	35
8)	49	21)	24
9)	64	22)	36
10)	81	23)	40
11)	908	24)	28
12)	712	25)	36
13)	802		

REMEMBERING NUMBERS

To increase your speed in most activities that require sight, you must build up speed in reading.

Numbers appear to be the same as letters: that is, they have meaning when they stand alone or when they are arranged in groups.

The difference between reading numbers and reading letters is that a letter can be read and pronounced in only one way, while the same number may be read in several ways.

For example: the group of numbers <u>4634427</u> may be expressed as

    a telephone number   463-4427
    a whole number   4,634,427
    dollars and cents $46,344.27

In solving a problem, is it necessary to know where a decimal point, a comma, or any other sign of division falls in a given group of numbers? The answer is, No. The only time it is important to know where the decimal point or the comma should go is when the answer is given. This rule always applies in multiplication and division operations. In addition and subtraction, however, the last digit must be expressed as a value to the same denominator in every group of numbers in the series.

That is, $17+7$ or $17-7$ is not the same thing as $17+.7$ or $17-.7$

When beginning an operation in addition or subtraction, scan the numbers first. After you have determined that all the final digits are values of the same denominator, read the numbers.

Another rule to remember: when you are reading a number, do not vocalize it. Read with the eyes, not with the lips and throat. For example: read the following number: <u>2339</u>. Now place your fingers on your throat, over the vocal cords, and read the number again. Was there any vibration? If so, then practice reading numbers until there is no vibration felt.

With practice, numbers will become mental pictures.

Memory Practice

A. Read each of the following numbers. After reading each number, look away from the page and repeat the number several times.

1)	23	14)	76
2)	326	15)	481
3)	3,241	16)	5,743
4)	51,873	17)	62,787
5)	467,567	18)	381,628
6)	5,761,842	19)	9,976,884
7)	47	20)	81
8)	638	21)	239
9)	7,893	22)	8,465
10)	37,222	23)	72,637
11)	734,898	24)	536,040
12)	8,235,625	25)	6,867,768
13)	1		

Repeat the above exercise, looking at each number for a shorter length of time before repeating it.

Try to remember the following numbers in sections. That is, section <u>735,825</u> as <u>(735)(825)</u>.

B. Read each of the following numbers. After reading each number, look away from the page and repeat the number several times.

1)	14	14)	5,423
2)	25	15)	8,238
3)	33	16)	73,481
4)	46	17)	38,842
5)	57	18)	97,653
6)	627	19)	65,121
7)	841	20)	42,836
8)	763	21)	875,435
9)	928	22)	257,929
10)	359	23)	471,183
11)	1,735	24)	555,525
12)	4,658	25)	787,686
13)	2,731		

IMPROVEMENT OF WORK HABITS

As we have stated in the preceding chapter, to increase your speed in activities that require sight, you must gain speed in reading. However, there is no advantage to be gained from building speed in reading if your comprehension of what you read is limited.

Before solving any mathematical problem, you must determine:

    1. The relationships expressed by the given numbers.

    2. What is required.

For example: John went to the market and bought 2 dozen eggs, 3 loaves of bread, and 1 pound of bacon. If eggs cost $.60 a dozen, bread $.29 a loaf, and bacon $.79 a pound, what is the amount John had to pay for this order?

1. The relationships are "number of units" and "cost per unit."

2. What is required is "total cost of order."

When reading a problem, do not concentrate on unnecessary information. That is, in the above problem, only the following information is necessary:

2 dozen eggs, 3 loaves bread, 1 pound bacon. Eggs: $.60 a dozen; bread: $.29 a loaf; bacon: $.79 a pound.

Exercises and Problems

In the following problems, determine: a) the relationships expressed by the numbers, b) what is required, and c) the necessary information. (Do not do the computation.)

1) John has 3 dozen oranges and he wants to divide them evenly among 6 people. How many oranges should each person get?

2) Gary went to the store and bought a harmonica for $1.95 and an instruction book for $.35. He gave the clerk $2.50. How much change did Gary get?

3) Jeff had $5.00. He saw a boat for $2.98, a car for $1, and a caboose for $1.25. Did Jeff have enough money to buy these three items?

4) Jean bought 4 pillow cases that cost $1.98 apiece, 2 fitted bottom sheets that cost $3.29 apiece, and 2 fitted top sheets that cost $3.09 apiece. What was her total bill?

5) Don and Frank started from the same point and drove in opposite directions. Don's rate of speed was 50 miles per hour. Frank's rate of speed as 40 miles per hour. How many miles apart were they at the end of 2 hours?

6) The local music shop had a record sale. The records normally cost $3.98 each. The sale price was $7.50 for 2 records. Pete bought 4 records at the sale price. How much money did Pete save by buying the records at the sale price?

7) Karen went to a department store and ordered curtains for 5 windows. One pair of curtains cost $14.28, 2 pairs cost $33.26 apiece, and the remaining 2 pairs cost $65.38 apiece. Would the total cost for the 5 pairs of curtains be under $200?

8) A pilot is going to fly a distance of 600 miles. The speed of his airplane is 150 miles an hour. How many hours will it take him to reach his destination?

9) How many square feet of carpeting will be needed to cover a floor that is 12 feet by 15 feet?

10) If John has $25, and a buffet luncheon costs $2.50 per person, how many people, including himself, can he take to this luncheon?

The following rules are to be followed when solving problems:

1. When working out a problem, do not write down anything that is not needed. If only the answer is required, and the basic data can easily be referred to, write down only the answer

That is, do not write down $25 \times 2 = 50$. Refer to $\underline{25 \times 2,}$ but write down only $\underline{50}$.

2. If the problem is too complex for you to be able to visualize the entire process, then write down, on a piece of scrap paper, only the information necessary for you to obtain the answer.

Problem: 2339
            $\times 45$

Refer to: 2339
            $\times 45$

Write on scrap paper:
11695
 9356

Write on answer paper: 105,255

Explanatory Solutions

1) a) Total number of items and number of ways items are to be divided.
   b) Number of items each way.
   c) Three dozen items are divided evenly among 6 people. How many items go to each person?

2) a) Quantity and cost per item. Amount given to pay for them.
   b) Difference.
   c) One item cost $1.95; one cost $.35. Gave $2.50. How much change?

3) a) Quantity and cost per item. Amount available.
   b) Comparison of total cost with amount available.
   c) He had $5.00. One item cost $2.98, one cost $1.00, and one cost $1.25. Did he have enough to buy the items?

4) a) Quantity and cost per item.
   b) Total cost.
   c) Four items cost $1.98 apiece, 2 cost $3.29 apiece, and 2 cost $3.09 apiece. What was the total bill?

5) a) Direction, rate of speed, and length of time traveled.
   b) How many miles apart at the end of the time?
   c) They started at the same point and moved in opposite directions. One moved at 50 miles per hour; one moved at 40 miles per hour. In 2 hours, how many miles apart were they?

6) a) Quantity and cost per item.
   b) Difference.
   c) Items normally costing $3.98 each were on sale at $7.50 for 2. Four were bought at this price. How much was saved?

7) a) Quantity and cost per item.
   b) Comparison of total cost to amount available.
   c) One item cost $14.28, 2 items cost $33.26 apiece, and 2 cost $65.38 apiece. Would the total cost be less than $200?

8) a) Distance covered and speed in miles per hour.
   b) Time required to cover distance.
   c) A distance of 600 miles was covered at a speed of 150 miles per hour. How many hours were needed to cover the distance?

9) a) Measurement of each side of area.
   b) Total square feet in area.
   c) How many square feet are there in an area 12 feet by 15 feet?

10) a) Amount available and cost per unit.
    b) Maximum number of units.
    c) He had $25. Luncheon cost $2.50 per person. For how many luncheons, including his own, could he pay?

Exercises In Improving Work Habits

A. Work out the following problems on a sheet of paper with a line down the center. Use the left side of the sheet for any necessary computations; use the right side for answers. In these problems, only the answers are required.

1) 2975×36

2) 45×2

3) $3\overline{)723}$

4) $285 - 193$

5) $279 + 172$

6) $376 - 107$

7) $50\overline{)78340}$

8) $4372 + 6629$

9) 327×113

10) $6489 + 1498$

11) $25\overline{)875}$

12) $189 + 981$

5) 564×231

6) 312×213

7) $4\overline{)2468}$

8) $3\overline{)2136}$

9) $6\overline{)726}$

10) $5\overline{)2605}$

11) $7849 - 6735$

12) $2375 - 1253$

13) $4638 - 3135$

14) $5687 - 2244$

15) $6234 - 3023$

16) $4791 + 3208$

17) $5369 + 4630$

18) $6470 + 3428$

19) $3443 + 2244$

20) $3210 + 3023$

B. Work out the following problems in the same manner as in *A* above.

1) 789×654

2) 987×321

3) 879×789

4) 645×546

In summary, the following rules are to be remembered when solving problems:

1. Determine the relationships expressed by the given numbers; determine what is required in the problem.

2. When reading a problem, concentrate on only the necessary information.

3. In solving a problem, refer to as much of the information as possible, writing down only what is needed.

Correct Answers For The Foregoing Questions

*(Please make every effort to answer the questions on your own before look-
ing at these answers. You'll make faster progress by following this rule.)*

A.
1) 107100
2) 90
3) 241
4) 92
5) 451
6) 269
7) 1566.8
8) 11001
9) 36951
10) 7987
11) 35
12) 1170

B.
1) 516006
2) 316827
3) 693531
4) 352170
5) 130284
6) 66456
7) 617
8) 712
9) 121
10) 521
11) 1114
12) 1122
13) 1503
14) 3443
15) 3211
16) 7999
17) 9999
18) 9898
19) 5687
20) 6233

Practice In Improving Work Habits

A. Answer a), b), and c) for each of the following questions.
   a) What relationships do the numbers express?
   b) What is required?
   c) What is the necessary information?

1) Gary bought a radio for $18.95. He gave the
clerk $20.00. How much change did Gary get?

2) John bought 20 records for $66.00 What was
the cost of each record?

3) Jeff had $5.00. He wanted to buy a bicycle
horn for $2.95 and a saddle bag for $2.50.
Could Jeff buy both items with the money he
had?

4) Jean bought a new dress for $17.95, a purse
for $10.95, and a hat for $7.95. What is the
total amount she had to pay for these items?

5) Patty bought 3 dozen oranges. The oranges
cost $.33 a dozen. What was the total cost of
the oranges?

B. Solve the following problems. Write down
only the answers.

1) 1375×5
2) $250 \div 2 =$
3) $125 + 234 =$
4) $482 - 291$
5) $60 + 40 - 20 - 10 =$

Correct Answers For The Foregoing Questions

A.
1) a) Quantity and cost per unit. Amount
available.
  b) Difference.
  c) The item cost $18.95. Twenty dol-
lars was given. How much change
was received?

2) a) Quantity and total cost.
  b) Cost per unit.
  c) Twenty items cost $66. What did
each item cost?

3) a) Quantity and cost per unit. Amount
available.
  b) Comparison.
  c) Five dollars was available. One item
cost $2.95; one cost $2.50. Could
both items be purchased?

4) a) Quantity and cost per unit.
  b) Total amount.
  c) One item cost $17.95, one cost
$10.95, and one cost $7.95. What
was the total bill?

5) a) Quantity and cost per unit.
  b) Total cost.
  c) If items cost $.33 a dozen, what
was the cost of 3 dozen?

B.
1) 6875
2) 125
3) 359
4) 191
5) 70

PROBLEM SOLVING

In addition to those explained in the previous chapters, there are several other rules that apply to problem solving.

The following two questions must be answered in the affirmative if there is to be a valid problem.

1. Are the elements in the *proper relationship* to allow for a meaningful answer?

That is, 2 apples and 2 pears cannot be added together.

2. Is there *sufficient relevant information* to let you arrive at the required answer?

For example: John bought 1 pound of bacon and 2 dozen eggs. The eggs cost $.60 a dozen. What was the total cost of John's order?

There is not sufficient relevant information. since the cost of the bacon is not given.

Speed In Problem Solving

A. Answer the following questions for each of the problems below. If the answer is No to any question, give the reason why. (Do not do the computation.)

    a) Is all the given information relevant to the problem?
    b) Is there sufficient information given?
    c) Is it a valid problem?

1) John went to the store and bought 2 dozen eggs, 1 pound of bacon, and 1 loaf of bread. If eggs cost $.60 a dozen, and bread $.29 a loaf, what was the total cost for this order?

2) Gary bought 2 records, 2 books, and 1 dictionary. Each record cost $2.98, each book cost $1.75, the dictionary cost $5.95, and a boat cost $3.98. How much did Gary spend?

3) Jeff had 2 dozen oranges, 1 dozen apples, 1 dozen pears, and 1 dozen onions. He wanted to divide his 5 dozen fruit evenly among 6 people. How many pieces of fruit would each person get?

4) John traveled at 40 miles an hour in one direction, and Bill traveled at 50 miles an hour in the opposite direction. At the end of 2 hours, how many miles apart were John and Bill?

5) If 70% of an order had a cost per unit of $1, and the remaining 30% had a cost per unit of $1.20, what is the average cost per unit of this order?

B. Answer the above 3 questions (a, b, and c) for the following problems. (Do not do the computation.)

1) Carol had to buy a dress, a pair of shoes, and a pocketbook. The dress cost $21.00, the shoes $14.98, and the pocketbook $4.97. Did she have enough money to pay for them?

2) Ray traveled 240 miles in 6 hours. How many miles per hour did Ray average?

3) Grandma and Grandpa traveled by bus from one point to another. The trip took 15 hours, and they left their point of origin at 8 A.M. What time did they arrive at their destination?

4) The Youth Fellowship decided to have a hayride. Five girls and five boys went on the trip. The parents of two of the children went along as chaperons. How many children went on the trip?

5) Bobby had to walk 2 miles to school. If he walked at an average of 3 miles per hour, how many minutes did it take him to walk to school?

After you have determined that there is sufficient relevant information given, you must choose a method to let you arrive at the required answer. At this point we shall introduce a deviation in method from those previously learned in school.

The following rules for solving problems in mathematics are taught in schools:

1. In solving a problem, always carry out the operation as indicated by the sign given in the problem.

That is, in the problem $A \times B =$, you would always multiply A by B to arrive at the proper answer.

2. When adding, subtracting, and multiplying, always work from right to left.

For example:
$$\begin{array}{r} 25 \\ \times 12 \\ \hline \end{array}$$

Multiply as follows:
5 by 2; 2 by 2; add 1 carried over
5 by 1; 2 by 1
Add from right to left.
The answer is 300.

If you wish to gain greater speed in mathematics, you must forget both the above rules. Whether you solve a problem by visualizing facts or by using a short-cut method, following these rules will cut down your speed.

In reading, the eyes move from left to right; this is their normal direction.

When you read the number 2339, you read the 2 first, then 3, 3, 9. Your eyes move from left to right. When you read the problem 25×2, you read it as 25 multiplied by 2, not as two times five-and-twenty. Again, your eyes move from left to right. Thus it can be assumed that reading from right to left, which is not the normal direction, causes a decrease in reading speed.

Substitute the following two rules for the ones stated above:

1. Solve a problem by using the method and the figures that are the easiest to work with in that problem.

Remember that mathematics is only a method of getting from one point to another. Starting with the basic information, and then working with that information or its equivalent, arrive at the required answer. Whether the method used is addition, subtraction, multiplication, or division does not matter. The answer should be arrived at by the fastest and most convenient means.

For example: $360 \times 25 =$
Two of the ways in which this problem can be solved are:
a) to multiply 360 by 25
b) to divide 360 by .04
If it is easier in this case to divide by .04 than to multiply by 25, then divide.

2. Where it is practical to do so, work from left to right.

For example: $25 \times 2 =$ write 50
To become proficient in solving problems in this way, you must gain speed in recalling the multiplication table. This speed will come with practice.

It must be remembered that when a sign is used in the statement of a problem, it is there only to tell you the relationship between the given numbers. The presence of a certain sign does not mean that to solve the problem you must perform the operation indicated by that sign.

A problem only states the relationship between the given facts and tells what is required as the answer. It does not tell you what operation you must perform to solve it.

For example: John bought 2 dozen eggs at a cost of \$.60 per dozen. What was the total cost of the eggs John bought?

What is stated: Quantity and cost per unit, and that the total cost is required.

Explanatory Solutions

A. 1) a) Yes.
   b) No—cost of bacon is not given.
   c) No.

2) a) No—cost of boat is not relevant.
   b) Yes.
   c) Yes.

3) a) No—onions are not fruit.
   b) Yes.
   c) No—there were 4 dozen fruit, not 5 dozen.

4) a) Yes.
   b) No—the starting point of each is not given.
   c) No.

5) a) Yes.
   b) Yes
   c) Yes.

B. 1) a) Yes.
   b) No—total amount available is not given.
   c) No.

2) a) Yes.
   b) Yes.
   c) Yes.

3) a) Yes.
   b) Yes.
   c) Yes.

4) a) No—chaperon information is not relevant.
   b) Yes.
   c) Yes.

5) a) Yes.
   b) Yes.
   c) Yes.

Practice In Problem Solving

A. Find what is stated in the following problems.

1) Don bought 10 handkerchiefs that cost $.10 apiece. What was the total cost of the handkerchiefs?

2) Frank bought 5 ties for a total cost of $7.50. What was the average cost per tie?

3) If Jean bought some pillow cases for a total cost of $8.46, and the average per unit cost was $2.82, how many pillow cases did she buy?

4) If Gary had $15 and spent $13.72, how much money did he have left?

5) Jeff has 2 dozen oranges and 2 dozen apples. How many dozen of the fruit does Jeff have?

B. Find what is stated in the following problems.

1) Pete traveled 1200 miles in 20 hours. How many miles per hour did Pete average?

2) Jean started a fire in the fireplace. Each log she put on burned for a half-hour. If she started with 10 logs, for how many hours could the fire burn?

3) Pam was planning a trip to Europe. She had a total of $700 available for expenses. If the plane tickets cost $372 how much money did she have left?

4) Fred had a coupon worth $2.00 on the purchase of one record. Each record cost $3.98, and Fred bought two records. How much did Fred have to pay?

5) On Wednesday it snowed 10 inches, and on Saturday it snowed 4 more inches. If that was the only snow that came in that week, what is the total snowfall for that week?

In summary, remember the following:

1. Analyze the problem to determine that there is:
   a) Relevant information.
   b) Sufficient information.
   c) A valid problem.

2. Forget these rules:
   a) Always do the problem in the manner shown.
   b) Always work from right to left.

3. Substitute for 2a and 2b:
   a) Solve problems by the method and with the figures that are the easiest to use.
   b) Where practical, work from left to right.

Explanatory Solutions

A. 1) Quantity and cost per unit and that the total cost is required.

2) Quantity and total cost and that the average cost per unit is required.

3) Cost per unit and total cost and that the quantity is required.

4) Amount available, amount spent, and that the difference is required.

5) Two quantities and that the total quantity is required.

B. 1) Distance and time and that the rate of speed is required.

2) Quantity and time per unit and that the total time is required.

3) Amount available, amount committed, and that the balance is required.

4) Quantity and cost per unit, discount, and that the balance is required.

5) Quantities, and that the total is required.

Exercises In Problem Solving

A. Answer a), b), and c) of each of the following questions.

> a) Is all the given information relevant to the problem?
> b) Is sufficient information given?
> c) Is it a valid problem?
>
> NOTE—If an answer is No to any questions, explain why.

1) Patty went to the store and bought a bottle of perfume, 2 tubes of lipstick, and 1 box of powder. The perfume cost $4.98 a bottle, lipstick $1.04, and the powder $1.57 a box. What was the amount Patty had to pay for these cosmetics?

2) Don had 36 books that he had to read in 3 months (13 weeks). He also had to write a thesis during this time. How many books did he have to read each week?

3) Alice bowled 3 games. Her scores were 136, 133, and 139. She had an average of 133 before bowling these 3 games. What is her average now?

4) To go from Poughkeepsie, New York, to West Palm Beach, Florida, you must travel 1,400 miles. If you can average a driving speed of 50 miles an hour, how many hours must you drive to make this trip?

5) Fifty per cent of an order had a cost per unit of $.53, 30 per cent of the order had a cost per unit of $.56, and 25 per cent of the order had a cost per unit of $.50. What is the average cost per unit of this order?

B. What do the following problems tell you?

1) Jeff bought 2 dozen eggs and 1 box of oatmeal. Eggs cost $.65 a dozen, and oatmeal costs $.29 a box. What was the total cost for these items?

2) Gary paid $12.00 for 6 records. What was the average cost per unit for each record?

3) Jean saw a dress for $15.95, a pair of gloves for $4.95, and a purse for $9.15. She had $30.00. Could she buy all the items she saw?

4) Patty bought a lamp for $37.50. She gave the clerk $40.00. How much change did Patty get?

5) John had $25.00. He saw some shirts that cost $4.95 apiece. How many of these shirts could John buy?

Correct Answers For The Foregoing Questions

(Please make every effort to answer the questions on your own before looking at these answers. You'll make faster progress by following this rule.)

A. 1) a) Yes.
  b) No—there is no *base* figure given for the cost of the lipstick.
  c) No.

2) a) No—thesis information is not relevant.
  b) Yes.
  c) Yes.

3) a) Yes.
  b) No—the number of games bowled to give the 133 average is not given.
  c) No.

4) a) Yes.
  b) Yes.
  c) Yes.

5) a) Yes.
  b) Yes.
  c) No—the percentages add up to 105 per cent.

B. 1) Quantity and cost per unit and that the total cost is required.

2) Quantity and total cost and that the average cost per unit is required.

3) Quantity and cost per unit, amount available, and that a comparison is required.

4) Cost, amount available, and that the difference is required.

5) Amount available, cost per unit, and that the quantity is required.

WORKING FROM LEFT TO RIGHT

This chapter discusses some of the rules to be used when deciding which direction to use when performing mathematical operations.

1. Simple Addition

Simple addition may be defined as addition of no more than 2 numbers, each of which may contain any number of digits.

In doing simple addition, always work from left to right.

When you have developed the habit of remembering the numbers in a problem, you will know ahead of time when there is a carry-over. This carry-over can never exceed +1 in simple addition.

For example:
$$\begin{array}{r} 9999 \\ +9999 \\ \hline 19998 \\ \longrightarrow \end{array}$$

2. Simple Subtraction

In simple subtraction, each of the two numbers may contain any number of digits.

Always work from left to right in simple subtraction. As with simple addition, you will learn to know ahead of time when there is to be a carry-over; this carry-over cannot exceed —1.

For example:
$$\begin{array}{r} 1111 \\ -999 \\ \hline 112 \\ \rightarrow \end{array}$$

3. Simple Multiplication

There is no real definition for simple multiplication. What is simple for one person may be difficult for another. Building up your speed in simple multiplication will depend on: a) your ability to recall the multiplication table and b) your ability to predict carry-overs accurately. In multiplication a carry-over can be any number.

Most people know the multiplication table up to and including 5. If this is true in your case, then a definition of simple multiplication for you would be multiplication of a number of any size by any number up to and including 5.

It must be remembered that working from left to right is supposed to help you increase your speed. It is natural for you to feel uncomfortable for a while when working in this way, because of your previous habit of working from right to left. To break a habit requires time, patience, and practice.

Practice in simple addition and subtraction can be started immediately. A review of the multiplication table may be necessary as preparation for simple multiplication. After you have completed this review, you can begin practice in multiplication.

Speeded Practice

Solve the following problems by working from left to right:

1. Simple Addition

A. 1)
$$\begin{array}{r} 235 \\ +644 \end{array}$$

2)
$$\begin{array}{r} 426 \\ +364 \end{array}$$

3)
$$\begin{array}{r} 72 \\ +38 \end{array}$$

4)
$$\begin{array}{r} 3217 \\ +6782 \end{array}$$

5)
$$\begin{array}{r} 4321 \\ +4687 \end{array}$$

6)
$$\begin{array}{r} 839 \\ +160 \end{array}$$

7)
$$\begin{array}{r} 438 \\ +621 \end{array}$$

8)
$$\begin{array}{r} 546 \\ +253 \end{array}$$

9)
$$\begin{array}{r} 762 \\ +569 \end{array}$$

10)
$$\begin{array}{r} 2327 \\ +678 \end{array}$$

B.
1) 623
   +111

2) 411
   +151

3) 975
   +368

4) 789
   +799

5) 158
   +968

6) 367
   +589

7) 639
   +984

8) 242
   +472

9) 435
   +835

10) 505
    +309

9) 935
   −375

10) 813
    −158

11) 721
    −484

12) 932
    −299

13) 623
    −155

14) 912
    −132

15) 763
    −164

2. Simple Subtraction

A.
1) 278
   137

2) 334
   129

3) 447
   152

4) 538
   439

5) 621
   367

6) 572
   −384

7) 628
   −546

8) 725
   −633

9) 483
   −256

10) 964
    −853

B.
1) 868
   −428

2) 944
   −587

3) 956
   −927

4) 498
   −463

5) 819
   −214

6) 951
   −719

7) 617
   −489

8) 721
   −576

3. Simple Multiplication

A.
1) 9
   ×5

2) 8
   ×3

3) 7
   ×4

4) 6
   ×2

5) 5
   ×8

6) 4
   ×9

7) 3
   ×9

8) 2
   ×7

9) 1
   ×7

10) 7
    ×3

11) 33
    ×4

12) 64
    ×5

13) 72
    ×2

14) 48
    ×3

15) 85
    ×2

16) 176
    ×3

17) 224
    ×2

18) 321
    ×5

19) 726
    ×4

20) 623
    ×5

B.
1) 954 ×1
2) 4 ×6
3) 145 ×4
4) 5 ×9
5) 923 ×3
6) 3 ×8
7) 578 ×5
8) 4 ×7
9) 827 ×1
10) 2 ×9
11) 391 ×2
12) 4 ×8
13) 89 ×4
14) 631 ×1
15) 5 ×3
16) 1 ×9
17) 2 ×8
18) 3 ×6
19) 5 ×7
20) 1 ×8
21) 5 ×6
22) 3 ×7
23) 1 ×6
24) 2 ×6
25) 9 ×4

Correct Answers For The Foregoing Questions

1. Simple Addition

A.
1) 879	2) 790	3) 110
4) 9999	5) 9008	6) 999
7) 1,059	8) 799	9) 1,331
10) 3,005		

B.
1) 734	2) 562	3) 1,343
4) 1,588	5) 1,126	6) 956
7) 1,623	8) 714	9) 1,270
10) 814		

2. Simple Subtraction

A.
1) 141	2) 205	3) 295
4) 99	5) 254	6) 188
7) 82	8) 92	9) 227
10) 111		

B.
1) 440	2) 357	3) 29
4) 35	5) 605	6) 232
7) 128	8) 145	9) 560
10) 655	11) 237	12) 633
13) 468	14) 780	15) 599

3. Simple Multiplication

A.
1) 45	2) 24	3) 28
4) 12	5) 40	6) 36
7) 27	8) 14	9) 7
10) 21	11) 132	12) 320
13) 144	14) 144	15) 170
16) 528	17) 448	18) 1,605
19) 2,904	20) 3,115	

B.
1) 954	2) 24	3) 580
4) 45	5) 2,769	6) 24
7) 2,890	8) 28	9) 827
10) 18	11) 782	12) 32
13) 356	14) 631	15) 15
16) 9	17) 16	18) 18
19) 35	20) 8	21) 30
22) 21	23) 6	24) 12
25) 36		

DROPPING FINAL ZEROS

At times you may find it advantageous to drop the final zero when solving a multiplication or division problem.

1. Multiplication by a Whole Number

In this form of multiplication, the final zeros in the multiplier and/or the multiplicand should be dropped. That is, the final zeros should not be used in the computation, but should appear only in the product.

You may wonder what advantage there is to be gained by dropping these final zeros. Mistakes are often made by placing numbers in the wrong columns when dealing with numbers that end in zero. If the final zero is not used in the computation at all, it cannot cause confusion.

For example:

```
  2310         129          1760
×150         ×210          ×205
────         ────          ────
 1155         129           880
 231          258           352
────         ────          ────
346500       27090        360800
```

Practice Problems

Solve the following multiplication problems, dropping the final zeros. Remember to write down only the necessary information as you solve these problems and to work from left to right.

A.

1) 230
   × 12

2) 175
   ×130

3) 203
   × 14

4) 621
   ×140

5) 430
   ×360

6) 132
   ×310

7) 350
   × 24

8) 520
   ×410

9) 634
   ×120

10) 431
   ×230

B.

1) 542
   × 50

2) 420
   × 15

3) 647
   × 20

4) 870
   × 21

5) 965
   × 30

6) 539
   ×110

7) 730
   × 34

8) 81
   × 40

9) 23
   ×530

10) 438
   ×210

Correct Answers For The Foregoing Questions

(Please make every effort to answer the questions on your own before looking at these answers. You'll make faster progress by following this rule.)

A.

1) 46
   23
   ———
   2760

2) 525
   175
   ———
   22750

3) 812
   203
   ———
   2842

4) 2484
   621
   ———
   86940

5) 258
   129
   ———
   154800

6) 132
   396
   ———
   40920

7) 140
   70
   ———
   8400

8) 52
   208
   ———
   213200

9) 1268
   634
   ———
   76080

10) 1293
   862
   ———
   99130

B.

1) 27100

2) 210
   42
   ———
   6300

3) 12940

4) 87
   174
   ———
   18270

5) 28950

6) 539
   539
   ———
   59290

7) 292
   219
   ———
   24820

8) 3240

9) 69
   115
   ———
   12190

10) 438
   876
   ———
   91980

2. Multiplication by Decimals

In miltiplication by decimals, other rules apply as to handling final zeros than in multiplication by whole numbers.

A. If there are one or more zeros immediately following the decimal point and no whole numbers preceding the decimal point in the multiplier, and there are one or more final zeros in the multiplicand, move the decimal point in the multiplier to the right the same number of places as there are final zeros in the multiplicand. Then cross out the final zero(s) in the multiplicand.

For example:

$$\frac{27500}{\times .05} = \frac{275}{\times 5} \qquad \frac{1250}{\times .005} = \frac{125}{\times .05}$$

B. If there are one or more final zeros in the multiplicand, and there are *no* zeros immediately following the decimal point in the multiplier, you may proceed as in *A,* above—that is, move the decimal point in the multiplier to the right the same number of places as there are final zeros in the multiplicand. Then cross out the final zeros in the multiplicand.

For example:

$$\frac{27500}{\times .25} = \frac{275}{\times 25} \qquad \frac{1620}{\times .16} = \frac{162}{\times 1.6}$$

If there are no final zeros in the multiplicand, there is no advantage in changing the problem.

Practice Exercises

Rewrite the following problems, dropping the final zeros. Do not compute.

A.
1) 240×2.5
2) $620 \times .04$
3) $724 \times .03$
4) $325 \times .26$
5) $2400 \times .02$
6) $8710 \times .56$
7) $400 \times .04$
8) $5300 \times .5$
9) $930 \times .3$
10) $484 \times .05$

B.
1) $820 \times .135$
2) $600 \times .002$
3) $340 \times .08$
4) $732 \times .12$
5) $800 \times .005$
6) $480 \times .4$
7) 870×2.3
8) 680×4.1
9) 76×3.3
10) $9000 \times .001$

Correct Answers For The Foregoing Questions

(Please make every effort to answer the questions on your own before looking at these answers. You'll make faster progress by following this rule.)

A.
1) 24×25
2) $62 \times .4$
3) $724 \times .03$
4) $325 \times .26$
5) 24×2
6) 871×5.6
7) 4×4
8) 530×5
9) 93×3
10) $484 \times .05$

B.
1) 82×1.35
2) $6 \times .2$
3) $34 \times .8$
4) $732 \times .12$
5) $8 \times .5$
6) 48×4
7) 87×23
8) 68×41
9) 76×33
10) 9×1

3. Division

The following rules apply to division:

A. When there are final zeros in the divisor but no final zeros in the dividend, move the decimal point in the dividend to the left as many places as there are final zeros in the divisor.

For example: 2700.) 37523. = 27) 375.23

B. When there are fewer final zeros in the divisor than there are in the dividend, drop the same number of final zeros from the dividend as there are final zeros in the divisor.

For example: 250.)45300. = 25.)4530.

C. When there are more final zeros in the divisor than there are in the dividend, move the decimal point in the dividend to the left as many places as there are final zeros in the divisor, then cross out the final zeros.

For example: 2300.)690. = 23.)6.9

D. When there are no final zeros in the divisor, no zeros can be dropped in the dividend.

For example: 23.)690. = 23.)690.

In the above statement, "final zeros in the divisor" refers only to those in a whole number. If there are final zeros following the decimal point, they are superfluous and should be dropped, with no effect on the dividend or the problem.

For example: 23.0)690. = 23.)690.

Speeded Practice

Rewrite the following problems, dropping final zeros. Do not compute.

A.
1) 20.)44.
2) 272.)5440.
3) 33.0)660.
4) 620.)12400.
5) 4100.)1230.
6) 400.)4824.
7) 30.)693
8) 330.)36300.
9) 200.)40.
10) 42.)840.

B.
1) 600.)72.
2) 310.)6200.
3) 7600)1520.
4) 46.)920.
5) 11.0)220.
6) 700.)84.
7) 90.)8100.
8) 8100.)1620.
9) 25.)5250.
10) 41.0)820.
11) 800.)96.
12) 650.)1300.
13) 5500.)110.
14) 36.)720.
15) 87.0)1740.

Correct Answers For The Foregoing Questions

A.
1) 2.)4.4
2) 272.)5440.
3) 33.)660.
4) 62.)1240.
5) 41.)12.3
6) 4.)48.24
7) 3.)69.3
8) 33.)3630.
9) 2.)4
10) 42.)840.

B.
1) 6.).72
2) 31.)620.
3) 76.)15.2
4) 46.)920.
5) 11.)220.
6) 7.).84
7) 9.)810.
8) 81.)16.2
9) 25.)5250.
10) 41.)820.
11) 8.).96
12) 65.)130.
13) 55.)1.1
14) 36.)720.
15) 87.)1740.

Multiplication Practice

A. Solve the following multiplication problems, dropping final zeros. Remember to write down only the necessary information when solving problems.

1) 189
    $\times$ 120

2) 240
    $\times$ 360

3) 309
    $\times$ 106

4) 430
    $\times$ 221

5) 643
    $\times$ 400

B. Rewrite the following multiplication problems, dropping the final zeros. Do not compute.

1) 370
    $\times$ 3.5

2) 530
    $\times$ .02

3) 823
    $\times$ .05

4) 426
    $\times$ .26

5) 4200
    $\times$ .02

C. Rewrite the following division problems, dropping the final zeros. Do not compute.

1) 240.)4800.

2) 460.)92.

3) 36.)1080.

4) 7200.)2160.

5) 27.0)540.

Correct Answers For The Foregoing Questions

(Please make every effort to answer the questions on your own before looking at these answers. You'll make faster progress by following this rule.)

A.

1) 378
    189

    22680

2) 144
    72

    86400

3) 1854
    3090

    32754

4) 43
    86
    86

    95030

5) 257200

B.

1) 37
    $\times$ 35

2) 53
    $\times$ .2

3) 823
    $\times$ .05

4) 426
    $\times$ .26

5) 42
    $\times$ 2

C.

1) 24.) 480.

2) 46.) 9.2

3) 36.) 1080.

4) 72.) 21.6

5) 27.) 540.

ARITHMETIC COMPUTATIONS

To add valuable points to your exam score you must master arithmetical computations. And by this we mean doing them quickly and with absolute accuracy. The computations themselves will be simple, although the form in which they are presented may rattle you if you're not prepared. In addition to calculation, they measure your ability to interpret and act on directions. Thus this chapter provides practice through a series of tests modeled on the different question types that have actually appeared on examinations. An important tip from our years of experience with the self-tutored test-taker: Study the Directions! We have included those you are most likely to meet on your exam. Control over them will gain precious minutes for you. This doesn't mean you can skip reading directions on your actual exam. It does mean that you will be ahead of the game for knowing the language examiners use. Then you can afford to play it cool. A misunderstood direction can lead to a run of incorrect answers. Avoid this costly carelessness.

TO SCORE HIGH ON MATH TESTS

1. SCHEDULE YOUR STUDY. Set a definite time, and stick to it, as explained in the chapter, STUDYING AND USING THIS BOOK. Enter Arithmetical Computations on your Study Schedule.

2. PLAN on taking different types of Computation Tests in each study period. Keep alert to the differences and complications. That will help keep you bright and interested.

3. DO YOUR BEST and work fast to complete each test before looking at our Correct Answers. Keep pushing yourself, and use the help this book provides, for checking purposes only.

4. RECORD YOUR TIME for each test next to your score. Your schedule may allow you to take the tests again. And you may want to see how your speed and accuracy have improved.

5. REVIEW YOUR ERRORS. This is a must for every study session. Allow time for redoing every incorrect answer. The good self-tutor is a good self-critic. He learns most from his mistakes. And never makes them again.

6. DON'T GUESS AT ANSWERS. Because each practice test, like the actual examination, requires a multiple-choice answer, you might be tempted to pick up speed by approximating the answers. This is fatal. Carefully work out your answer to each question. Then choose the right answer. Any other way is certain to create confusion, slow you down, lower your score.

7. CLARITY & ORDER. Write all your figures clearly, in neat rows and columns. And this includes the figures you have to carry over from one column to another. Don't make mistakes because of lack of space and cramped writing. Use scratch paper wherever necessary.

8. **SKIP THE PUZZLERS.** If a single question gives you an unusual amount of trouble, go on to the next question. Come back to the tough one after you have done all the others and still have time left over.

9. **STUDY THE SAMPLE SOLUTIONS.** Note how carefully we have worked out each step. Get into this habit in doing all the practice tests. You'll quickly find that it's a time-saver . . . a high-scoring habit.

Sample Questions and Detailed Solutions

DIRECTIONS: Each question has five suggested answers lettered A, B, C, D, and E. Suggested answer E is NONE OF THESE. Blacken space E only if your answer for a question does not exactly agree with any of the first four suggested answers. When you have finished all the questions, compare your answers with the correct answers at the end of the test.

Sample 1. Divide:

$$4.6 / \overline{233.404}$$

(A) 50.74
(B) 52.24
(C) 57.30
(D) 58.24
(E) None of these

Sample II. Multiply:

$$\begin{array}{r} 2\ 946 \\ \times\,7.007 \\ \hline \end{array}$$

(A) 21,642.622
(B) 20,642.622
(C) 41,244.001
(D) 20,641.622
(E) None of these

SOLUTION 1.

$$\begin{array}{r} 5\,0.74 \\ 4/6. / \overline{233/4.04} \\ 230 \\ \hline 340 \\ 322 \\ \hline 184 \\ 184 \end{array}$$

Since the answer is clearly 50.74, blacken A on the answer sheet. Do not mark any of the other letter choices. There is only one correct answer.

SOLUTION II.

$$\begin{array}{r} 2\ 946 \\ \times\,7.007 \\ \hline 20622 \\ 0000 \\ 0000 \\ 20622 \\ \hline 20{,}642.622 \end{array}$$

The answer is 20,642.622, which is answer choice B. This answer is similar to answer choices A and D, but it is not the same. So you must be careful not to let the A and D choices confuse you. Blacken only B on your answer sheet.

Now, push forward! Test yourself and practice for your test with the carefully constructed quizzes that follow. Each one presents the kind of question you may expect on your test. And each question is at just the level of difficulty that may be expected. Don't try to take all the tests at one time. Rather, schedule yourself so that you take a few at each session, and spend approximately the same time on them at each session. Score yourself honestly, and date each test. You should be able to detect improvement in your performance on successive sessions.

ARITHMETIC SUMMATION TEST ONE

Time Allowed: 10 minutes

DIRECTIONS: In this test you are asked to do two of the fundamental operations in arithmetic: addition and multiplication. They are closely related in that multiplication is really a succession of additions. For the multiplication problems, blacken the space under A if the given answer is correct. Blacken the space under B if the answer is incorrect. For the addition problems, blacken the space under D if the given answer is correct. Blacken the space under E if the answer is incorrect. We suggest that you do all of the multiplication problems before going on to addition. You should be able to work more accurately and quickly that way.

MULTIPLICATION

```
1)   16        2)   69
   ×  4           ×  8
   ────           ────
     64            552

3)   27        4)   46
   ×  3           ×  5
   ────           ────
     71             51

5)   79        6)   58
   ×  2           ×  4
   ────           ────
    158            222

7)   15        8)   28
   ×  3           ×  6
   ────           ────
     35            168

9)   49       10)   89
   ×  7           ×  9
   ────           ────
    343            801
```

ADDITION

```
1)   68        2)   44
     30             57
     46             60
   + 52           + 32
   ────           ────
    206            193

3)   37        4)   24
     63             43
     12             72
   + 78           + 57
   ────           ────
    190            197

5)   20        6)   48
     59             42
     66             77
   + 81           + 16
   ────           ────
    236            184

7)   34        8)   94
     28             36
     65             89
   + 41           + 64
   ────           ────
    168            283

9)   25       10)   52
     40             17
     66             25
   + 31           + 64
   ────           ────
    152            158
```

WORK SPACE

Answer Sheet

	A	B	C	D	E
1					
2					
3					
4					
5					
6					
7					
8					
9					
10					

MULTIPLICATION

11) 67
× 3
191

12) 54
× 7
378

13) 67
× 6
412

14) 29
× 8
222

15) 36
× 5
190

16) 78
× 4
312

17) 18
× 4
72

18) 25
× 7
165

19) 47
× 6
282

20) 88
× 4
352

21) 68
× 5
330

22) 53
× 8
414

23) 64
× 3
192

24) 28
× 9
242

25) 82
× 8
656

WORK SPACE

ADDITION

11) 44
68
75
+38
225

12) 26
64
39
+24
163

13) 58
64
27
+67
216

14) 65
34
48
+92
249

15) 11
18
85
+42
156

16) 33
26
94
+35
178

17) 88
64
38
+46
226

18) 29
63
11
+84
187

19) 54
36
29
+63
182

20) 48
75
63
+68
254

21) 75
62
32
+64
223

22) 38
82
46
+54
220

23) 12
43
65
+57
187

24) 46
58
42
+23
179

25) 28
94
35
+32
199

WORK SPACE

Answer Sheet

	A	B	C	D	E
11					
12					
13					
14					
15					
16					
17					
18					
19					
20					
21					
22					
23					
24					
25					

SCORE

%

NO. CORRECT

NO. OF QUESTIONS ON THIS TEST

Correct Answers

*(You'll learn more by writing your own an-
swers before comparing them with these.)*

1. A-E	8. A-D	15. B-D	22. B-D
2. A-D	9. A-E	16. A-E	23. A-E
3. B-D	10. A-D	17. A-E	24. B-E
4. B-E	11. B-D	18. B-D	25. A-E
5. A-E	12. A-E	19. A-D	
6. B-E	13. B-D	20. A-D	
7. B-D	14. B-E	21. B-E	

ARITHMETIC DIMINUTION TEST TWO

Time Allowed: 10 minutes

DIRECTIONS: Subtraction and division are two of the basic operations in arithmetic. This test will help you gain proficiency in both these diminution processes, and thereby in many others. For the division problems, blacken the space under A if the given answer is correct. Blacken the space under B if the answer is incorrect. For the subtraction problems, blacken the space under D if the given answer is correct. Blacken the space under E if the answer is incorrect. For this test the space under C will not be blackened. We suggest that you do all the division problems before going on to subtraction. Although the processes are related, you should be able to work more accurately and quickly if you do the test this way.

SUBTRACTION

1) 95 −48 = 37
2) 76 −38 = 48

3) 59 −23 = 36
4) 39 −23 = 17

5) 63 −48 = 15
6) 89 −42 = 47

7) 49 −13 = 37
8) 82 −67 = 15

9) 62 −29 = 32
10) 84 −68 = 15

11) 27 −16 = 11
12) 51 −27 = 24

13) 92 −46 = 56
14) 37 −18 = 29

15) 41 −25 = 16
16) 74 −35 = 38

DIVISION

1) $3\overline{)21}$ = 8
2) $8\overline{)360}$ = 45

3) $9\overline{)36}$ = 4
4) $2\overline{)10}$ = 5

5) $4\overline{)36}$ = 8
6) $7\overline{)231}$ = 34

7) $3\overline{)24}$ = 9
8) $6\overline{)12}$ = 2

9) $8\overline{)64}$ = 7
10) $5\overline{)205}$ = 41

11) $7\overline{)497}$ = 71
12) $3\overline{)102}$ = 35

13) $2\overline{)12}$ = 6
14) $6\overline{)48}$ = 9

15) $9\overline{)828}$ = 82
16) $2\overline{)54}$ = 27

WORK SPACE

Answer Sheet

	A	B	C	D	E
1					
2					
3					
4					
5					
6					
7					
8					
9					
10					
11					
12					
13					
14					
15					
16					

SUBTRACTION

17) 65 —26 39	18) 81 —29 62	19) 67 —38 39
20) 85 —37 48	21) 52 —23 29	22) 42 —13 38
23) 26 —15 11	24) 34 —17 27	25) 32 —19 13
26) 46 —17 39	27) 71 —59 22	28) 90 —48 42
29) 58 —39 19	30) 96 —49 47	31) 56 —28 38
32) 75 —37 38	33) 54 —18 34	34) 91 —43 49
35) 72 —48 24	36) 45 —27 18	37) 33 —17 25
38) 68 —29 39	39) 24 —15 19	40) 44 —19 25

WORK SPACE

Answer Sheet

	A	B	C	D	E
17	⁞	⁞	⁞	⁞	⁞
18	⁞	⁞	⁞	⁞	⁞
19	⁞	⁞	⁞	⁞	⁞
20	⁞	⁞	⁞	⁞	⁞
21	⁞	⁞	⁞	⁞	⁞
22	⁞	⁞	⁞	⁞	⁞
23	⁞	⁞	⁞	⁞	⁞
24	⁞	⁞	⁞	⁞	⁞
25	⁞	⁞	⁞	⁞	⁞
26	⁞	⁞	⁞	⁞	⁞
27	⁞	⁞	⁞	⁞	⁞
28	⁞	⁞	⁞	⁞	⁞
29	⁞	⁞	⁞	⁞	⁞
30	⁞	⁞	⁞	⁞	⁞
31	⁞	⁞	⁞	⁞	⁞
32	⁞	⁞	⁞	⁞	⁞
33	⁞	⁞	⁞	⁞	⁞
34	⁞	⁞	⁞	⁞	⁞
35	⁞	⁞	⁞	⁞	⁞
36	⁞	⁞	⁞	⁞	⁞
37	⁞	⁞	⁞	⁞	⁞
38	⁞	⁞	⁞	⁞	⁞
39	⁞	⁞	⁞	⁞	⁞
40	⁞	⁞	⁞	⁞	⁞

SCORE

%

NO. CORRECT

NO. OF QUESTIONS ON THIS TEST

DIVISION

43 17) 4 / 172	33 18) 7 / 224	32 19) 9 / 288
9 20) 3 / 27	8 21) 6 / 42	86 22) 4 / 336
6 23) 9 / 45	52 24) 2 / 104	64 25) 5 / 370
73 26) 7 / 504	5 27) 3 / 15	41 28) 4 / 164
84 29) 8 / 752	84 30) 2 / 168	63 31) 7 / 371
3 32) 9 / 18	2 33) 5 / 10	76 34) 4 / 264
73 35) 9 / 657	4 36) 6 / 30	9 37) 2 / 16
8 38) 8 / 72	85 39) 7 / 595	55 40) 5 / 275

Correct Answers

(You'll learn more by writing your own answers before comparing them with these.)

1.B-E	11.A-D	21.B-D	31.B-E
2.A-E	12.B-D	22.B-E	32.B-D
3.A-D	13.A-E	23.B-D	33.A-E
4,A-E	14.B-E	24.A-E	34.B-E
5.B-D	15.B-D	25.B-D	35.A-D
6.B-D	16.A-E	26.B-E	36.B-D
7.B-E	17.A-D	27.A-E	37.B-E
8.A-D	18.B-E	28.A-D	38.B-D
9.B-E	19.A-E	29.B-D	39.A-E
10.A-E	20.A-D	30.A-D	40.A-D

COMPUTATIONAL SPEED TEST THREE

Time Allowed: 10 minutes

DIRECTIONS: Each question has five suggested answers lettered A, B, C, D, and E. Suggested answer E is NONE OF THESE. Blacken space E only if your answer for a question does not exactly agree with any of the first four suggested answers. When you have finished all the questions, compare your answers with the correct answers at the end of the test.

ANSWERS

1) Add:
$27.602 + 19.27 =$
- (A) 467.72
- (B) 47.872
- (C) 468.72
- (D) 46.872
- (E) None of these

2) Convert $27/64$ to %.
- (A) 40.625%
- (B) 42.188%
- (C) 43.750%
- (D) 45.313%
- (E) None of these

3) 15 is 20% of?
- (A) 18
- (B) 3
- (C) 75
- (D) 35
- (E) None of these

4) Multiply:
$23 \times 9\frac{3}{4} =$
- (A) $191\frac{2}{3}$
- (B) $224\frac{1}{4}$
- (C) $213\frac{3}{4}$
- (D) $32\frac{3}{4}$
- (E) None of these

5) 55% of 15 =
- (A) 82.5
- (B) 0.825
- (C) 0.0825
- (D) 8.25
- (E) None of these

ANSWERS

6) Convert .0625 to a fraction.
- (A) 1/16
- (B) 1/15
- (C) 1/14
- (D) 1/13
- (E) None of these

7) Convert $0.16\frac{3}{4}$ to a %.
- (A) $16\frac{3}{4}$%
- (B) $.16\frac{3}{4}$%
- (C) $.016\frac{3}{4}$%
- (D) $.0016\frac{3}{4}$%
- (E) None of these

8) The equivalent of $0.03125 =$
- (A) 3/64
- (B) 1/16
- (C) 1/64
- (D) 1/32
- (E) None of these

9) Divide:
$1.75\overline{)21.70}$
- (A) 124
- (B) 12.4
- (C) 1.24
- (D) .124
- (E) None of these

10) Subtract:
$410.07 - 38.49 =$
- (A) 372.58
- (B) 371.68
- (C) 381.58
- (D) 382.68
- (E) None of these

Answer Sheet

	A	B	C	D	E
1					
2					
3					
4					
5					
6					
7					
8					
9					
10					

ANSWERS   **ANSWERS**

11) Multiply:
20.16
$\times$ 7¾

(A) 15.12
(B) 151.20
(C) 141.12
(D) 156.24
(E) None of these

16) Add:
3 5/16 + 2 ½ =

(A) 5 13/16
(B) 5⅜
(C) 5 7/16
(D) 5 9/16
(E) None of these

12) Add: 90.79
79.09
97.90
+ 9.97

(A) 277.75
(B) 278.56
(C) 276.94
(D) 277.93
(E) None of these

17) Subtract:
349.198
— 52.3791

(A) 296.817
(B) 295.8187
(C) 297.9189
(D) 296.8189
(E) None of these

13) Divide:
.035 / 49

(A) 1.4
(B) 14
(C) 140
(D) 1400
(E) None of these

18) Divide:
.56 / 44.55528

(A) 78.563
(B) 795.63
(C) 7.9563
(D) 7956.30
(E) None of these

14)
$$\frac{5/4}{4\,⅝ - 2\,¾} =$$

(A) 1
(B) 2
(C) 1 7/10
(D) 2 3/10
(E) None of these

19) Add:
372.58
371.68
381.58
+382.68

(A) 1509.42
(B) 1508.52
(C) 1718.52
(D) 1508.53
(E) None of these

15) Multiply:
1.25 × 72.964 =

(A) 912.05
(B) 9120.50
(C) 91.205
(D) 9.1205
(E) None of these

20) Multiply:
4 5/12 × 7 ¾ =

(A) 24 11/48
(B) 35⅓
(C) 34 11/48
(D) 33 5/48
(E) None of these

Answer Sheet

	A	B	C	D	E
11	⁞	⁞	⁞	⁞	⁞
12	⁞	⁞	⁞	⁞	⁞
13	⁞	⁞	⁞	⁞	⁞
14	⁞	⁞	⁞	⁞	⁞
15	⁞	⁞	⁞	⁞	⁞
16	⁞	⁞	⁞	⁞	⁞
17	⁞	⁞	⁞	⁞	⁞
18	⁞	⁞	⁞	⁞	⁞
19	⁞	⁞	⁞	⁞	⁞
20	⁞	⁞	⁞	⁞	⁞

SCORE

%

NO. CORRECT

NO. OF QUESTIONS
ON THIS TEST

WORK SPACE   **WORK SPACE**

Correct Answers

*(You'll learn more by writing your own an-
swers before comparing them with these.)*

1. D	6. A	11. D	16. A
2. B	7. A	12. A	17. D
3. C	8. D	13. D	18. E
4. B	9. B	14. E	19. B
5. D	10. E	15. C	20. C

WORD PROBLEMS TEST ONE

Time Allowed: 10 minutes

DIRECTIONS: The following arithmetic word problems have been devised to make you think with numbers. In each question, the arithmetic is simple, but the objective is to comprehend what you have to do with the numbers and/or quantities. Read the problem carefully and choose the correct answer from the five choices that follow each question.

Correct key answers to all these test questions will be found at the end of the test.

1. Add the following: 40¢, $2.75, $186.21, $24,865, $.74, $8.42, $2,475.28, $11,998.24.

   (A) $38,537.04   (B) $39,537.04
   (C) $38,533.40   (D) $39,573.40
        (E) None of these

2. Perform the indicated operations and express your answer in its simplest form: 5/8 divided by 20/3 times 7/19 divided by 63/38 times 16/21 divided by 1/14.

   (A) 2/9   (B) ½
   (C) ⅓   (D) 5/9
        (E) None of these

3. Perform the indicated operations: .020301 times 2.15 divided by .00000063.

   (A) 69218.19   (B) 69821.19
   (C) 69281.91   (D) 69281.19
        (E) None of these

4. Add the following fractions: 1½, 2 1/16, 9⅓, 2¼, 6 1/5.

   (A) 21 8/20   (B) 21½
   (C) 20   (D) 20 9/20
        (E) None of these

5. Perform the indicated operations and express your answer in inches: 12 feet, minus 7 inches, plus 2 feet 1 inch minus 7 feet, minus 1 yard, plus 2 yards 1 foot 3 inches.

   (A) 130 inches   (B) 128 inches
   (C) 129 inches   (D) 131 inches
        (E) None of these

6. Add:

      7 years, 3 months
      5 years, 6 months
      8 years, 11 months

   (A) 20 yrs.   (B) 20 yrs. 8 mos.
   (C) 21 yrs. 9 mos. (D) 21 yrs. 8 mos.
        (E) None of these

7. Find the cost of 2 dozen boxes of pencils at $3.60 per ¼ dozen boxes.

   (A) $28.80   (B) $29.50
   (C) $20.88   (D) $28.08
        (E) None of these

8. When 5.1 is divided by 0.017 the quotient is

   (A) 30   (B) 300
   (C) 3,000   (D) 30,000
        (E) None of these

9. One percent of $23,000 is

   (A) $.023   (B) $2.30
   (C) $23   (D) $2300
        (E) None of these

10. The sum of $82.79; $103.06 and $697.88 is, most nearly,

   (A) $1628   (B) $791
   (C) $873   (D) $1395
        (E) None of these

11. The sum of 2345 and 4483 is

   (A) 6288   (B) 6828
   (C) 6882   (D) 8628
        (E) None of these

12. The difference between 2876 and 1453 is

    (A) 1342   (B) 1324
    (C) 1234   (D) 1423
          (E) None of these

13. If each of 5 sections has 15 cans, the total for all five sections is

    (A) 70   (B) 65
    (C) 60   (D) 80
          (E) None of these

14. The area of a street 100 yards long and 30 yards wide is

    (A) 3,000 sq. yds.   (B) 3,500 sq. yds.
    (C) 2,500 sq. yds.   (D) 130 sq. yds.
          (E) None of these

15. Five tons of snow will weigh how many pounds?

    (A) 1,000 lbs.   (B) 10,000 lbs.
    (C) 100 lbs.   (D) 5,000 lbs.
          (E) None of these

16. If a man earns $3000 a year, approximately how much is his weekly pay?

    (A) $45   (B) $50
    (C) $55   (D) $60
          (E) None of these

17. A man who works 8 hours a day for 6 days will work a total of how many hours?

    (A) 40 hrs.   (B) 45 hrs.
    (C) 50 hrs.   (D) 47 hrs.
          (E) None of these

18. If a load of snow contains 3 tons, it will weigh how many lbs.?

    (A) 3,000 lbs.   (B) 1,500 lbs.
    (C) 12,000 lbs.   (D) 6,000 lbs.
          (E) None of these

19. A section of pavement which is 10 feet long and 8 feet wide contains how many square feet?

    (A) 80 sq. ft.   (B) 92 sq. ft.
    (C) 800 sq. ft.   (D) 18 sq. ft.
          (E) None of these

20. If a man mops 13 halls each day for 15 days, he will have mopped a total of how many halls?

    (A) 165 halls   (B) 190 halls
    (C) 200 halls   (D) 175 halls
          (E) None of these

21. If you divided 56 pounds of soap powder equally among 8 men, each man would get how many pounds of soap powder?

    (A) 6 lbs.   (B) 7 lbs.
    (C) 8 lbs.   (D) 5 lbs.
          (E) None of these

22. The sum of 284.5, 3016.24, 8.9736, and 94.15 is, most nearly,

    (A) 3402.9   (B) 3403.0
    (C) 3403.9   (D) 4036.1
          (E) None of these

23. If 8394.6 is divided by 29.17, the result is most nearly

    (A) 288   (B) 347
    (C) 2880   (D) 3470
          (E) None of these

24. If two numbers are multiplied together, the result is 3752. If one of the two numbers is 56, the other number is

    (A) 41   (B) 15
    (C) 109   (D) 76
          (E) None of these

25. The sum of the fractions ¼, ⅔, ⅜, ⅚, and ¾ is

    (A) 20/33   (B) 1 19/24
    (C) 2¼   (D) 2⅞
          (E) None of these

Correct Answers

1. B	8. B	15. B	22. C
2. A	9. E	16. C	23. A
3. D	10. C	17. E	24. E
4. E	11. B	18. D	25. D
5. C	12. D	19. A	
6. D	13. E	20. E	
7. A	14. A	21. B	

SCORE

.... %

NO. CORRECT ÷
NO. OF QUESTIONS ON THIS TEST

WORD PROBLEMS TEST TWO

Time Allowed: 10 minutes

DIRECTIONS: The following arithmetic word problems have been devised to make you think with numbers. In each question, the arithmetic is simple, but the objective is to comprehend what you have to do with the numbers and/or quantities. Read the problem carefully and choose the correct answer from the five choices that follow each question.

Correct key answers to all these test questions will be found at the end of the test.

1. The fraction 7/16 expressed as a decimal is

   (A) .1120   (B) .4375
   (C) .2286   (D) .4850
         (E) None of these

2. If .10 is divided by 50, the result is

   (A) .002   (B) .02
   (C) .2   (D) 2.
         (E) None of these

3. The number 60 is 40% of

   (A) 24   (B) 84
   (C) 96   (D) 150
         (E) None of these

4. If ⅜ of a number is 96, the number is

   (A) 132   (B) 36
   (C) 256   (D) 156
         (E) None of these

5. The sum of 637.894, 8352.16, 4.8673 and 301.5 is, most nearly,

   (A) 8989.5   (B) 9021.35
   (C) 9294.9   (D) 9296.4
         (E) None of these

6. If 30 is divided by .06, the result is

   (A) 5   (B) 50
   (C) 500   (D) 5000
         (E) None of these

7. The sum of the fractions ⅓, 4/6, ¾, ½, and 1/12 is

   (A) 3¼   (B) 2⅓
   (C) 2⅙   (D) 1 11/12
         (E) None of these

8. If 96934.42 is divided by 53.496, the result is most nearly

   (A) 181   (B) 552
   (C) 1819   (D) 5520
         (E) None of these

9. If 25% of a number is 48, the number is

   (A) 12   (B) 60
   (C) 144   (D) 192
         (E) None of these

10. The number 88 is 2/5 of

   (A) 123   (B) 141
   (C) 221   (D) 440
         (E) None of these

11. If the product of 8.3 multiplied by .42 is subtracted from the product of 156 multiplied by .09, the result is most nearly

   (A) 10.6   (B) 13.7
   (C) 17.5   (D) 20.8
         (E) None of these

12. Add the following lengths: 4 yards, 2 feet, 3 inches; 4 feet, 11 inches; 6 yards, 8 inches; 6 yards; and give the answer in feet and fractions thereof.

   (A) 39'   (B) 38½'
   (C) 38¾'   (D) 39¼'
         (E) None of these

13. What is the net amount of a bill of $428 after a discount of 6% has been allowed?

    (A) $401.10   (B) $402.32
    (C) $401.23   (D) $402.23
         (E) None of these

14. What number decreased by 3/7 of itself is equal to 56?

    (A) 97   (B) 100
    (C) 96   (D) 91
         (E) None of these

15. The length of time from 8:23 A.M. to 2:53 P.M. is

    (A) 6 hours 16 minutes
    (B) 6 hours 30 minutes
    (C) 7 hours 16 minutes
    (D) 6 hours 40 minutes

16. The sum of 9/16, 11/32, 15/64 and 1 3/32 is most nearly

    (A) 2.234   (B) 2.134
    (C) 2.334   (D) 2.214
         (E) None of these

17. At 4 cents each, the cost of 144 fuses would be

    (A) $.48   (B) $5.76
    (C) $4.00   (D) $8.00
         (E) None of these

18. Oil sells at 42½ cents a quart. The cost of 4 gallons of oil is

    (A) $6.50   (B) $6.60
    (C) $6.70   (D) $6.80
         (E) None of these

19. The sum of the numbers 38806, 2074, 48761, 9632, 7899, 4628, is

    (A) 111,800   (B) 112,000
    (C) 14,900   (D) 111,700
         (E) None of these

20. If a piece of wood measuring 4 feet 2 inches is divided into three equal parts, each part is

    (A) 1 foot 4⅔ inches   (B) 1 foot 2⅓ inches
    (C) 1 foot 4 inches   (D) 1 foot 7/18 inch
         (E) None of these

21. If gaskets are sold at the rate of 3 for 7 cents, then 21 gaskets will cost

    (A) 21 cents   (B) 50 cents
    (C) 70 cents   (D) $1.41
         (E) None of these

22. A worker receives $18.35 per day. After working 13 days his total earnings should be

    (A) $238.65   (B) $238.60
    (C) $238.55   (D) $238.70
         (E) None of these

23. 1/7 changed to a two-place decimal is

    (A) .15   (B) 14.29
    (C) 15.00   (D) .14
         (E) None of these

24. A square has an area of 49 sq. in. The number of inches in its perimeter is

    (A) 7   (B) 28
    (C) 14   (D) 98
         (E) None of these

25. 126 ÷ 189 reduced to lowest terms equals

    (A) ⅔   (B) 4/9
    (C) 8/18   (D) ¾
         (E) None of these

Correct Answers

(You'll learn more by writing your own answers before comparing them with these.)

1. B	8. E	15. B	22. C
2. A	9. D	16. A	23. D
3. D	10. E	17. B	24. B
4. C	11. A	18. D	25. A
5. D	12. E	19. A	
6. C	13. B	20. A	
7. B	14. E	21. E	

SCORE

%

NO. CORRECT ÷

NO. OF QUESTIONS ON THIS TEST

ARITHMETICAL REASONING TEST ONE

Time Allowed: 10 minutes

DIRECTIONS: Each problem in this test involves a certain amount of logical reasoning and thinking on your part, besides the usual simple computations, to help you in finding the solution. Read each problem carefully and choose the correct answer from the five choices that follow. Mark E as your answer —— if none of the suggested answers agree with your answer. When you have finished, check your answers with the correct answers at the end of the test.

1. Find the interest on $25,800 for 144 days at 6% per annum. Base your calculations on a 360-day year.

  (A) $619.20   (B) $619.02
  (C) $691.02   (D) $691.20
     (E) None of these

2. A court clerk estimates that the untried cases on the docket will occupy the court for 150 trial days. If new cases are accumulating at the rate of 1.6 trial days per day (Saturday and Sunday excluded) and the court sits 5 days a week, how many days' business will remain to be heard at the end of 60 trial days?

  (A) 168 trial days   (B) 185 trial days
  (C) 188 trial days   (D) 186 trial days
     (E) None of these

3. The visitors section of a courtroom seats 105 people. The court is in session 6 hours of the day. On one particular day 486 people visited the court and were given seats. What is the average length of time spent by each visitor in the court? Assume that as soon as a person leaves his seat it is immediately filled and that at no time during the day is one of the 105 seats vacant. Express your answer in hours and minutes.

  (A) 1 hr. 20 min.   (B) 1 hr. 18 min.
  (C) 1 hr. 30 min.   (D) 2 hr.
     (E) None of these

4. If paper costs $1.46 per ream and 5% discount is allowed for cash, how many reams can be purchased for $69.35 cash? Do not discard fractional part of a cent in your calculations.

  (A) 49 reams   (B) 60 reams
  (C) 50 reams   (D) 53 reams
     (E) None of these

5. How much time is there between 8:30 a.m. today and 3:15 a.m. tomorrow.

  (A) 17¾ hrs.   (B) 18 hrs.
  (C) 18⅔ hrs.   (D) 18½ hrs.
     (E) None of these

6. How many days are there between September 19th and December 25th, both inclusive?

  (A) 98 days   (B) 96 days
  (C) 89 days   (D) 90 days
     (E) None of these

7. A clerk is requested to file 800 cards. If he can file cards at the rate of 80 cards an hour, the number of cards remaining to be filed after 7 hours of work is

  (A) 40   (B) 250
  (C) 140   (D) 260
     (E) None of these

8. An officer's weekly salary is increased from $80.00 to $90.00. The per cent of increase is, most nearly,

  (A) 10 per cent   (B) 11 1/9 per cent
  (C) 12½ per cent   (D) 14 1/7 per cent
     (E) None of these

9. If there are 245 sections in the city, the average number of sections for each of the 5 boroughs is

(A) 50 sections   (B) 49 sections
(C) 47 sections   (D) 59 sections
     (E) None of these

10. If a section had 45 miles of street to plow after a snow storm and 9 plows are used, each plow would cover an average of how many miles?

(A) 7 miles   (B) 6 miles
(C) 8 miles   (D) 5 miles
     (E) None of these

11. If a crosswalk plow engine is run 5 minutes a day for ten days in a given month, it would run how long in the course of this month?

(A) 50 min.   (B) 1½ hrs.
(C) 1 hr.   (D) 30 min.
     (E) None of these

12. If the department uses 1500 men in manual street cleaning and half as many more to load and drive trucks, the total number used is

(A) 2200 men   (B) 2520 men
(C) 2050 men   (D) 2250 men
     (E) None of these

13. If an inspector issued 186 summonses in the course of 7 hours, his hourly average of summonses issued was

(A) 23 summonses   (B) 26 summonses
(C) 25 summonses   (D) 28 summonses
     (E) None of these

14. If, of 186 summonses issued, one hundred were issued to first offenders, then there were how many summonses issued to other than first offenders?

(A) 68   (B) 90
(C) 86   (D) 108
     (E) None of these

15. A truck going at a rate of 20 miles an hour will reach a town 40 miles away in how many hours?

(A) 3 hrs.   (B) 1 hr.
(C) 4 hrs.   (D) 5 hrs.
     (E) None of these

16. If a barrel has a capacity of 100 gallons, it will contain how many gallons when it is two-fifths full?

(A) 20 gal.   (B) 60 gal.
(C) 40 gal.   (D) 80 gal.
     (E) None of these

17. If a salary of $3000 is subject to a 20 percent deduction, the net salary is

(A) $2,000   (B) $2,400
(C) $2,500   (D) $2,600
     (E) None of these

18. If $1000 is the cost of repairing 100 square yards of pavement, the cost of repairing one square yard is

(A) $10   (B) $150
(C) $100   (D) $300
     (E) None of these

19. If a man's base pay is $3000 and it is increased by a bonus of $350 and a seniority increment of $250, his total salary is

(A) $3,600   (B) $3,500
(C) $3,000   (D) $3,700
     (E) None of these

20. If an annual salary of $2160 is increased by a bonus of $720 and by a service increment of $120, the total pay rate is

(A) $2,960   (B) $3,960
(C) $2,690   (D) $3,000
     (E) None of these

Correct Answers

(You'll learn more by writing your own answers before comparing them with these.)

1. A	6. A	11. A	16. C
2. D	7. E	12. D	17. B
3. B	8. C	13. B	18. A
4. C	9. B	14. C	19. A
5. E	10. D	15. E	20. D

SCORE

%

NO. CORRECT ÷

NO. OF QUESTIONS ON THIS TEST

ARITHMETICAL REASONING TEST TWO

Time Allowed: 10 minutes

DIRECTIONS: Each problem in this test involves a certain amount of logical reasoning and thinking on your part, besides the usual simple computations, to help you in finding the solution. Read each problem carefully and choose the correct answer from the five choices that follow. Mark E ————————— if none of the suggested answers agree with your answer. When you have finished, check your answers with the correct answers at the end of the test.

1. If the average cost of sweeping a square foot of New York City street is $.75, the cost of sweeping 100 square feet is

   (A) $7.50 (B) $750
   (C) $75 (D) $70
   (E) None of these

2. If a Sanitation Department scow is towed at the rate of three miles an hour it will need how many hours to go 28 miles?

   (A) 10 hrs. 30 min. (B) 12 hrs.
   (C) 9 hrs. 20 min. (D) 9 hrs. 15 min.
   (E) None of these

3. If a truck is 60 feet away from a Sanitation Man, it is how many feet nearer to him than a truck which is 100 feet away?

   (A) 60 ft. (B) 40 ft.
   (C) 50 ft. (D) 20 ft.
   (E) None of these

4. A clerk divided his 35 hour work week as follows: 1/5 of his time in sorting mail; ½ of his time in filing letters; and 1/7 of his time in reception work. The rest of his time was devoted to messenger work. The percentage of time spent on messenger work by the clerk during the week was most nearly

   (A) 6% (B) 10%
   (C) 14% (D) 16%
   (E) None of these

5. A city department has set up a computing unit and has rented 5 computing machines at a yearly rental of $140 per machine. In addition, the cost to the department for the maintenance and repair of each of these machines is $10 per year. Five computing machine operators, each receiving an annual salary of $3,000, and a supervisor, who receives $3,800 a year, have been assigned to this unit. This unit will perform the work previously performed by 10 employees whose combined salary was $32,400 a year. On the basis of these facts, the savings that will result from the operation of this computing unit for 5 years will be most nearly

   (A) $50,000 (B) $64,000
   (C) $66,000 (D) $95,000
   (E) None of these

6. Twelve clerks are assigned to enter certain data on index cards. This number of clerks could perform the task in 18 days. After these clerks have worked on this assignment for 6 days, 4 more clerks are added to the staff to do this work. Assuming that all the clerks work at the same rate of speed, the entire task, instead of taking 18 days, will be performed in

   (A) 9 days (B) 12 days
   (C) 17 days (D) 16 days
   (E) None of these

7. Six gross of special drawing pencils were purchased for use in a City department. If the pencils were used at the rate of 24 a week, the maximum number of weeks that the six gross of pencils would last is

   (A) 6 weeks (B) 12 weeks
   (C) 24 weeks (D) 36 weeks
   (E) None of these

8. A stock clerk had 600 pads on hand. He then issued ⅜ of his supply of pads to

Division X, ¼ to Division Y, and ⅙ to Division Z. The number of pads remaining in stock is

(A) 48 (B) 125
(C) 240 (D) 475
(E) None of these

9. If a certain job can be performed by 18 clerks in 26 days, the number of clerks needed to perform the job in 12 days is

(A) 24 clerks (B) 30 clerks
(C) 39 clerks (D) 52 clerks
(E) None of these

10. After gaining 50% of his original capital, a man had a capital of $18,000. Find the original capital.

(A) $12,200.00 (B) $13,100.00
(C) $12,000.00 (D) $12,025.00
(E) None of these

11. A cog wheel having 8 cogs plays into another cog wheel having 24 cogs. When the small wheel has made 42 revolutions, how many has the larger wheel made?

(A) 14 (B) 20
(C) 16 (D) 10
(E) None of these

12. A man worked 30 days. He paid 2/5 of his earnings for board and room and had $81 left. What was his daily wage?

(A) $4.75 (B) $5.00
(C) $5.50 (D) $4.25
(E) None of these

13. A dealer bought some motorcycles for $4000. He sold them for $6200, making $50 on each motorcycle. How many motorcycles were there?

(A) 40 (B) 38
(C) 43 (D) 44
(E) None of these

14. A firm had ¼ of its capital invested in goods, ⅔ of the remainder in land, and the remainder, $1224, in cash. What was the capital of the firm?

(A) $4,986.00 (B) $4,698.00
(C) $4,896.00 (D) $4,869.00
(E) None of these

15. A and B together earn $2100. If B is paid ¼ more than A, how many dollars should B receive?

(A) $1,166.66⅔ (B) $1,161.66⅔
(C) $1,616.66⅓ (D) $1,166.66⅓
(E) None of these

16. If a house is bought for $2150 and sold again for $2365, what is the gain per cent?

(A) 8% (B) 15%
(C) 20% (D) 10%
(E) None of these

17. A person owned 5/6 of a piece of property and sold ¾ of his share for $1800. What was the value of the property?

(A) $2,808.00 (B) $2,880.00
(C) $2,088.00 (D) $2,880.80
(E) None of these

18. A house costing $11,250 rents for $1200 a year. The taxes and other expenses are $300 per year. Find the per cent of net income on the investment.

(A) 8% (B) 6%
(C) 4% (D) 10%
(E) None of these

19. B owned 75 shares of stock in a building association, worth $50 each. The association declared a dividend of 8%, payable in stock. How many shares did he then own?

(A) 81 shares (B) 80 shares
(C) 90 shares (D) 85 shares
(E) None of these

20. It requires four men three days to take an inventory and the monthly salary of each is as follows: A-$250, B-$130, C-$120, D-$90. Calculate the cost of taking the inventory, assuming that there are 25 full working days in a month.

(A) $80.70 (B) $87.00
(C) $70.80 (D) $70.08
(E) None of these

Correct Answers

1. C	6. E	11. A	16. D
2. C	7. D	12. E	17. B
3. B	8. B	13. D	18. A
4. D	9. C	14. C	19. A
5. B	10. C	15. A	20. C

SCORE

%

....

NO. CORRECT ÷

NO. OF QUESTIONS ON THIS TEST

INTRODUCTION TO NEW MATH

NEW MATH SYMBOLS

Symbols	Meaning
{ }	Indicates a set.
$a \in A$	a is an element of the set A.
$a \notin A$	a is not an element of the set A.
$\emptyset$ or { }	The null set or the empty set.
$n(S)$	The cardinal number of the set S.
$A \subset B$	A is a subset of B, or A is contained in B.
$A \not\subset B$	A is not a subset of B.
U	A universal set.
$A \cup B$	The union of the sets A and B; A "cup" B.
$A \cap B$	The intersection of the sets A and B; A "cap" B.
W	The set of whole numbers.
N	The set of natural numbers.
I	The set of integers.
GCF	The greatest common factor.
LCM	The least common multiple.
$\lvert x \rvert$	The absolute value, or magnitude, of x.
$a < b$	a is less than b.
$a > b$	a is greater than b.
$a \leq b$	a is less than or equal to b.
$a \geq b$	a is greater than or equal to b.
$a \neq b$	a is not equal to b.
$-a$	The additive inverse of a; the opposite of a.
a^{-1} or $1/a$	The multiplicative inverse of a; the reciprocal of a.
(x, y)	The ordered pair of x and y; the co-ordinates x, y.

ONE OF THE MOST useful and important concepts in mathematics is that of *sets*. A set is any collection or group of objects or ideas that are accurately described and placed together. Thus, we can talk about the set of chairs in a room, or the set of golf clubs, or the set of numbers between one and one hundred.

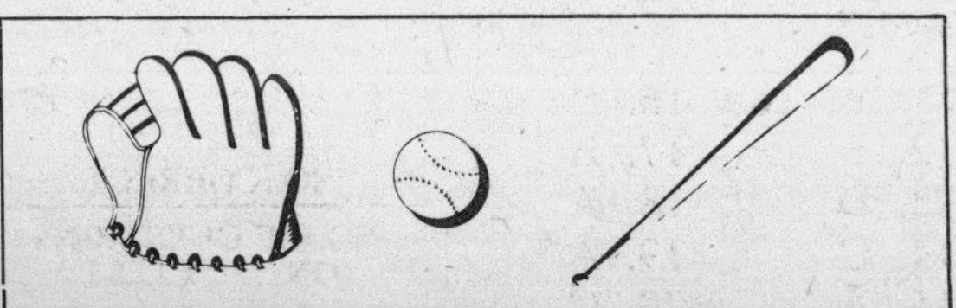

We use the idea of a set in many ways every day. The objects or ideas that compose a set are called the *elements* or members of the set. For example, two would be considered a member of the set of even numbers. An important characteristic of sets is that we must be able to determine whether or not a given object or idea is in the set. To the mathematician this means that the set must be *well-defined,* so that we can easily tell what the members of a given set are.

Consider the set of "all the good books in the town library." This would not be a well-defined set since people may differ as to whether or not certain books are good. "Good book" means different things to different people. In addition, the phrase, "the town library," is also not very precise since one might ask, "Which town?" or if the town is large and has more than one library, "Which library?" The set of all girls in Mr. Smith's sixth period History class would be a well-defined set, whereas the set of pretty girls in Mr. Smith's sixth period class would not be well-defined.

Use of Brackets

In mathematics we usually name a set by a capital letter and indicate the members of the set by placing the elements within a set of braces. Thus, we could represent the set of seasons of the year as

$$B = \{\text{summer, winter, spring, fall}\}.$$

Notice that a set may be indicated by *listing* the elements or by *describing* its elements. Hence:

$$C = \{1, 2, 3, 4, 5, 6, 7, 8, 9\} = \{\text{natural numbers less than 10}\}$$

would be two way of representing this particular set. Natural numbers are *counting numbers*. The natural numbers and zero make up the set of whole numbers.

Consider the set $A = \{1, 2, 3. 4\}$. To indicate that 1 is an element of the set A we use the Greek letter epsilon ($\in$) and write $1 \in A$. This would be read as, 1 is a member of (or an element of) the set A. To show, for example, that 5 is not a member of the set A, we write $5 \notin A$.

Null Sets

Suppose you were asked to list the elements of the set of nine-legged bears. Obviously there exist no members of this set and the result is a special set which is called the *null* or *empty set*. The empty set is the set which contains no members and another Greek letter ϕ (phi) is used to designate this set. Sometimes the empty set is represented by simply writing a set of braces with no elements in between.

$$D = \phi \text{ or } D = \{\ \}$$

and D may be, for example, the set of all odd numbers that are divisible by two.

SHOW YOU KNOW

Exercise 1 *

1. List the elements in each of the following sets:
   a. A = {Presidents of the United States from 1932 to 1964}
   b. B = {the capital of the State of Illinois}
   c. C = {the odd natural numbers less than 10}
   d. D = {the positive natural numbers greater than zero}

2. Describe the following sets in words:
   a. A = {a, b, c, d, e, f}
   b. B = {1/4, 2/4, 3/4}
   c. C = ϕ
   d. D = {4, 8, 12, 16}

3. Why are each of the following statements false?
   a. If A = {2, 4, 6, 8}, $2 \notin$ A.
   b. {0} is the same as ϕ.
   c. T = {tall men on the New York Yankees' team} is well defined.

Equal Sets

Having introduced the idea of a set, we now wish to examine some of the concepts that are associated with sets. First of all, two sets are said to be *equal* if they each contain the same elements. Thus, if A = {2, 3, 4} and B = {4, 2, 3} then we can say that A = B. Notice that when we refer to equal sets, the order of the elements is not important. The sets, A and B, are equal because each element of A is also an element of B and vice versa.

Cardinal Number

Consider, now, the two sets S = {a, b, c, d} and T = {1, 2, 3, 4}. Certainly S and T are not equal (which we can say symbolically as S $\neq$ T) since they do not contain the same elements. Yet the sets S and T do have one property in common and that is that they

each contain the same number of elements. The number of elements in a given set is referred to as the *cardinal number* of the set. The cardinal number of the set S is 4 since S contains four elements and we would indicate this fact by writing n(S) = 4, or #(S) = 4.

The cardinal number of a set can be determined by matching the elements of the set with the set of natural (or counting) numbers beginning with one. Hence

$$S = \{a, b, c, d\}$$
$$\updownarrow \ \updownarrow \ \updownarrow \ \updownarrow$$
$$T = \{1, 2, 3, 4\}$$

shows how the elements of the set S can be paired with the set T of the first four natural numbers.

Equivalent Sets

When the elements of two sets are matched in this manner, we say that we have established a *one-to-one correspondence* between the members of the two sets. When such a one-to-one correspondence can be formed between two sets, the sets are called *equivalent*. For example, consider the sets A = {Jim, Dane, George} and B = {apple, pear, plum}. We can match the elements of A and B as follows:

$$A = \{\text{Jim, Dane, George}\}$$
$$\updownarrow \qquad \updownarrow \qquad \updownarrow$$
$$B = \{\text{apple, pear, plum}\}$$

and, hence, we can say that the sets A and B are equivalent. We can say, also, that n(A) = n(B) = 3. Thus, to say that a one-to-one correspondence exists between the elements of two sets is the same as saying that the two sets are equivalent or that the cardinal numbers of the two sets are equal. Notice that if we were to consider all possible sets that contain three elements the only thing that these sets would have in common would be the property of "three-ness." The same statement can be made for all sets with one, two, one hundred and twenty, etc.: hence, cardinal numbers constitute a property of sets. We may also say that cardinal numbers answer the question: "How many?"

The cardinal number of the empty set ϕ would, of course, be 0 since the empty set contains no elements. The set of all cardinal numbers is {0, 1, 2, 3, 4, . . .} where the three dots indicate that the string of numbers continues on without end.

Infinite Sets

The set of all cardinal numbers (sometimes also called the set of whole numbers) is an example of an *infinite* set. An infinite set is a set whose elements can-

---

* Answers to all problems on this and following pages will be found in the section, *Solutions to the Exercises,* starting on Page 315.

not be counted. If you attempted to count the elements in an infinite set, you would go on and on counting forever, for there is no last element in the set. A set whose elements can be counted is called a *finite* set. Thus, if A = {Presidents of the United States} then A would be a finite set; whereas, the set B = {even natural numbers} would be an example of an infinite set.

SHOW THAT YOU KNOW

Exercise 2

1. If A = {5, 6, 7, 8, 9} and B = {9, 6, 7, 8, 5}:
    a. Does $A = B$?
    b. Is A equivalent to B?
    c. $n(A) = ?$
    d. $n(B) = ?$
    e. Establish a one-to-one correspondence between the elements of A and B.

2. Can you establish a one-to-one correspondence between the set of states of the union and the set of state governors? What is the cardinal number of each set?

3. Tell whether the following sets are finite or infinite, and, if possible, list the elements in each set:
    a. {odd natural numbers}
    b. {all people in the world at a given moment}
    c. {∅}
    d. {the multiples of 5}

4. Can you establish a one-to-one correspondence between the set of cardinal numbers, {0, 1, 2, 3, 4, 5, . . .} and the set of even cardinal numbers, {0, 2, 4, 6, 8, 10, . . .}?

What Is A Subset?

Consider the two sets A = {1, 2, 3, 4} and B = {1, 3}. Notice that each element in set B is also contained in the set A. We would say, then, that B is a *subset* of A. Thus, a subset can be thought of as a set within a set. In general, one set is a subset of another if it contains some, all, or none of the elements of the given set, and that it contains only elements of the given set. If A is a subset of B, then we write $A \subset B$, which is read: "A is a subset of B" or "A is contained in B."

Suppose we were asked to find all of the subsets of A = {1, 2, 3}. Certainly each of the following would be a subset: {1}, {2}, {3}, {1, 2}, {1, 3}, {2, 3}.

But also the set {1, 2, 3} is a subset according to our definition. Thus, every set is a subset of itself. Also the empty set is a subset of A. In fact, the empty set is a subset of every set. Thus, the set A above has a total of 8 subsets. The set itself and the empty set are called *improper* subsets, while the other possible subsets are referred to as *proper*.

Let us summarize the important facts about subsets thus far.

1. A is a subset of B $(A \subset B)$ if every element of A is an element of B.

2. Every set is a subset of itself.

3. The empty set is a subset of every set.

4. If a subset contains some (but not all) of the elements of a given set, then it is called a proper subset. The empty set and the set itself are improper subsets.

If A is not a subset of B, then we write $A \not\subset B$ (just as we would write $A \neq B$ if A and B do not contain the same elements).

Universal Set

It is sometimes convenient to refer to the set of all possible elements under consideration in a particular problem. Such a set is called the *universal set* or the *universe* or the *domain* for that problem. That is, all possible elements that can be discussed in a given situation form the universal set for that situation.

Suppose we are considering the set A = {Woodrow Wilson, Harry S. Truman, John F. Kennedy}. Then we could consider as our universal set the set of Democratic Presidents of the U. S.; or perhaps the set of all Presidents of the U. S.; or, to make it even larger, the set of all past and present citizens of the U. S. Hence, the universal set is a changing concept and what is taken as the universal set will depend on the situation. We should be able to define the universal set for any given problem. Generally, the capital letter U is used to represent the universal set. Notice that the set we wish to refer to automatically is a subset of the universal set for a problem.

Venn Diagrams

It is sometimes helpful when working with sets to represent the sets and the concepts involved with diagrams or pictures. These are generally referred to as *Venn diagrams* or *Euler circles*. For example, suppose we have the following sets:

U = {natural numbers}
A = {even natural numbers}
B = {2, 4, 6, 8}

We can represent this situation by the following Venn diagram:

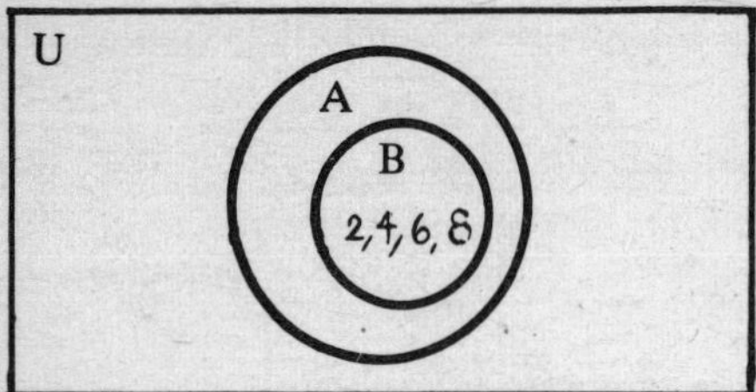

Notice that B ⊂ A since each element that is in B is also in A.

SHOW THAT YOU KNOW

Exercise 3

1. List all possible subsets of the following sets:
    a. {∅}
    b. {a}
    c. {1, 2}
    d. {Jim, John, Jack}
    e. From your experience with parts a, b, c, and d, can you determine how many subsets a set with four elements will have? Can you generalize this concept to a set containing elements?

2. Referring to 1 a, b, c, d above, which of the subsets would be improper subsets?

3. Again referring to 1 a, b, c, d above, list a possible universal set for each of the sets given.

4. Given:
    $$U = \{natural\ numbers\}$$
    $$R = \{1, 3, 5, 7, \ldots\}$$
    $$S = \{1, 3, 5, 7, 9\}$$
    $$T = \{1\}$$
    a. Which of the following are false statements? Why?
       1. R ⊂ S
       2. T ⊄ R
       3. T ⊂ S
    b. Construct a Venn diagram to represent the sets given above.
    c. Describe the sets R and S.

Binary Operations

We are all familiar with the fundamental operations with numbers—addition, subtraction, multiplication and division—which are called *binary operations* because they involve working with two numbers at a time. We wish now to examine the binary operations with sets.

Suppose we have the following two sets:

$$A = \{1, 2, 3, 4\}$$
$$B = \{2, 4, 6, 8, 10\}$$

If we join these two sets to form a new set containing only the members of A and B, then this new set is called the *union* of A and B. This amounts to performing a binary operation on the two sets and the result is a new set. The union of two sets is denoted by A ∪ B and this can be read as "the union of set A and set B" or "A union B." Sometimes the union symbol is called *cup* and hence we might read this sentence as "A cup B." Thus, for the two sets above, A ∪ B = {1, 2, 3, 4, 6, 8, 10}. Notice that each element appears only once in the union.

The union of two sets, then, is a set formed by considering all of the elements in each of the two given sets. If the two given sets are equal, then the union of the two sets will equal one of the given sets. Thus, for example, if S = {Tom, Jim, Joe} and T = {Jim, Tom, Joe}, then S ∪ T = {Joe, Jim, Tom}.

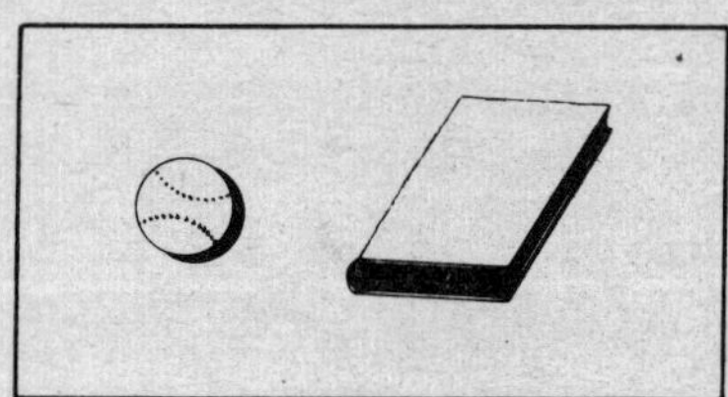

Intersection

A second binary operation on sets is that of *intersection of sets*. The intersection of two or more sets is the set of elements common to both sets and is represented by A ∩ B. In the sets A and B used in the above section A ∩ B = {2, 4}. The symbols A ∩ B would be read as "the intersection of set A and set B" or "A intersect B" or "A cap B." Let us look at another example. Suppose that R = {Mary, Sue, Joan} and V = {Sue, Sally}. What would R ∩ V be? Well, to determine the intersection we look for elements that appear in both sets. In this case, Sue is the only member of both R and V and hence R ∩ V = {Sue}. The union of R and V would be {Sue, Mary, Joan, Sally}.

Disjoint Sets

If two sets do not have any elements in common, then these sets are called *disjoint*. If we apply the set operation of intersection to disjoint sets the result is the empty set. Hence, if $A = \{1, 2, 3\}$ and $B = \{9, 10, 11, 12\}$ then $A \cap B = \phi$.

Venn diagrams are a convenient device for representing set unions and intersections. For example, if

$U = \{$natural numbers$\}$

$X = \{$all even natural numbers$\}$ or $\{2, 4, 6, 8, \ldots\}$

$Y = \{$all natural numbers less than 10$\}$ or $\{1, 2, 3, \ldots, 9\}$ then we can represent these sets as follows:

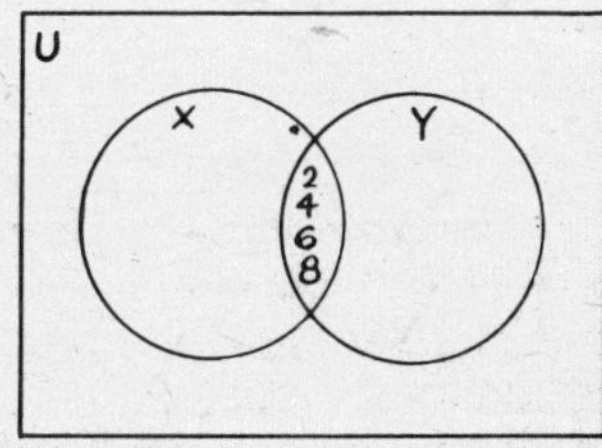

Notice that

$X \cup Y = \{$all even natural numbers and 1, 3, 5, 7, 9$\}$ and

$X \cap Y = \{2, 4, 6, 8\}$

Another example of the use of Venn diagrams to picture set relationships is the following involving quadrilaterals. If $U = \{$quadrilaterals$\}$, then

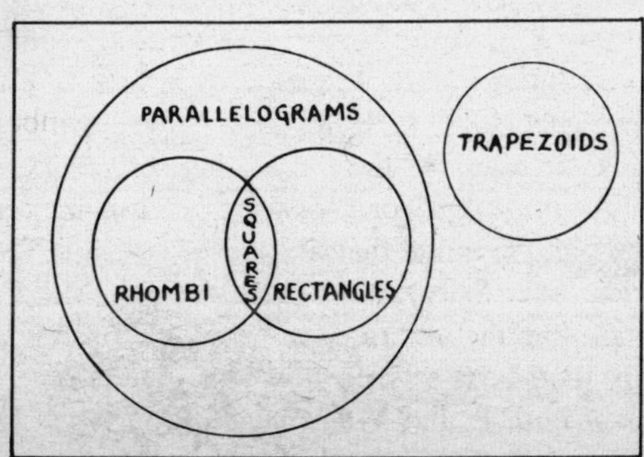

Notice that the set of rectangles is represented as a subset of the set of parallelograms and the set of rhombi (quadrilaterals with four equal sides) is also a subset of the set of parallelograms. Also, from the diagram we can conclude that a square is a rectangle and also a rhombus, since the set of squares is the intersection of these other sets. Notice also that the set of trapezoids and the set of parallelograms are disjoint sets.

Exercise 4

1. If $A = \{1, 2, 3, 4, 5, 6, 7, 8, 9\}$ and $B = \{1, 3, 5, 7, 11, 13, 17, 19\}$, then
   a. $A \cup B =$
   b. $A \cap B =$
   c. $n(A) =$
   d. $n(B) =$
   e. $n(A \cup B) =$
   f. $n(A \cap B) =$
   g. Represent the sets A and B using Venn diagrams. What would a universal set be for this situation?

2. If $S = \{$even natural numbers$\}$ and $T = \{$odd natural numbers$\}$, find $S \cup T$ and $S \cap T$.

3. If $Q = \{a, b, c, d\}$ and $R = \{e, f, g, h, i, j\}$, then
   a. $Q \cup R =$
   b. $Q \cap R =$
   c. $n(Q) =$
   d. $n(R) =$
   e. $n(Q \cup R) =$
   f. $n(Q \cap R) =$
   g. $n(Q) + n(R) =$

Note: When two sets are disjoint, then the cardinal number of the union set is equal to the sum of the cardinal numbers of each set. That is, $n(Q \cup R) = n(Q) + n(R)$. This is one possible way to introduce or define the process of addition.

4. If A is any set and U a universe for A, find the following unions and intersections.
   a. $A \cup O =$
   b. $A \cap O =$
   c. $A \cup A =$
   d. $A \cap A =$
   e. $A \cup U =$
   f. $A \cap U =$

Systems Of Numeration

As a student progresses through school, he becomes more acquainted with numbers and the properties of numbers. In fact, we become so used to working with numbers that we often forget what makes this marvelous invention of man function.

What exactly is a number? Well, a number is nothing more than an idea in the minds of men. It is an abstract concept; we can't see a number nor touch it. Suppose you and I are cavemen sitting around a fire and I am talking about the number of sheep that I have. How do I convey this idea to you?

Just as with the relating of any other concept, this becomes a problem of communication. If I have three sheep, then I can tell you this by holding up three fingers and perhaps saying, "Ugh, ugh, ugh." By doing so, I am trying to convey to you the idea of *three-ness* and am giving this idea a name. Perhaps I may even draw three lines | | |, to represent this concept. Probably now you can begin to see how man started to develop a number system. We have come a long way since the time of the caveman.

To summarize, then, a number is an idea. Just as truth, love, justice, etc., are abstract concepts, so is a number. Man has given these ideas names in order to communicate with other men. Thus, when I say I have three sheep, a picture is formed in your mind concerning the quantity of sheep involved. If I wish to communicate a number to you in writing, then I use a *numeral* or symbol to represent the particular number idea. Thus, 3, III, 9 - 6, 12/4, etc., are all numerals for the number *three*. Notice that you could write many more symbols representing threeness, and, in fact, for any given number. There are infinitely many symbols that can be used to represent that number. The collection of symbols used to communicate number ideas is called a *system of numeration.*

NUMBER SYSTEMS

The number system that we use is called the Hindu-Arabic system. Actually, in the comparative history of man, this is a fairly new system, having been widely used only in the past four or five hundred years. As we shall see, our number system was a great improvement over those that preceded its invention.

Egyptian

One of the earliest systems of numeration was the Egyptian system. The Egyptians used the following symbols to name their numbers:

1	10	100
Vertical staff	heel bone	coiled rope
1,000	10,000	100,000
lotus flower	bent finger	tadpole
1,000,000		
astonished man		

The Egyptian numerals could be repeated and were additive. So that to represent forty-two thousand, three hundred seventy-six, the Egyptians would write:

Evaluating from right to left yields:

$$\begin{aligned}
\text{(bent fingers)} &= 10,000 + 10,000 + 10,000 + 10,000 = 40,000 \\
\text{(lotus)} &= 1,000 + 1,000 = 2,000 \\
\text{(coiled rope)} &= 100 + 100 + 100 = 300 \\
\text{(heels)} &= 10 + 10 + 10 + 10 + 10 + 10 + 10 = 70 \\
\text{(staffs)} &= 1 + 1 + 1 + 1 + 1 + 1 = 6 \\
\hline
&= 42,376
\end{aligned}$$

Roman

Of the many older systems of numeration, that of the Romans is the most familiar to us—next to our own, of course.

ROMAN NUMERAL	Hindu-Arabic Numeral
I	1
IV	4
V	5
VIII	8
X	10
L	50
LXVII	67
XCVI	96
C	100
D	500
M	1000

Roman numerals are still often used today. As we compare these two systems of representing numbers, what differences do we find? First of all, it is obvious that the Romans had to invent a new symbol for a number as they needed it. Thus, as a Roman counted and arrived at, say, 49, a new symbol was needed to make 50. They happened to select the letter L to convey this information. The Hindu-Arabic system doesn't have this problem, for it is what is called a *base-place system*. Let us examine this idea more closely.

Hindu-Arabic

Consider the numeral 333. Because of the position of each digit, each 3 has a different value. Each digit has a *face value* of 3 but a *place value* of 300, 30, and 3, respectively. Thus, the position that a digit occupies in relation to the rest of the digits is important. We may write 333 in extended notation as follows:

$$333 = 3 \text{ x } 100 + 3 \text{ x } 10 + 3$$
$$= 3 \text{ x } 10^2 + 3 \text{ x } 10 + 3$$

Notice that 10 plays an important role in our system. Indeed, this is why we refer to this as the *decimal system* or why we say that we are operating in *base 10*.

The base of any place-value system of numeration is determined by the method of grouping used. In base 10, when we reach a count of 9 ones, the next number will be recorded as 1 group of tens; the following number is then one group of ten plus one 1, or 11, and so forth until we get to 1 group of ten and 9 ones which is then followed by 20, or 2 groups of 10 and no ones. When we get to 9 groups of ten and 9 ones, we add another place to indicate the number of 100's or 10^2's and thus get

$$1 \ 0 \ 0$$

one group / no \ no ones
of 100   tens

We could proceed like this indefinitely, adding another place when we need it to indicate a succeeding power of ten. Thus, we can think of 4,538 as

$$(4 \text{ x } 1000) + (5 \text{ x } 100) + (3 \text{ x } 10) + 8 \text{ or}$$
$$(4 \text{ x } 10^3) + (5 \text{ x } 10^2) + (3 \text{ x } 10) + 8$$

or 578,062 as $(5 \text{ x } 10^5) + (7 \text{ x } 10^4) + (8 \text{ x } 10^3) + (0 \text{ x } 10^2) + (6 \text{ x } 10) + 2$. Notice that the zero in 578,062 tells us that no 10 x 10's are used in this number. The use of zero is another difference to be noted from the Roman system, for they had no symbol to denote "nothing." Can you see why zero plays an important role?

Solutions to New Math Exercises

Exercise 1

1. a. A = {Roosevelt, Truman, Eisenhower, Kennedy, Johnson}
    b. B = {Springfield}
    c. C = {1, 3, 5, 7, 9}
    d. D = {1, 2, 3, 4, . . .}

2. Most of these sets can be described in a variety of ways. Here are some examples:
    a. A = {the first six letters of the alphabet}
    b. B = {fractions between 0 and 1 with denominators of 4}
    c. Since C is the null set, there are many possible answers. For example, C = {all human beings 50 feet tall} or C = {all odd numbers divisible by 4}
    d. D = multiples of 4 greater than 0 and less than 20

3. a. 2 *is* an element of the set A.
    b. {0} contains the element 0 and hence, since it contains an element, it is not empty.
    c. Opinions may vary as to whether or not a particular player is tall.

Exercise 2

1. a. yes
    b. yes
    c. n(A) = 5
    d. n(B) = 5
    e. 5, 6, 7, 8, 9
       ↕ ↕ ↕ ↕ ↕
       9, 6, 7, 8, 5

2. yes: 50

3. a. infinite; {1, 3, 5, 7, 9, . . .}
    b. finite
    c. finite
    d. infinite; {0, 5, 10, 15, . . .}

4. yes

    0, 1, 2, 3, 4, 5, . . ., n, . . .
    ↕ ↕ ↕ ↕ ↕ ↕   ↕
    0, 2, 4, 6, 8, 10, ... 2n, . . .

Exercise 3

1. a. ∅
    b. ∅ , {a}
    c. ∅ , {1} , {2} , {1, 2}
    d. ∅ , {Jim,}, {John}, {Jack}, {Jim, Jack},

{Jim, John}, {John, Jack}, {Jim, Jack, John}

e. A set with no elements has $2^0 = 1$ subsets.
A set with 1 element has $2^1 = 2$ subsets.
A set with 2 elements has $2^2 = 4$ subsets.
A set with 3 elements has $2^3 = 8$ subsets.
Therefore, a set with 4 elements will have $2^4 = 16$ subsets.

In general, a set with n elements will have 2^n subsets.

2. a. $\emptyset$
b. Both subsets are improper.
c. $\emptyset$ and {1, 2}
d. $\emptyset$ and {Jim, Jack, John}

3. There are many possibilities for each case. Here are some examples:
a. Any set you would name could be a universal set.
b. U = {letters of the alphabet}
c. U = {natural numbers}
d. U = {names of boys beginning with the letter J}

4. a. 1. false, $S \subset R$
2. false, $T \subset R$
3. true
b.

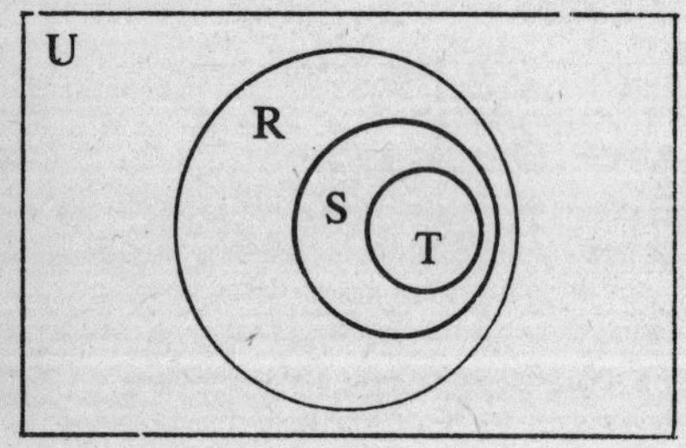

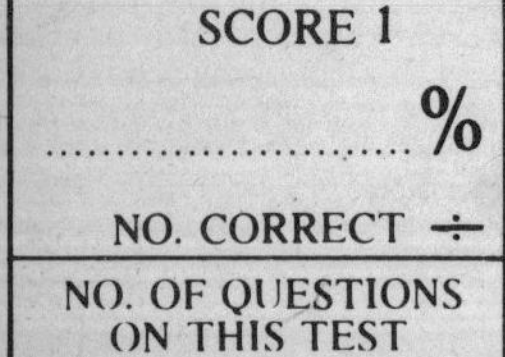

c. Possible answers are:
R = {odd natural numbers}
S = {add natural numbers less than 10}

Exercise 4

1. a. A $\cup$ B = {1, 2, 3, 4, 5, 6, 7, 8, 9, 11, 13, 17, 19}
b. A $\cap$ B = {1, 3, 5, 7}
c. n(A) = 9
d. n(B) = 8
e. n(A $\cup$ B) = 13
f. n(A $\cap$ B) = 4

g.

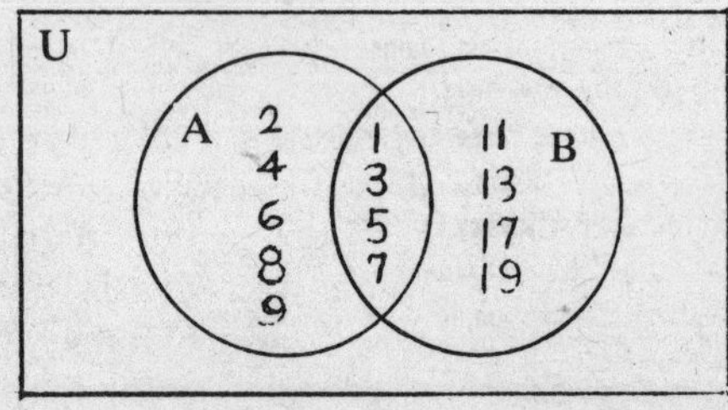

U = {natural numbers}

2. S $\cup$ T = {natural numbers}
S $\cap$ T = $\emptyset$

3. a. Q $\cup$ R = {a, b, c, d, e, f, g, h, i, j}
b. Q $\cap$ R = $\emptyset$
c. n(Q) = 4
d. n(R) = 6
e. n(Q $\cup$ R) = 10
f. n(Q $\cap$ R) = 0
g. n(Q + n(R) = 4 + 6 = 10 = n(Q $\cup$ R)

4. a. A $\cup$ $\emptyset$ = A
b. A $\cap$ $\emptyset$ = $\emptyset$
c. A $\cup$ A = A
d. A $\cap$ A = A
e. A $\cup$ U = U
f. A $\cap$ U = A

SCORE 1	SCORE 2	SCORE 3	SCORE 4
%	%	%	%
NO. CORRECT ÷	NO. CORRECT ÷	NO. CORRECT ÷	NO. CORRECT ÷
NO. OF QUESTIONS ON THIS TEST	NO. OF QUESTIONS ON THIS TEST	NO. OF QUESTIONS ON THIS TEST	NO. OF QUESTIONS ON THIS TEST

ARCO BOOKS FOR MORE HELP

*Now what? You've read and studied the whole book, and there's
still time before you take the test. You're probably better prepared
than most of your competitors, but you may feel insecure about
one or more of the probable test subjects.*

HIGH SCHOOL AND COLLEGE PREPARATION

American College Testing Program Exams	04363-6	5.00
Arco Arithmetic Q & A Review, Turner	02351-1	4.00
Arco's Handbook of Job and Career Opportunities	04328-8	3.95
Better Business English, Classen	04287-7	2.95
California High School Proficiency Examination	04412-8	6.00
Catholic High School Entrance Examination	00987-X	5.00
The College Board's Examination, McDonough & Hansen	02623-5	5.00
College By Mail, Jensen	02592-1	4.00
College Entrance Tests, Turner	01858-5	5.00
College-Level Examination Program (CLEP), Turner	04150-1	6.00
The Easy Way to Better Grades, Froe & Froe	03352-5	1.75
Elements of Debate, Klopf & McCroskey	01901-8	5.00
Encyclopedia of English, Zeiger	00655-X	3.95
English Grammar: 1,000 Steps	02012-1	6.00
English Grammar and Usage for Test-Takers, Turner	04014-9	5.00
The Florida Literacy Test, Morrison	04669-4	6.00
Good English with Ease, revised edition, Beckoff	03911-6	4.00
High School Entrance and Scholarship Tests, Turner	00666-8	5.00
High School Entrance Examinations—Special Public and Private High Schools	02143-8	5.00
How to Prepare Your College Application, Kussin & Kussin	01310-9	2.00
How to Use a Pocket Calculator, Mullish	04072-6	4.95
How to Write Reports, Papers, Theses, Articles, Riebel	02391-0	5.00
Letter-Perfect:The Accurate Secretary, Gilson	04038-6	6.00
Mastering General Mathematics, McDonough	03732-6	5.00

GED PREPARATION

Comprehensive Math Review for the High School Equivalency Diploma Test, McDonough	03420-3	4.00
High School Equivalency Diploma Tests, Turner	00110-0	5.00
New High School Equivalency Diploma Tests, Turner	04451-9	4.95
Preliminary Arithmetic for the High School Equivalency Diploma Test	02165-9	4.00
Preliminary Practice for the High School Equivalency Diploma Test	01441-3	5.00
Preparation for the Spanish High School Equivalency Diploma (Preparacion Para El Exam De Equivalencia De La Escuela Superior—En Espanol)	02618-9	6.00
Step-By-Step Guide to Correct English, Pulaski	03402-5	3.95

General Education Development Series

Correctness and Effectiveness of Expression (English HSEDT), Castellano, Guercio & Seitz	03688-5	4.00
General Mathematical Ability (Mathematics HSEDT), Castellano, Guercio & Seitz	03689-3	4.00
Reading Interpretation in Social Sciences, Natural Sciences, and Literature (Reading HSEDT), Castellano, Guercio & Seitz	03690-7	4.00
Teacher's Manual for the GED Series, Castellano, Guercio & Seitz	03692-3	2.50

ARCO LITERARY CRITIQUES

Blake, Gardner	01951-4	1.95
Byron, Doherty	01942-5	1.95
Charlotte and Emily Bronte, Sherry	02185-3	1.95
Chaucer, Grose	01890-9	1.95
D.H. Lawrence, Slade	02177-2	1.95
E.M. Forster, Rose	02357-0	1.95
Fielding, Macallister	02359-7	1.95
George Bernard Shaw, Brown	02365-1	1.95
George Orwell, Oxley	01894-1	1.95
Jane Austen, Sherry	01949-2	1.95
Joseph Conrad, Newhouse	01888-7	1.95
Keats, Inglis	01886-0	1.95
Matthew Arnold, Thorpe	02361-9	1.95
Milton, Carey	02179-9	1.95
Robert Browning, Williams	02183-7	1.95
Scott, Calder	02355-4	1.95
Shakespeare, Grose & Oxley	01892-5	1.95
Swift, Speck	02175-6	1.95
Tennyson, Steane	01947-6	1.95
Thackeray, Williams	01953-0	1.95
Thomas Hardy, Johnson	02363-5	1.95
T.S. Eliot, Pearce	01884-4	1.95
W.B. Yeats, Cowell	02181-0	1.95
Wordsworth, Drabble	01944-1	1.95

CIVIL SERVICE AND TEST PREPARATION—GENERAL

LR—Library Reinforced Binding

CIVIL SERVICE AND GENERAL TEST PREPARATION

MILITARY EXAMINATION SERIES

PROFESSIONAL CAREER EXAM SERIES

ARCO SCHOLARSHIP EXAMINATION SERIES

COLLEGE BOARD ACHIEVEMENT TESTS/CBAT

American History and Social Studies Achievement Test, Altman	01722-8	1.45
American History and Social Studies Achievement Test—Second Edition	04337-7	3.95
Biology Achievement Test—Second Edition, Solomon & Spector	04094-7	3.95
Chemistry Achievement Test	04101-3	3.95
English Composition Achievement Test	04338-5	3.95
English Composition Achievement Test	01247-1	.95
French Achievement Test, Biezunski & Boisrond	01668-X	1.45
German Achievement Test, Greiner	01698-1	1.45
Latin Achievement Test	01743-0	1.45
Mathematics: Level I Achievement Test, Bramson	03847-0	3.00
CBAT Mathematics Level II, Bramson	04284-2	3.95
Physics Achievement Test, Bruenn	01265-X	1.95
Spanish Achievement Test, Jassey	01741-4	1.45

AP/CBAT

Advanced Placement and College Board Achievement Tests in Physics (B-C)	04493-4	5.95

AP/CLEP

Advanced Placement and College Level Examinations in American History, Woloch	03804-7	4.95
Advanced Placement and College Level Examinations in Biology	04415-2	5.95
Advanced Placement and College Level Examinations in Calculus	03802-0	8.95
Advanced Placement and College Level Examinations in Chemistry	04484-5	4.95
Advanced Placement and College Level Examinations in English—Analysis and Interpretation of Literature	04406-3	4.95

AP/CLEP/CBAT

Advanced Placement, College Level Examinations and College Board Achievement Tests in European History	04407-1	5.95

CLEP

College Level Examination in Composition and Freshman English	03798-9	4.95
College Level Examinations in Mathematics: College Algebra, College Algebra-Trigonometry, Trigonometry	04339-3	5.95

1,000 IDEAS FOR TERM PAPERS SERIES

1,000 Ideas for English Term Papers, Farmer	01548-9	1.95
1,000 Ideas for Term Papers in American History, Farmer	01925-5	1.95
1,000 Ideas for Term Papers in Economics, Arc Ed. Brd.	01964-6	1.95
1,000 Ideas for Term Papers in World Literature, Farmer	01970-0	1.95
1,000 Ideas for Term Papers in Philosophy and Religion, Uttal	02701-0	1.95
1,000 Ideas for Term Papers in Social Science, Farmer	01966-2	1.95
1,000 Ideas for Term Papers in Sociology, Arc Ed. Brd.	01968-9	1.95

S3709